# SLUMS, URBAN DECLINE AND REVITALIZATION

Concept's International Series in Geography

1. Perspectives in Agricultural Geography (In Five Volumes)
   Edited by NOOR MOHAMMAD

2. Perspectives in Geomorphology (In Four Volumes)
   Edited by H. S. SHARMA

3. Perspectives in Urban Geography
   Edited by C. S. YADAV

1. New Directions in Urban Geography
2. Comparative Urban Research
3. Comparative Urbanization : City Growth and Change
4.A Models in Urban Geography (Theoretical)
4.B Models in Urban Geography (Mathematical)
5. Urban Research Methods : Central Place, Hierarchical and City Size Models
6. Contemporary City Ecology
7. Slums, Urban Decline and Revitalization
8. Contemporary Urban (Issues)
9. Rural-Urban Fringe
10. Morphology of Towns
11. Cities and Housing
12. Perceptual and Cognitive Image of the City
13. Urban Economics
14. City Planning : Problems and Prospects
15. City Planning : Administration and Participation
16.A City Planning and Policies
16.B City Planning and Policies

*Concept's International Series in Geography No. 3*

Perspectives in Urban Geography

Volume Seven

# SLUMS, URBAN DECLINE AND REVITALIZATION

*Edited by*

C.S. YADAV

CONCEPT PUBLISHING COMPANY, NEW DELHI

ISBN: 81-7022-080-7 (Set)
ISBN: 81-7022-018-1 (Vol. VII)

First Published 1987



*Published and Printed by*
Ashok Kumar Mittal
**Concept Publishing Company**
A/15-16, Commercial Block, Mohan Garden
New Delhi-110059 (INDIA)
*Phones* : 25351460, 25351794 *Fax* : 091-11-25357103
*Email* : publishing@conceptpub.com

## PREFACE

### NATURE OF URBAN GEOGRAPHY

There are several studies on urban geography which reveal that, as a major sub-discipline, it has a long tail but a short body. However, the spectrum is so vast and broad that researchers are able to make general statements in defence of its conception, philosophy, nature and orientation. Urban geography today encompasses and interfaces with various disciplines which are interested in urban studies. As an introduction to this series, our task here is to make an attempt to briefly review the development of geographical interest in various aspects of cities.

There are several reviews of the early development of urban geography which have been dealt with by Berry and Harton (1970)[1] and Carter (1974).[2] Berry and Harton in their book, **Geographical Perspective on Urban System**, have made an attempt to introduce readers to its present-day status. They have clearly resolved that "the formative years of the social science in the late nineteenth century and early twentieth century were also the years in which urban studies first developed,"[3] thus providing the context for geography's emerging interest in cities. However, the emergence of urban studies dates back to the writings of Greek scholars, but as a sub-discipline, it has reached its present-day status only in the past 30 years.

In their historical perspective the works on urban geography show that the pre-20th century studies primarily concerned themselves with themes of location, size and shape of the cities. The initial findings were strongly subjective, descriptive and dependent more on observation such as the works of Hassert (1907)[4] and Blanchard (1911).[5] In the succeeding years the conceptual framework of site and situation was criticized by Aurousseau (1924)[6] and Crowe (1938)[7], their conception being that cities were not inanimate objects in landscape, but also organic elements which involved people and their movements. The morphologist, later in 1960, truly brought the indigenous line of evolution in the sphere of urban geography and studies on the build-up fabric of cities (Conzone, 1960).[8] Smails (1955)[9] constituted the prime base of urban geography, which remained articulated without any major conceptual change till early 1960s. The studies on the morphological aspects of the urban system were influenced by external forces, consequently the methodological frameworks got impetus within the discipline. At this juncture the evolution of concepts was not based on environment but took shelter under the umbrella of economics of location, and incorporated analysis of land values and rents, and the concept of nodality and accessibility. These concepts were derived from the economic theories of Cooley (1394)[10], Weber (1899),[11] and Hurd (1903).[12]

The Chicago School of Urban Ecology hastened the evolution of urban geography. In his monumental work Park (1925)[13] developed the idea of order and analysis of towns. Further, a powerful thrust and much of the rationale was provided to the studies of urban geography by the Central Place Theory of Christallar (1933).[14]

The impact of the statistical method was powerful and it brought rapid and enormous changes in the field of urban geography. It also brought new insights into the development and application of urban geography towards increased quantification. Brian J. Berry, a pioneer in the field, analysed the spatial order, size and location of towns and cities. There was widespread use of innovative techniques to explore the nature of urban problems, hypotheses were tested, new theories propounded and old theories remodelled. The statistical methods were put to a variety of uses. Smith (1965)[15] evaluated the classification of settlements; Berry and Garrison (1956)[16] examined the utility of the rank-size rule for urban populations. The models of Park and Burgess (1925),[17] Harris and Ullman (1945)[18] and Homar Hoyt (1939)[19] were tested and re-examined by various geographers.

A new impetus to urban geography came from social area analysis which was initially propounded by Shevky and Bell (1955)[20] and later on this provided a basis for factorial ecology. The collaboration of this stream in urban geography was offered by Berry (1971)[21], Herbert (1972)[22] and Johnston (1971).[23] As a consequence of these thrusts in geography after

1960, the techniques of investigation were sharpened and this has provided the basis for a scientific explanation of cities. Attempts were made to introduce new theories and frame laws to make the explanation of events more rational and logical. Sophisticated models were propounded as urban geography entered a new era of rationalizing the subject matter of urban studies on the basis of new philosophies, new concepts, new theories, new methodologies and applications.

However, the status of contemporary urban geography has been elevated only recently by the behavioural approach. The studies of perception and cognition which have a long tradition in physiology were first introduced into the field of geography by Lynch (1960)[24] Dowson and Stea (1973)[25], Gould and White (1974).[26] At present there is a sudden spurt in the studies on the subject with a new paradigm. But the full impact of behavioural approaches upon urban geography has yet to be realized.

The aim of this series is to seek reorientation of the discipline strengthened by new philosophies, methodologies, subject matters or application. The series has been arranged in such a way that all contemporary viewpoints are covered comprehensively. Hopefully, this series will inspire researchers to appreciate the work already done by geographers in studying cities. Geography by nature seems to be a synthesizing field of inquiry. As such we have made an endeavour to combine some of the otherwise disparate facts garnered by other disciplines in such a manner that we can gain a better understanding of the urban system. The study of urban geography is essential if we are to analyse the human consequences of the settlements in which we live. It is useful to planners, decision makers in government and corporations and also to each one of us as citizens. Finally, it gives us a perspective on what may be happening to our cities and to the nature.

To achieve the above goal only those contributions with originality and contrasting viewpoints were selected for inclusion in this series. In doing so the editor does not wish to compete with the journals in the field in which innovative research and methodological aspects are presented. But he does wish to convey, and convey with conviction, that significant researches are being undertaken in the different branches of urban geography and in other allied disciplines. The present series is an attempt to provide a selective reappraisal and rigorous examination of the assumptions and the urge to disseminate new knowledge created by the mutual interaction. Emphasis is also placed on the conceptualization and theorization of the subject matter so that general laws may emerge. A conscious effort has been made to organize the series in such a way that it reflects the philosophical approach parallel to that of the behavioural school. Finally, a vigorous attempt has been made to demonstrate throughout the series how geographers are basically involved in solving the urban problems.

C. S. YADAV

## REFERENCES


1. Berry and Harton, **Geographic Perspectives on Urban Systems: With Integrated Readings**, New Jersey, Prentice Hall, Inc, Englewood Cliffs, 1970.
2. Carter, **The Study of Urban Geography**, Edward Arnold, London, 1974.
3. Berry and Harton, 1970.
4. Hassert, K., **Die Stadte Geographisch Betrachect**, Leipzig, 1907.
5. Blanchard, R., **Grenoble: Etude de Geographic Urbanine**, Paris, 1911.
6. Aurousseau, M., "Recent Contributions to Geography: A Review," **Geographical Review**, 1924, 14, p.444.
7. Crowe, P.R., "On Progress in Geography," **Scottish Geographical Magazine**, 1938, 54,1-19.
8. Conzone, M.R.G., "The Plan Analysis of an English City Centre," Ink. Norkorg (Ed), **Proceedings of I.G.U. Symposium on Urban Geography**, C.W.K. Gleerup, Lund, 1962.
9. Smails, A.E., "The Urban Mess of England and Wales," **Transactions and Papers**, Institute of British Geographers, 1946, 11, 85, p.101.
10. Cooley, C.H., "The Theory of Transportation," **Publications of the American Economic Association**, 1894, 9, p.5-7.
11. Weber, A.F., The **Growth of Cities in the Nineteenth Century: A Study in Statistics**, New York, 1899.
12. Hurd, R., **Principles of City Land Values: New York Record and Guide**, 1903, p.19-21.
13. Park, R.E., "Suggestions for the Investigation of Human Behaviour in an Urban Environment," in R.E. Park, E.W. Burgess, R.D. Mackenzie (eds), **The City**, University of Chicago Press, 1925.
14. Christallar, W., **Central Place in Southern Germany**, Gustar Fischer, Teno, 1933.
15. Smith, R.M.T., "Method and Purpose in Functional Town Classification," **Annals of the Association of American Geographers**, 1965, 55, pp.539-548,
16. Carrison, W.L., "Applicability of Statistical Inference to

Geographical Research," **Geographical Review**, 1956, 46, 427, 429.

17. Burgess, E.W., "The Growth of City," in R.E. Park, E.W. Burgess and R.D. Mackenzie (eds), **The City**, University of Chicago Press, 1925.
18. Ullman, E.L., "The Nature of Cities," **Annals**, American Academy of Political and Social Science, 1945, 242, 7-17.
19. Hoyt, H., **The Structure and Growth of Residential Neighbourhoods in American Cities**, Washington, Federal Housing Administration, 1939.
20. Shevky, E. and Bell, W., **Social Area Analysis**, Stanford University Press, Stanford, 1955.
21. Berry, B.J.L. (ed), "Comparative Factorial Ecology," **Economic Geographic (Supplement)**, 1971,47.
22. Herbert, D.T., **Urban Geography: A Social Perspective**, David and Charles, Newton Abbot, 1972.
23. Johnston, **Urban Residential Pattern**, Bell, London, 1971.
24. Lynch, **Image of the City**, Massachusetts, Cambridge, 1960.
25. Dowson and Stea, "Image and Environment", Chicago and London, 1973.
26. Gould and White, R., **Mental Maps**, London, 1974.

**ACKNOWLEDGEMENTS**

We Thank Editors Gerd-Michael Hellstern, Frithjof Spreer Hellmut Wollmann, **Heft 2 Vol. II and III** for their permission to use material from "Applied Urban Research", Proceedings of the European Meeting on Applied Urban Research, Essen, 2-4, Oct. 1981.

## CONTENTS

**SECTION TWO**
**Slumification in Third World Cities**

## LIST OF CONTRIBUTORS

**Pushpa Agnihotri**: Lecturer in Geography, Government Post-Graduate College, Hoshangabad (M.P.) (India).

**Joseph P. Beaton**: Assistant Professor, Department of Geography, University of Denver, Denver, Colorado-80208

**K. S. O. Beavon**: Department of Geography and Environmental Studies, University of the Witwatersrand, 1, Jan Smuts Avenue, Johannesburg, South Africa-2001.

**Hermann Borghorst**: Geisbergstr. 11, 1000 Berlin 30 (West Germany).

**DeWitt Davis, Jr.**: Department of Elementary Education, University of Arkansas at Pine Bluff, Pine Bluff, Arkansas-71601.

**Eberhard von Einem**: Institut fur Stadtforschung, Berlin, Schoneberger Ufer 65, 1000, Berlin 30

**Andreas Falke**: Seminar Wissenschaft von Der Plitik Georg-August Universitaet Goetting Center for Urban Programmes, Saint Louis University, U.S.A.

**Farhat Gulzar**: Assistant Professor, Department of Geography, Punjab University, New Campus, Lahore (Pakistan).

**Lutz Holzner**: University of Wisconsin, Milwaukee

**Detlev Ipsen**: University of Kacsel.

**Kevin C. Kearns**: Associate Professor of Geography, University of Northern Colorado, Greeley, Co 80639

**Jean-Paul Levy**: Maitre Assistant, Universite de Toulouse Le Mirail, 109, Bis rue Vauguelin, 31081, Toulouse Cedex (France)

**S. Gregory Lipton**: University of Kansas and HUD, U.S.A.

**Peter Marcuse**: University of Columbia, New York

**H. S. Mathur**: Assistant Professor, Department of Geography, University of Rajasthan, Jaipur (India).

**Nicholas N. Patricios**: Professor and Director, University of Miami, Coral Gobles, Florida-33124

**B. Guy Peters** : Center for Public Policy Studies, Tulane University, U.S.A.

**C. M. Rogerson**: Department of Geography and Environmental Studies, University of the Witwatersrand, 1, Jan Smuts Avenue, Johannesburg, South Africa-2001.

**Rickie Sanders**: Department of Geography, Indiana University, Bloomington, Indiana-47401

**H. M. Saxena**: Department of Geography, Govt. Post-Graduate College, Sriganganagar, Rajasthan (India).

**Michael P. Smith**: Center for Public Policy Studies, Tulane University, U.S.A.

**D. S. Shrivastava**: Lecturer in Geography, University of Saugar, Sagar (M.P.) (India).

**C. S. Yadav**: Department of Geography, Bhagat Singh College, Delhi University, New Delhi (India).

ONE

C. S. Yadav

# INTRODUCTION

## SLUMS IN PERSPECTIVE

Twentieth century urbanization has brought in its wake an alarming, inevitable and persistent problem of slums. Slum life punctuates every city of the world. Today's metropolitan cities are in "widerness" and at the verge of "explosion" because of the "cancerous outgrowth" of the "misery belts" in the form of slums as a consequence of which cities are running into their sorry state. The problem of slums has become so massive and vital that it has compelled the attention of several social scientists, planners and administrators to the pathetic plight of their dewellers and the sub-human conditions prevailing in them.

## DEFINITION

The idea of slum is very variable. Many attractive diffinitions have been formulated, showing the need of precise, logical and concise definitions which may support the various dimensions of the "big beast". There is a wealth of conflicting opinions, with a detailed exposition of the vital problem of slums: methods of finding and defining, delimiting and describing. However, it is very difficult to reconcile them into one philosophy because the idea of a slum is so nebulous and is often so personal and peculiar to each social scientist that they have agreed not to agree to a common, single definition of the slum. Thus the prevalent definitions of a slum have not succeeded in offering a satisfactory answer. Nevertheless, they have certainly thrown some light on how the idea has grown, varied, has been adopted and distorted.

It is from this observation that our prime concern arises to find out a most desirable, common and authoritative definition of a slum and what constiutes a slum. It is an acceptable fact that a comprehensive and logical or empirical definition of a slum is of considerable value to the local authorities and researchers to determine which part of the city should be declared as a slum and taken up for improvement. From the following discussion it seems that irrespective of the diverse opinions about the definition of a slum, there is common agreement on the dictum that a slum is an area in which the social and physical environment is so unhealthy as to constitute a menace to every aspect of wellbeing be, it physical, mental, social or psychological. However, looking at the evidence, it has become quite obvious that different cities or regions have different notions and every city has its own nomenclature for its slums. Some examples of the many local terms are: Bustees in Calcutta, Jhuggis and Jhonpris in Delhi; Cheris and Chawls in Bombay. In Latin America they are known as Jaealas or Colonias proletarias, in Mexico as Favelas, Mocanihas, Algados or Vilasde Maloras in Brazil as Calumpass, in Chile as Buessosairies Barrios clandetinos and in Colombia and Peru as in Andra Chos Miserias. Relatively recently sociologists have coined some terms such as "Blight Areas", "Renewal Areas", "Deteriorated Areas", "Gray areas", "Lower Class Neighbourhood ", "Low Income Areas", and "Innercore Areas". Apart from these terms and adjectives labelled to designate slums, there are some academic terms also, such as "Marginal Areas", "Transitional Areas", "Uncontrolled Settlements", "Spontaneous Settlements", "Substandard Settlement", "Unplanned Settlements", "Provisional", "Unconventional" and "Autonomous Settlements". Thus any attempt to summarize all these characteristics is bound to get into trouble, some fundamentals would be untouched, some principles would overlap. Some may even ask, Well then, what to call it? The word "Slum" has been long in use, almost since the 18th century when it was used as a term for squalid housing in densely populated districts of industrial cities. Eric Patridge (1958) in his A Short Etymological Dictionary of Modern English[1] reveals that the word slum probably originated from "slumber" which apparently had been conceived by a majority of scholars as unkown back streets or alleys which were wrongly presumed to be "sleepy" and "quiet". Some of the popular definitions reflect emotional attitudes towards slums. These value laden terms emphasized the seamy aspects of a slum, its filth and squalor, its poor social conditions and presence of vicious characters Marshal B. Clinard. (1966)[2]. These old value-laden, less scientific and imprecise descriptions of a slum have, however, provided a better impression of the reality. John Robertson (1920)[3] fully supports this and has commented that, "A town slum may be structurally good and yet, from its darkened surroundings and its filthy environment, absence of free air supply, its soot-laden atmosphere, it may be one of the most unwholesome dwellings".

A brief historical review of the study of slums indicates that the definition of a slum has anticedents stretching over many years. There have been many volumes which have made a positive contribution in the right perspective. One of the monumental studies is that of Ford (1936)[4] who has provided a comprehensive definition of the word "slum". A slum tends to be defined in terms of more or less accurately observed consequences. To conform to contemporary usage, the emphasis instead should be upon conditions of structure, age and upkeep. We may, therefore, better define a "blighted district as any area in which the large majority of buildings, whether commercial, industrial or residential, are old and in which fundamental repairs are no longer being made. Any area of deteriorating housing in which there is poor upkeep of houses and premises is a lighted district and a potential slum. Any area of old, neglected and deteriorating housing is a slum as soon as it becomes insantitary or otherwise injurious to its occupants".

These definitions of Ford undeniably explicitly generalize too broadly the physical characteristics of a slum in the city. There seems to be a complete lack of social and economic elements which are so vital in their influence. Nevertheless, the definition of a slum as a common indicator of reality is given in the Oxford University Dictionary (1955)[5] as "a street, alley, court, etc., situted in a crowded district of a town or city and is inhabited by people of low income classes or by very poor. A number of these streets and alleys forming a thickly populated neighbourhood of a squalid and wretched character".Socio logists of the Chicago school, in the 1920s, implied that slums are social units. Harvey Zorbough (1929)[6], an eminent socio logist of this school, has made a significant contribution towards the difinition of a slum. He states with conviction that, "The common denominator of the slum is its submerged aspects and its detachment from the city as a whole. The slum is a bleak area of segregation of the sediments of society, an area of extreme poverty, tenements, ramshakle buildings of eviction and evaded rents, an area of working mothers and children, of high rates of birth, infant mortality, illegitimacy and death, an area of pawn shops and second-hand stores, of gangs, of flops . . . slum is an area which has reached the limit of decay and is on the verge of reorganization . . . The slum harbours many sorts of people, the criminal, the radical, the bohemian, the migratory workers, the immigrants, the unsuccessful, the queer and the unadjusted.

The above difinition has led to confusion and misguided

action. The latter part of the definition speaks too strongly about the slums as a place of social evil which is not the right perspective universally accepted. Commonsense knowledge of slums of the Third World clearly shows that all slum areas are not vice areas.

The conference summoned by President Hoover (Ford 1936)[7] in 1931 on "House Building and Home Ownership" defined slums as residential areas where "a mass of more or less non-descript individual houses, tenements, stables, dilapidated shops, an absence of paint, accumulation of dirty tin cans and rubbish . . . malodour intermingled with the smell of decaying matter... A slum was considered "as the abode of half-starved, filthil clothed children, of diseased and criplled individuals, a place of poverty, wretchedness, ignorance and vice". It further speaks about the slum "as a recession from the normal standard of sound society". It also says that a slum is "a distinct area of disorganization and disintegration". These definitions are contrary to the present day definitions which do not consider the slum as a place of decaying and dilapidated houses, filthy alleys and streets, nor an area where the number of uncared for children and poverty-striken adults live. It is considered as more than an economic condition, it is a social phenomena in which the attitudes, ideas, ideals and practices play an important role. This conviction seems to come from the observation of David R. Hunter (1968)[8] who thought that, "Slum is more than a crowded building, it is more than the dirty streets, the lack-llustre people sitting on the stems, the shrieking children running up and down, the sullen boys hanging at the corners, the stupefied addits leaning against... It is a way of life and it run on a way of looking at the future or is perhaps looking away from it".

More recently some vigorous attempt has been made to define a slums by many committees commissions and individuals who have analysed the real perspective of the slums. Some feel that a slum is more than an aggregation of buildings and people. They argue on its identity in relation to urban change and growth. It may be an interstitial area of apparently static character, surrounded by areas in the process of change or in time perspective. It may be a habitation area in between a former better use and a coming new use of the space. Thus only recently, the attitude towards the slum problem has undergone a considerable change. Despite the fact that slums are the locus of poverty, the people of these settlements make a substantial contribution to the economy of the urban places. It is rather ridiculous to think that they do not have a sense of community and a stimulation for social improvement as indicated in a report of the U.N.[9] that "slums and squatters are uncontrolled settlements whose marginal inhabitants are not fully integrated, socially and economically, into the development process". This statement about slum community is a rather subjective generalization. It reflects that slum-dwellers are not capable to contribute in terms of stimulation to econmic growth, intellectual leadership, scientific or cultural creativity. They are considered just plain citizens. Neverthless, John R. Seely[10] has remarked and most truely analysed the role of slum dwellers. "The slum is not just a dumping ground, nor just a way station in the city, it also is a provider of goods and services that are demanded by non-slum population". In this respect slum-dwellers are required for the survival of the affluent society becuase they render services to these communities. It is, therefore, very wrong to assert that slum inhabitants are passive workers. rather they are actually engaged in the econmic and social development of the city. Shri Sri Prakasa,[11] a prominent citizen and one-time Governor of Bombay, in his inaugural address at a seminar on slum clearance in 1957, has said that "the slums with which we have to deal, generally speaking, are those that are formed by various humble folk who congregate in cities to supply the daily needs of the well-to-do and for which there are no strict regulations because of which their haphazard and unsatisfactory nature continues".

On the basis of available evidence it can be ascertained that slums are enormous pools of potential human and social resources and there is a high degree of resourcefulness in slum communities which is reflected by their invasion of vacant land, even remotely suitable, infiltration and successively moving to an area, adapting to a new environment, generally hostile, and socializing newcomers in the ways of city life. To ascertain the role of slums it has been found that slums are the areas where poverty-striken rural migrants find their first home at a cheaper rent, from where they begin a search for their work and employment and make necessary adjustments with the city life. It is a firm conviction that slums shelter all those who are rejected elsewhere for reasons of poverty and low socio-economic status. If this is so, then slums are the areas where the degraded, the destitute, the downtrodden and the outcaste get an opportunity to obtain a secure base so that they can face the large and highly diversified urban communities. Thus slums provide an identity and social base to the new coming migrants. The slums as such are considered as unique entities which are inhabited by communities with relatively young families, with a potential for economic growth and for long-term development, if they are not allowed to dissipate into helplessness. What is needed is a little motivation to make them aware about their potentialities which will rejuvenate and restructure social concepts and spark a chain of improvement among slum-dwellers.

It is very wrong to claim that slum-dwellers are not their own masters because their destiny is shaped by others. On the contrary, slums are defined as the areas of self-generating communities who strive to achieve a stable social life by adapting themselves to congestion, insanitation and to scant basic services. They build their homes themselves, they make a search for employment and try to stabilize themselves as far as possible. Thus, as a process, slums are a direct response to the lack of housing in the fast-growing cities where people choose and build their own shelters to save themselves from an inhospitable environment and obtain an identity. A slum is, therefore, in ecological terms, a process of invasion in which slum dwellers in groups invade vacant lands in the city and occupy them illegally. In terms of bare necessity inadequate housing breeds slums and slums are a blot on a city housing facilities which are due to the failure of the administrative efforts, lack of resources and forethought. Thus it is evident that slums are a man-made phenomena and are the unmistakable symbol of our neglect of a primary necessity: housing. The slums are nothing but only one part of human struggle for shelter.

All that has been said above only reveals that slum is an evaluative term and not an analytic concept. The definitions, however, reflect clearly the physical and social image of the slums. It is a well-established notion that slums are part and parcel of the city life. Their existence is not a curse for cities, rather with their specific functions the slum communities are a blessing in disguise for the elite and other strata of the city population, inasmuch as they provide a wide variety of services and contribute greatly to the survival of the rich. It is to be noted here that academicians while defining the term slum have adopted two distinct approaches: Traditional vs Environmental. The traditional approach highlights the negative and incomplete view and the environmental approach pertains to the way in which housing effort tries to shelter the shelterless. The first approach obviously deals with the insufficient standards and norms of modern housing units. It largely deals with the negative connotations of slums as "vice areas", "cancerous areas", "delinquent areas", etc., whereas the second approach envisages the ability of existing housing which facilitates access to areas where family activities occur daily. It demonstrates how adequately it provides protection from a hostile environment. In other words traditionalists are more aware of the appearance of the housing while environmentalists are concerned with the way in which housing accommodates the residents in relation to their situation (U.N.).

## NATURE AND CHARACTER OF SLUMS

There are various characteristic features of a slum: its appearance, economic status, overcrowding, congestion, health and sanitary conditions, morals, ways of living, attitudes, isolation and permanancy. Although most definitions have pointed out that slum areas are punctuated by inadequate housing, insufficient structural and basic amenities, overcrowding and congestion, to a large extent, however, it is a community in process, it is a way of living and moreover it is a sub-system in a large urban system which is characterized by attributes of poverty, insanitation, deviant behavior and social isolation and apathy. The people who live in slums are looked down upon by the so-called elite people, they are considered inferior, socially outcaste and, administratively, are kept out of the power structure. Furthermore, slums in their eyes harbour suspicious characters and as such these are designated as "evil areas" and "vice areas". But alas, slum is a child of our own wrong doings. What are you going to do about it? is the buruing problem of today. It is high time for a researcher to think that the negative connotations which envisage something evil have to be shunned, the derogatory terms and adjectives avoided, and one has to look at the problem with an open mind and with a broad outlook.

## HOUSING CONDITIONS

The physical appearance of slums has been most often characterized by its aspects of housing and street patterns. In most of the slums housing is crowded, neglected, old, deteriorated and obsolete. The buildings are poorly arranged, there is inadequate lighting and air circulation, there is poor architectural design, lack of sanitary facilities and a general deficiency of civic amenities. There is poor maintenance of the buildings; the condition is further aggravated when among the buildings are the shacks, corrugated-tin and thatch-and-mud huts. This shows that slum housing the world over is not fit for human habitation. Some of the following examples of physical conditions of the slums give us a clearer picture of the reality that exists. Frederick Engels (1936)[12] evaluated the conditions in Manchester in the following way: "The streets are generally unpaved, rough, dirty, filled with vegetable and animal refuse, without sewers and gutters but supplied with foul stagnant pools instead. Moreover ventilation is impeded by the bad confused method of building of the whole quarter, and since many human beings here live crowded into a small space the atmosphere that prevails in these working man's quarters may readily be imagined." Another example with a bitter impression is offered by John Robertson[13]: "A town slum dwelling may be structurally good and yet from its darkened surroundings, its absence of free air supply, its soot-laden atmosphere and its filthy environment, it may be one of the most unwholesome dwellings." B. S. Toron Roe (1928)[14] further substantiates the existing reality by evaluating thus, "windows dirty, broken and patched with white or brown paper, curtains dirty and frayed and blinds half drawn. The street doors are open, showing bare passages and stairs lacking hannisters while door jambs are generally brown with dirt and rubbed shiny by the coats of the leisured class, whose habit is to lean up against them".

A comprehensive account of slum dwellings with an appropriate degree of fitness for human habitation is given in the U.S. Census of Housing, (1960)[15]: "Dilapidated housing does not provide safe and adequate shelter. It has one or more critical defects or has a combination of intermediate defects in sufficient number to require extensive repair of buildings, or is of inadequate original construction, critical defects resulting from continued neglect or lack of repairs indicating serious damage to structure...."

The deteriorating housing needs more repair than would be provided in the course of reguler maintenance. It has one or more defects of intermediate nature that must be corrected if the units are to continue to provide safe and adequate shelter. The deterioration and dilapidation of buildings make the area unwholesome because such type of buildings are a menace to health, safety, morality or welfare of the occupants. They pose the danger of collapse during hostile weather. The cracks and holes in the buildings harbour rats, reptiles, lizards and dirty insects which make a living horrible. Thus this type of housing is most undesirable and needs correction Mumfold (1961).[16]

## OVERCROWDING AND CONGESTION

Most of the slums of the world are characterized by overcrowding and congestion. Overcrowding in a broader sense means accumulation of small buildings in an area whereas congestion denotes overcrowding of people in buildings. Congestion is the key housing factor that produces a profound effect on the slum communities in various ways. There are three distinct physiological consequences of overcrowding: (i) challenge to the sense of individuality, (ii) challenge to the child's illusions about other people, and (iii) challenge to any illusion about sex.

The inadequacy of housing has a profound effect on the physique of slum dwellers. Fatigue and lack of sleep are the visible symptoms of inadequate housing which causes irritation and wastage of energy. Slum dwellers, due to lack of space, spend most of their free time outside the house which seriously jeopardizes the home life. Inadequate housing seriously affects the behaviour of children. Obviously, the slum children are uncontrolled, indisciplined, violent and do not pursue their studies, and are observed to be in open rebellion against their parents. Also inadequate housing creates a lot of stress and strain in the minds of slum dwellers as a consequence of which there are frequent quarrels between husband and wife. Thus overcrowding puts many obstacles in the path of a sound personality or moral growth. This seriously affects their privacy. In other words, inadequate housing greatly hinders a slum dweller's chances of orientation towards individual responsibility and achievement. A real picture of this apathy is outlined by Charles Abram (1964)[17]: "In Delhi above 400,000 people live to a square mile, whereas in Bombay tenements ten persons are crowded in a room of ten to fifteen square feet. In Panama, shelters bulge at the seams with as many as twenty people in a room of fifteen square feet. In Kingston, Jaimaica, nine people may live in a simple tiny hut six by ten feet. In Accra, Ghana, occupany per single house in 1960 was 19.3 people and it was even higher in Kumasi. In Hong Kong five or six human beings share single cubicles measuring forty square feet."

## NEIGHBOURHOOD FACILITIES

The sub-standard housing is inevitably correlated with inadequate basic and civic amenities. In slums the stagnant water or open drains add bad odour and create pollution. The heaps of rubbish and garbage make the environment of the locality unhealthy. In slum localities of developing countries there is no electricity and there is a shortage of bathrooms, latrines and other sanitary facilities. Innumerable people share one water tap which leads to frequent quarrelling among ladies. Common latrines are shared by hundreds of families. In some localities where there are no public latrines, the night soil remains accumulated for weeks. Charles Abram (1964) illustrated the consequences of these inadequcies thus: "In Lagos, Nigeria, for example, 85 per cent of 4,759 schoolchildren whose stools were examined were found to be infected with intestinal parasites, roundworms and hookworms." He further demonstrates that "dysentery and diarrhoea accounted for 10 per cent of all deaths in Nigeria's capital city which occurred among children under the age of five".

## POOR SANITATION AND HEALTH

A universal characteristic of most of the slums is their spoil outlook due to dirty, unclean surroundings. Most of the slum dwellers who are rural migrants have brought their inherited quality of adapting themselves to insanitary conditions. Insanitation causes ill health. Due to prevalent dirt, heaps of garbage and refuse on the roadside there is an acute respiratory infection amongst the dwellers. Due to lack of toilets, infectious diseases like measles, chickenpox, whooping cough and some minor digestive diseases are most common in slum areas. It is a truism that mortality rates are quite high in these areas as compared to those which are cleaner.

## POVERTY

The substandard housing and poverty are interlinked and interrelated concepts. Slum is the locus of poverty (Hunter) and poverty determines the personality of slum dwellers. It is a denial of self-respect, privacy and the enlargement of the self; moreover because of poverty slum-dwellers are socially degraded, disorganized and excluded from the normal community. Poverty always correlates to a high degree of incidence of illness and death, mental illness, juvenile and adult delinquency. The causation goes from poverty to bad morals, mental and physical health.

## ATTITUDE TOWARDS SLUMS

There is no doubt that the slums of our cities, no matter how they are defined, are percieved to be a problem. Here the question arises to what extent it is necessary to regard slums as a problem even though majority of the slum-dwellers opt to live in such areas and are content to remain there. In the first place, "The problem is thus primarily a state of mind D. A. Kirby, (1976)".[18] It seems it is a situation that worries members of society either as individuals or groups. Thus the problem exists only when it is perceived. Second, the slum problem may be perceived differently by different individuals and different sectors of society.

Friedman (1967)[19] proposes that in majority of the countries a slum is perceived as a problem by at least three groups of people--those, possibly a minority, who live in the slum areas and the local and national governments. Each of these groups perceives the slum problem quite differently. Those who live in the slum itself perceive the slum as a problem by focussing their attention on the deficiencies in the living standards and the comforts, on the stigma and pain associated with life in a slum. The non-slum dwellers see the slum as a threat both to them as individuals and to society to which they belong. They visualize slum as the breeding ground for crime, violence, disease and other anti-social disorders. According to Friedman government's, perception of the slum problem is a reaction to the problem as perceived by the electorate.

## ABOUT THE VOLUME

Despite technological innovations urban renewal programmes and rapid suburbanization, slums remain a persistent problem of the major cities of the world. The aim of this volume is, therefore, to examine their nature and residential obsolescence, the processes that cause occurrence and socio-economic consequences of renewal programmes. The volume is divided into two sections. Section I introduces the problem of slums in the Western countries and contains those articles which provide to readers a critical review of the major empirical and theoretical research into slum housing and residential renewal and neighbourhood revitalization. In this section attention is focussed on the conflicting attitudes towards housing renewal and urban decline in developed countries. Section II presents case studies of slums in Pakistan and India. The intention is that the study will provide an empirical analysis of certain factors and theories in different cultural groups. This Section will also provide the reader with an insight into the difficulties involved in resolving the slum problems.

Accordingly, Section I is introduced by an article by Joseph P. Beaton entitled, "The Problematic Assessment of Urban Blight". In this he ascertains that virtually every city in the world has at least one sector that might be labelled as "blighted", and the focus of this paper is on the meaning of the urban blight, the nature of blight perception and the consequences of an official public pronouncement that an urban area is blighted. The author feels that the term blight is complicated in that during the past few years it has experienced many different applications. Many a scholar has made liberal use of the term blight without actually defining it. However, the author in this paper has made a vigorous attempt to provide a comprehensive definition of the term. He has tried to demonstrate that a public blight declaration is most effective when it is rendered in conjunction with a realistic revitalization or redevelopment scheme.

Peter Marcuse, in his article, "The decline of cities in the United States: Inevitable or Deliberate", clearly reveals that many older central cities in the United States show evidence of serious decay, with declining public services, abandoned housing, high unemployment and all the problems that accompany these phenomena. The policies of the current administration are based on an explanation of this decay that sees it as the inevitable accompaniment of inevitable technological and economic changes. Policies consequently should be designed not to fight, but to take into account such decay. The contrast with European developments and policies is striking indeed. The explanation for the contrast lies not in differences in the underlying forces or trends, which are indeed the same internationally, but in differences in explicit government policies, in turn accounted for by differences in the constellations of forces determining such policies. Some details of how government policies in the USA lead to the decay of certain cities are provided.

During the 1970's millions of Americans have moved from cities in the industrial North West and Mid West to the so-called sunbelt states in the South and South West of the country. The population migration has been accompanied by an equally hasty south Ward mobility of industrial, wholesale and retail firms and other service establishment. The author Lutz Holzner in his article "Cultural Foundations for the Decline of American Cities", expects that the North South migration will swell during the current decade and may assume the character prosperous and booming cities such as Boston, New York, Detroit or Chicago are caught in the demographic squeese and can afford to maintain only intolerably minimal staffs on their police, fire fighter, and refuse collector operations. The author analyses, the effects of national character and cultural foundation and improvisation, greed and profiteering and violence for the constant decline of American cities.

Today the need to tackle the problems of the inner city is keenly felt and the demand for improvement is not new. In 19th century industrial towns, the deterioration in the living, working and environmental conditions has resulted in widespread social unrest. The possibility that discontent of the urban poor would turn to something more dangerous in the absence of improvement in health and housing made commentators anxious. They feared violence and possible revolutionary consequences of appalling living conditions reacting to this situation. N. N. Patricios, in his article, "Consensual and Conflict Perspective of Inner City Decline and Revitalization", outlined the problems of decline in inner city residential areas. He has briefly described the different approaches to how to tackle the problem in an effective manner. The process of decline and revitalization are then examined from the point of view of two theoretical perspectives, Consensual Theory and Conflict Theory. Because of the difficulties with the consensual perspective of decline and revitalization, a planning strategy based on the conflict perspective is proposed.

The revitalization of declining and deteriorated inner city neighbourhoods is a stated political goal in most of the Western industrialized nations, as is the minimization of its social costs. Eberhardvon Einem, in his article, "Comparing Urban Revitalization in the United States and West Germany", postulates that the revitalization of declining and deteriorated inner city neighbourhoods is a stated political goal in most of the urban industrialized nations. In this paper the author concentrates on and examines urban revitalization in two countries, the United States and West Germany. First, the author compares private market revitalization including the demographic characteristics of the "renovators" and the factors influencing the level of private market renovations. Secondly, the author discusses public policies employed in the two countries that aim at stimulating rehabilitation and coping with displacement.

The transformation of community organizations, representing the poorest areas of American cities, into community development corporations in the aftermath of the war on poverty is probably the clearest indication that community mobilization is not sufficient to revitalize the ghetto. Protest and confrontation tactics serve well to get the attention of the public. The media, the politician and an unresponsive bureaucracy never consider poor and minority residents as equal partners in clientele relationships. Andreas Falke, in his article, "Community Mobilization: A Strategy For Inner-City Revitalization: The Recent U.S. Experience", assesses the role of community organizations in the process of inner city revitalization in the USA with reference to community development corporations, and argues that the outright use of mobilization tactics has markedly declined as the Community Development Corporations (CDC) have moved into programme development, but their contribution to city revitalization has been small. Since much of the recent community-based organizational activity has to be understood in the light of private market investment, attention is focussed on groups that want to take advantage of the reinvestment, but are determined to protect the interests of lower-income residents too. Far more typical and widespread than organizational activity pursuant to gentrification displacement conflict, it is argued that these groups play a crucial role in bringing about a socially balanced revitalization.

Yet another attempt about revitalization is made by Michael P. Smith and B. Guy Peters, who in their paper, "The Uses of Neighbourhood Revitalization", seek to clarify the competing and sometimes contradictory meanings that have been given to the concept of "Neighbourhood Revitalization" in the literature on urban politics, administration and planning. Neighbourhoods are at once social areas, areas of collective consumption and social service delivery, units of political organization and focal points of the political economy of urban land use. Proponents of Neighbourhood Revitalization often differ on the functions of urban neighbourhoods that they would build into revitalized neighbourhoods. The possible forms of neighbourhood economic development can be arranged along a continuum from the neighbourhood as a laboratory for an indigenous economic entrepreneurship to the neighbourhood as a focus of a plan to redistribute resources geographically to low-income locales. Normative models of neighbourhood social development range from Richard Sennelt's conflictual "Survival Community", promising personal growth through conflict and risk, to the subjective security of the classical folk community. Models of neighbourhood political development range from class analytical treatments of the urban neighbourhoods as the emergent arena of social movement policies and class conflict to more conservative views of the neighbourhood as an instrumental of social control calls for neighbourhood decentralization by organizational theorists also can be arranged along this continuum of change and stability. Proponents of greater administrative equity and responsiveness envisage local neighbourhood organizations as potential bureaucratuc clientele groups capable of generating dmeands and supports for new models of urban service delivery. At the other end of the spectrum advocates of greater administrative efficiency accept existing urban services, but to seek to deliver them more efficiently through neighbourhood decentralization. The authors suggest that stable and dynamic ends should not be confused with stable and dynamic means. Some dynamic changes may be undertaken for the purpose of stablizing a community. For example, in a destabilized neighbourhood undergoing forced relocation, it may be necessary to employ dynamic means in order to produce stable neighbourhoods. Conversely, the dynamic changes in economic development by entrepreneurship may have extremely destablizing effects on a community. After comparing and contrasting several salient perspectives on neighbourhood development policy is, of course, a political question. The incompatabilities of values, goals and theories of social development that underly the competing models of neighbourhood revitalization suggest that the issue will remain conflictual and politically problematic for the foreseable future.

Demographers and urban researchers have reported on the movement of people from the centre of cities to the suburbs. There is a conflicting trend that middle class people are moving to the central city neighbourhoods who fix up the housing, increase demand for housing and determine housing prices. This trend has resulted in a conflict between some classes with the high incomes and the indigenous poor population. Gregory Lipton in his article, "The Future Central City: Gentrified or Abandoned", reveals the fact that displacement of minorities and low income individuals has been reported in the popular Press and in a number of scholarly case studies. Whether displacement is a major national problem or limited to a number of isolated neighbourhoods is the subject of national debate. Urban scholars point to a decreasing overall demand for central city properties and an overall decrease in the number of white individuals living in the Central City to discount the significance of the reports of displacement. This article analyses both migration by race and housing trends in central cities. The analysis proceeds from nationally aggregated data to central city level data. It is argued that while the population is decreasing in central cities, the number of middle class individuals is increasing in many central city neighbourhoods and the number of available housing units is decreasing. This is increasing the competition for existing units. If these trends continue and overall housing costs continue to increase, displacement is likely to become widespread.

Squatting is most commonly associated with developing countries in which rural-to-urban migration has led to the creation of shantytown type settlements on the urban periphery. However, squatting is now well advanced in Great Britain, Italy, France, Denmark and the Netherlands and it is increasing in Sweden and West Germany. Kevin C. Kearns, in his article, "Intra-Urban Squatting in London", demonstrates that intra-urban squatting in the Western industrialized society differs significantly from Third World squatting. As a human adaptive mechanism for coping with intensified housing stress this variant involves the occupation, renovation and revitalization of existing inner urban buildings. It serves a practical function in urban ecology and conservation and is increasingly accepted by housing authorities on its economic merits. Squatting in Britain emerged a decade ago, closely paralleling similar movements in other European countries. London, where the squatter population has grown to 30,000, has become the quintessential model. Squatting has become a viable alternative form of tenure which fills a distinctive gap in London's increasingly exclusive housing structure.

Squats may be typed according to their ownership, legal status and mode of habitation. Large squatting communities often function democratically and have an enduring, stable social organization. Some squatter communities are authorized and eventually become legal housing corporations with permanent Institutionalized sociology and with it, the minority theory is regarded as the reaction of liberal Americans in the middle and upper classes to the problem connected with immigration, urbanization and industrialization. The preoccupation of German authors with minorities is also linked to the concern about social conflicts. As history shows discrimination of individuals for a long duration because of a certain group afflliation or more precisely because of the common characteristics of this group which became the source of discrimination leads to a social conflict. If no possible solutions can be found the accumulation of unsolved problems can give rise to social dynamite which could shake the foundations of our society. Deltev Ipsen, in his article, "Housing Conditions and Interests of Foreign Workers in the Federal Republic of Germany", treats foreigners as minority. While analysing the character of foreigners the author's perspective is limited to an individualizing view of social facts. The author concentrates on five relevant themes within the frame of the minority theory. (In Section I, a short description is given of the particular disadvantage of the foreign worker as regards housing conditions.) Secondly, the author examines as to what extent the situation of deprivation is a question of time which can be solved by the ability of the Individual to adapt. Thirdly, the author explores whether or not the housing situation is accepted by those concerned and wether the situation can ultimately be traced back to particular cultural standards. Fourthly, the author evaluates some of the mechanisms of deprivation and raises the question whether the mechanisms are particular to the group of foreign workers or not. Finally, the author incorporates the foreigners' housing situation into the stratified structure of the general housing provision.

For years, many economists who were and are a part of the neoclassical school have strongly advocated human capital and marginal productivity. In recent years much has been written regarding labour market segmentation in the United States and other more developed countries with similar economic structures. The formal and informal labour market theory applied to the less developed countries of Africa, Asia and Latin America is a similar form of labour market segmentation. Dewitt Davis and Rickies Sanders in their article, "Employment Problems for Blacks: Labour Segmentation and Different Geographic Scales", put forth the idea that there is a need to analyse the causes of illegal employment and migration among the blacks at different geographic scales by utilizing the structure of the formal and informal labour activites carried out in most less developed countries compared to the most developed countries. The paper is constructed around the black population because that group has the largest unemployment problem.

The authors in this paper indentify that during the 1960s and 1970s unemployment and underemployment among the minorities and women have been one of the paramount problems which the American society has faced and continues to struggle with at the beginning of the 1980s. The paper focusses on the existence of unemployment specifically among the blacks inside and outside metropolitan areas, and regional differences in terms of migration. There is discussion and conceptualization of the dual labour market theory in relation to unemployment, illegal employment and migration. Constantly, the paper treats, in depth, the various circles in secondary and illegal employment. It also shows the parallel between the dual labour market in less developed countries and black urban and rural ghettos.

It is no doubt amusing to compare, as some writers have, the rehabilitation of the old neighbourhoods in France to an Spanish inn. Each potential protagonist, each social group, arrives with its own motives and intentions which are numerous and possibly contradictory. The policy of rehabilitation of old quarters/neighbourhoods offers today a line of observation of great interest in understanding the remoulding of local private protagonists in a national context no longer resembling that of 15 or 20 years ago. Jean Paul Lery, in his article, "The Rehabilitation of Town Centres and Old Quarters/Neighbourhoods in France", rationally interprets the rehabilitation plan of Toulouse in France. Section I of the paper deals with Toulouse background in terms of Urbanization, a slowing down process, development of the teritiary sector, the construction of neighbourhood and local urban politics. Section II deals with spontaneous private rehabilitation in terms of the "Rehabilitation Connection"; the local community in the face of rehabilitation. Section III deals with rehabilitation in Toulouse, interpretations.

Urban renewal started in many West German cities as well as in Berlin in the sixties after the removal of the large-scale war destruction. Extensive renewal projects, however, were carried out in the seventies on the basis of the urban promotion law of 1971. The resident participation in the planning process was a central component of this federal law. The purpose was to thereby increase the democratization of urban planning on the one hand and to secure a more efficient procedure on the other. Dr. Hermann Borghorst, in his paper, "Citizen Participation in Urban Renewal in Berlin", tries to postulate in Section I a new form of citizen participation in urban renewal. In Section II, the author interprets the experience with citizen participation in urban renewal. In section III the author has made an attempt to formulate strategies for Krensberg: Grassroot initiative. In Section IV the author summarizes his findings. The author has come to the conclusion that in a deteriorating neighbourhood a stable and active citizen with growing expertise arises, who in the process of a dialogue with the administration and experts is able to articulate and to successfully enforce its perspectives to the renovation of its living quarters. The author advises the administrative experts, planners and local politicians to learn from the dialogue with citizens to take arguments of the citizens seriously and not try to force upon them prefabricated planning concepts.

## SECTION II

In common with the situation in many Third World cities there occurs a broad spectrum of street occupations in the latter day South African cities. The pavement people of South Africa engage variously in a range of low-income earning activities which span retail distribution, production, transport ation, begging and crime. Amongst an array of work activities which are conducted off the pavements are included the vending of fruits, vegetables and flowers, street barbering, shoe-shining, hustling and prostitution. These precarious value generating niches have been recognized and recorded in many contemporary South African cities. However, geographers have largely eschewed this significant facet of the national urban milieu.

K. S. O. Beavon and C. M. Rogerson, in their article, "Aspects of Hawking in the Johannesburg Central Business District", focus their attention upon one component of the many and varied street occupations that presently are manifest in the South African cities. More specifically the objective here is to delineate the characteristics, and conditions of existence of the street hawkers who ply their trade in the downtown or the CBD of Johannesberg. Their investigation seeks to find out the working and living conditions of the "informal sector" or, more correctly, "the casual poor". The authors reveal that in the context of the racial structuring of South Africa's forced "labour" economy, almost all the participants in street occupations are members of the country's black subordinate race groupings. They struggle hard for survival amidst the constraints of the apartheid economy.

In the growing cities of Pakistan millions of people are settling on public and private land, have raised temporary haphazard structures thereon popularly known as "slums". The increasing numbers of people who have taken up residence in Lahore and the large-scale urbanization that has gained momentum due to the multifunctional character of the city has created serious problems in respect of urban facilities but the housing is worst affected. A large portion of the population which falls in the low-income bracket has no alternative but to live in improvised shelters which are devoid of even minimal facilities. Dr. Farhat Gulzar in his article, "Slumification of Lahore", analyses the character and development of slums in Lahore. He brings out a comprehensive list of the possible localities termed as slums which more or less resemble villages. The author finds that the inhabitants of the slums live in all sorts of makeshift dwellings using any kind of building material which they can lay their hands upon. Their dwellings are made of katcha bricks, mud, wood, straw, bamboo and pucca bricks. The author reveals that some of the slum inhabitants live in dilapidated abandoned Hindu temples. The common amenities like drinking water, sewage, electricity, latrines, bathrooms virtually do not exist. The author is pained to find that most of the slum-dwellers in Lahore live in sub-human conditions.

In the developed world the problem of slums is generally associated with big cities, but in the developing countries slum problem is associated not only with big cities but also with medium and small cities. In India most of the small towns even are highly congested and unhygienic. Dr. H. N. Saxena, in his article, "The Problems of Slums in Small Towns: A Case Study of Sriganganagar", specifically explains the salient features of slums in the small town under study. He examines the nature of slums, their spatial distribution, housing and street patterns, occupational and social structure and suggests remedies for the improvement of slums.

It is a truism that today slums punctuate almost every city of the world. The problem of slums has attracted the attention of planners, administrators and social workers who are consciously or unconsciously worried about the big beast. Dr. H. S. Mathur, in his article, "Socio-economic Profile of Urban Slums: A Case Study of Jaipur City", analyses the nature and character of slums in the city. He deals with the socio-economic conditions, family composition, housing conditions, employment, literacy, and health problems. Finally, he postulates that in order to evolve an integrated plan of action for the social and economic betterment of slum areas, total assessment of the problems of slum dwellers has to be made. The redevelopment plans should be so framed and executed as to cause no harassment, no coercion and no adverse effect on the status of the slum-dwellers.

The process of urbanization deeply affects the future of a city and therefore it has become an object of great concern to the urban planners. In India the rate and scale of urbanization have been increasing fast since the early sixties. Population increase in urban centres is much faster than in rural areas. This phenomenal change has resulted in slumification in the Indian cities. Pushpa Agnihotri and D. S. Srivastava, in their article, "Geographical Survey of Slums: A Case Study of Cities of Madhya Pradesh", provide a comparative analysis of the slums of Indore, Bhopal and Sagar. They demonstrate that industrialization gives impetus to urbanization. New job opportunities are created and a rush from rural areas follows. This leads to overcrowding in the cities because of a slow pace of residential development. Slums grow quickly in many parts of the cities to accommodate this influx of immigrants.

Like most other States of the country cities in Madhya Pradesh also have slums in all their degrading forms. Here resides the poorest class of society, sprinkled with social parasites of varied descriptions. Congestion, filth and insanitary conditions breed diseases of body and mind and create a situation which is both physically and morally degrading.

Urban slums are generally understood as places where conditions of housing fall much below the general standards of living. This term, therefore, is comparative and means various things in different contexts. If the American definition of a slum is applied to India the traditional parts of the cities with narrow lanes, cramped houses, unhealthy living conditions, etc., would have to be designated as slum areas.

This paper reports the results of a study of the causes of slum living in three cities of the State and attempts to describe the nature of adjustments within an urban area. An attempt has also been made to determine the factors that contribute to or influence these adjustments. The data upon which this study is based were collected by means of interviews with 200 slum dwellers of three cities within the age group of 18 to 60 years who had lived at least for five years or more in the slum area. Indore (1982, population 827.071), Bhopal (672,329) and Sagar (207,401) were selected for this study because of their relatively large and rapidly growing slum areas and also because they are good examples of industrial service, function and diversified cities, respectively. A schedule was used for collecting information which included such questions as reasons for coming to the city, background of their homeland, their contacts with homes, questions related to caste, religion, economic status and social organization of slums.

## REFERENCES


1. Eric Patridge, 1958, **A Short Etymological Dictionary of Modern English,** Mcmillan, New York.
2. Marshall B. Clinard, 1966, **Slums and Community Development,** The Free Press, New York, p. 4.
3. John Robertson, 1920, **Housing and Public Health,** Frank and Wagnalls, Co., p. 181.
4. James Ford, 1936, **Slums and Housing, History, Conditions and Policy,** Harward University Press, Cambridge, p. 11.
5. **Oxford University Dictionary,** 1955 edn., Oxford University Press, New York.
6. Harvey Zorbough, 1929, **The Gold Coast and the Slums,** Chicago University Press, p. 19.
7. Hoover, 1931, Conferences on Home Building and Home Ownership, Washington D.C., quoted in Ford, ibid.
8. David R. Hunter, 1968, **The Slum's Challenge and Response,** The Free Press, New York, p. 10.
9. U.N., "Extent of Slums and Squatters in Selected Cities in Developing Countries".
10. Seely, J. R., 1959, "The Slum, its Nature, Use and Users", **Journal of the American Institute of Planners,** 1959, XXV, 7-14.
11. Sri Prakasa, 1957, Seminar on Slum Clearance.
12. Frederick Engels, 1936, "Early Slum Conditions in Manchester in 844" in A. R. Desai and S. Devdas Pillai (eds.), **Slums and Urbanization,** Popular Prakashan, Bombay, 1970.
13. John Robertson, Housing and Public Health.
14. B. S. Toron Roe, 1928, **The Slum Problem.**
15. U.S. Census of Housing, 1960, Washington D.C., Department of Commerce, Bureau of the Census, p. 111.
16. Lewis Mumfold, 1961, **The City in History,** Harcourt Brace and Wood, Inc., New York.
17. Charles Abram, 1964, **Man's Struggle for Shelter in an Urbanization World,** HIT, Press, Cambridge, Mass.
18. D. A. Kirby, 1976, **Slum Housing and Residential Renewal: The Case in Urban Britain,** Longman Inc., New York.
19. Friedman, 1967, "Government and Slum Housing—Some General Considerations", **Law and Contemporary Problems,** Spring, pp. 357-70.

TWO

Joseph P. Beaton

# THE PROBLEMATIC ASSESSMENT OF URBAN BLIGHT

## URBAN BLIGHT DEFINITION

In writing of Urban Blight and Slums in 1938, Mabel L. Walker opened her book with a declaration that no satisfactory definition had yet been devised for the term blight.[1] Four and a half decades later, scholars are still struggling to concoct a comprehensive definition of the term.

Blight can be an affliction, a condition or both. As an affliction, blight can retard growth or foster deterioration, even to the point of destruction. As a condition, blight can exist as a state in which decline or ruin has been promoted.[2] Certainly, the affliction can persevere throughout the most extreme stages of the condition. Indeed, the very condition can be a blighting factor and so an element of the affliction.[3] This multidimensional nature of blight adds ambiguity to an already complicated term.

The term blight is complicated in that during the past few years it has experienced many different applications. Beginning in the thirties, students of the city began applying "blight" to myriad afflictions and troubled conditions of urban areas.[4] Their use of this description or classification has expanded its scope so broadly as to make a precise definition difficult.

The two main problems in selecting a suitable definition of urban blight are that it can take on a variety of forms and can occur in varying degrees. Among other things, urban blight may involve dwellings, commercial and professional establishments, industrial plant and equipment, institutions, the communications infrastructure and the social climate. The extent of the blight can range from that which is so negligible as to demand no immediate corrective action to that which requires the bulldozer of complete renewal.

Many scholars have made liberal use of the category of urban blight without actually defining it. Some simply presume the reader will draw the needed inferences from the term, while others discuss it in relation to other phenomena. By way of example, planner Harry W. Richardson demonstrates his preoccupation with economic elements by suggesting[5]:

> Urban blight is associated most of all with a decline in the income of central areas and with a tendency for this decline to become cumulative. This trend displays itself in the familiar phenomena: failure to maintain property, a widening gap between neighborhood tax receipts and expenditures on services, out-migration of high income residents, and urban poverty.

Some students of urban blight have opted to concern themselves with subordinate categories such as residential or commercial blight, rather than the entirety of the urban affliction-condition. For instance, economist Fred E. Case offers the following definition of residential blight[6]:

> total housing units in a city minus sound units with all plumbing facilities, on the assumption that a sound unit is much more easily identified than one with some dilapidation or deterioration.

Although this interpretation is logical, it is less than functional without the specific definition of the key words: sound, dilapidation, and deterioration.

Geographer Brian J. L. Berry provides considerably more detail in defining commercial blight. He divides the category into four types of blight: "economic blight", "physical blight", "functional blight or technological obsolescence" and "frictional or environmental blight". Berry further notes that various combinations of these blight types also exist as forms of commercial blight.[7]

However, despite the lengths Berry goes to in subdividing commercial blight, his multiphase definition is still very generalized. He requires the balance of the fifth chapter of his monograph, Commercial Structure and Commercial Blight, to complete his classification of the term that is just one element of urban blight.[8]

The definition dilemma is neatly epitomized by the explanation rendered in 1953 by Allen A. Twitchell of the American Public Health Association. In his words, blight[9]:

> usually refers to an area or district of some size. It refers to no one characteristic or condition, nor even to any one set of conditions or characteristics that are always found in the same combination. Instead, it covers a fairly wide range of conditions and characteristics that from example to example are found in differing combinations, and with or without certain secondary features.

It would seem impossible, then, to prepare a comprehensive working definition of urban blight that would satisfy everyone.

**Blight Perception: Image vs. Reality**

Compounding the problem of an almost limitless suite of definitional parameters is the diverse manner in which blight appraisal is achieved. Usually, blight is ascertained through visual perception, a medium discussed in some detail by geographers David Lowenthal, Yi-Fu Tuan and Pierce Lewis, among others.[10] When employed by a city agency, this form of appraisal may be as simple as a one-pass wind shield survey or as sophisticated as a multifaceted sidewalk survey.

Long Beach, California is a municipality with one of the most elaborate systems of visual blight appraisal in the country. The long Beach system is called Data Analysis Retrieval Targeting (DART) and is administered by the Long Beach Community Development Department. It has been in use only a few years, but is considered by the Long Beach City Council to be an invaluable tool in planning city redevelopment strategy.[11]

Under the DART programme, the Community Development Department subcontracts for building inspectors who assess the external building condition, landscape condition, and ambiance of all but the newest developments in Long Beach.[12] For an example of DART thoroughness, we might look at the manner in which building condition is appraised. Using six condition codes ranging from excellent to irreparable, the inspectors rate the following components of buildings that are visible from the sidewalk: foundation, walls, roof, patio, garage, porch, fireplace, driveway, windows, paint and trim. Six codes each are also employed in rating the condition of the landscape and the ambiance of the area.[13] All of these ratings are subsequently compiled by computer to produce a report as massive as it is detailed.

On first examination, this system is impressively comprehensive, but due consideration finds it quite incomplete as a means of appraising urban blight. In the first place, it ignores most elements of social and infrastructural blight. Secondly, since this is a sidewalk survey, it is an inadequate measure of building condition. The inadequacy is based on the fact that the method provides no possibility for the appraisal of the interior condition of the structures surveyed. Such important factors as the condition of interior walls, ceilings, floors, stairs, plumbing, electrical wiring and fixtures, and mechanical devices (e.g., air-conditioning, heating and elevators) cannot be determined in DART surveys. Furthermore, the inspectors cannot rate the condition of exterior features such as roofs and walls that are not visible from the sidewalk. The DART system is hardly all-encompassing.

The glaring inadequacies of even the most sophisticated visual appraisal techniques only serve to emphasize the potentially controversial basis upon which most evaluations of urban blight are based. However, it is not only the techniques that can produce debatable conclusions; the appraisers of blight cannot all be expected to be of one mind.

In discussing the formation of urban images, Kevin Lynch suggests that[14]:

> The creation of an environmental image is a two-way process between the observer and the observed. What he sees is based on exterior form, but how he interprets and organizes this, and how he directs his attention, in its turn affects what he sees. The human organism is highly adaptable and flexible, and different groups may have widely different images of the same outer reality.

Economist Scott Greer concurs succinctly in writing that[15]:

> There is considerable likelihood that the terms "blight" and "nonblight" will not be mutually exclusive. Thus, one man's blight may be another man's nonblight, depending upon how important he thinks a given condition or characteristic to be.

The wide range of values that permit observers to perceive urban environments so differently and to construct highly personalized realities are best exemplified by the contrasting perspectives of locals and visitors, or insiders and outsiders.[16] In <u>Topophilia: A Study of Environmental Perception, Attitudes, and Values</u>, Tuan explains that[17]:

> The outsider judges by appearance, by some formal canon of beauty. A special effort is required to empathize with the lives and values of the inhabitants.

and

> (The outsider's) main contribution is the fresh perspective. The human being is exceptionally adaptable. Beauty or ugliness—each tends to sink into his subconscious mind as he learns to live in his world. The visitor is often able to perceive merits and defects in an environment that are no longer visible to the resident.

Pocock and Hudson, authors of Images of the Urban Environment, add further emphasis to the difference in the perspective of the outsider and touch upon a cause of this diversity in suggesting that[18]:

> Visitors possess another distinctive viewpoint and image compared with any resident subgroup. They see the environment, not through the filter of habituation in which meaning and social engagement have dulled alertness to physical appearance, but in a highly perceptive state.

These observations properly add another dimension to the nature of perception. They acknowledge that, for the insider especially, the image of an urban environment is not formed exclusively by visual appreciation. As Lynch explains, "There are other influences on imageability, such as social meaning of an area, its function, its history, or even its name.[19] Psychologist William Ittelson adds that[20]:

> Environmental perception is not only dependent upon the physical, interpersonal, and cultural aspects of the environment, but also upon the status of the person, including needs, actions, motives, cognitive processes, and so on.

Aspects such as these help to explain why an inhabitant of an area may disagree with a blighted appraisal rendered by an outsider.

The classic example of the importance of this insider perspective in blight perception appears in Herbert Gans' oft-cited study of the West End of Boston.[21] Gans suggests that before the district structures were razed as part of a 1959 urban renewal effort, the perception of the visitor to the West End was that of[22]:

> many poorly maintained structures, some of them unoccupied or partially vacant, some facing on alleys covered with more

> than an average amount of garbage, many vacant stores; and enough of the kinds of people who are thought to inhabit a slum area.

However, to the residents of the area, the West End was not a decaying slum. It was a district they enjoyed, particularly because of the neighbourly attitude of the population and the comforts of secure and familiar surroundings. Their image of the West End was not one of blight, but rather one of a warm hearth and a vital human community.[23]

These comparisons say nothing of the fact that the image held by one insider can differ radically from that of another, even when the two share a neighborhood.[24] Different attitudes and value systems promote diverse perspectives.

Furthermore, no single observer adequately considers all possible factors contributing to the condition of a particular environment. As a result, the individual images conceived by the respective observers of an area are the products of only partial evaluations.

The images observers formulate are based on their personal images of reality and not on reality itself. Economist Kenneth Boulding contends that "images can only be compared with (other) images. They can never be compared with any outside reality.[25] Psychologist Ulric Neisser elaborates on such an evaluation of images in asserting that[26]:

> The vividness, the reality-status of an image is not well correlated with its usefulness or accuracy. The psychic reality of images is like the subjective reality of deep-trance hypnotic experience: it is genuine for the person himself, but it does not endow him with any special capacities. In other words, images can be dramatic as subjective phenomena, and can be valuable cognitive tools, but these two dimensions of imagery are not the same.

Therefore, no matter how sophisticated the method of evaluation of the urban condition might be, blight is still a subjective appraisal, an opinion. However, since most observers assume that their images of an area reflect reality, blight appraisals flow freely. Many of these opinions are rendered with little thought to their possible negative consequences.

**Symbolic Public Messages of Blight**

According to Boulding, a widely publicized pronouncement,

or a "symbolic public message," is capable of generating waves of optimism or pessimism.[27] Therefore, a widespread declaration to the public that an area is blighted can have positive or negative repercussions. The positive consequences result from the deliberate attempt by city authorities to expose the blighted area to public scorn. The intent is to garner enthusiastic citizen support for a city plan to upgrade the area and to establish justification for the expenditure of public funds for redevelopment.[28] The second major consequence is negative. This occurs when public response to a declaration of blighted is either to oppose redevelopment or revitalization or to give up on the district or neighbourhood.[29] There are numerous examples of each of these consequences.

Perhaps the most colourful example of a widely publicized blight verdict that had a positive result is that which took place in Philadelphia. As the initial step in a concerted effort to enlist public support for the redevelopment of Philadelphia, a citizens' advisory committee staged a fascinating exhibit at Gimbels Department Store in 1947. In the space of two months, approximately four hundred thousand persons visited this "Better Philadelphia Exhibition". What they saw was a multi-media presentation that graphically portrayed both the blighted condition of the city at that time and the appearance of a bright future. The highlight of the exhibit was a fourteen-by-thirty foot scale model of the central city. One at a time, the various deteriorated city sections depicted in the model were automatically displaced by improved versions designed by redevelopment planners.[30] According to political scientist Conrad Weiler[31] :

> A visual image of a new physical structure of the city was created that had a subtle but important political effect. By showing what Independence Hall would look like when the blocks of grimy, run-down stores, factories, and warehouses were removed and the historical buildings offset by large malls to the north and east, by showing a reconstructed waterfront with a marina and a promenade and a restored colonial area between the two, the model subtly eroded the fatalistic Philadelphia acceptance of urban decline and created a positive, tangible goal by which to judge political events.

While specific redevelopment programmes did not get underway until well into the ensuing decade, most students of the scene contend that since that very convincing exhibition of 1947, the citizenry of Philadelphia have generally been most supportive of redevelopment efforts.[32]

Without question, a political reform movement initiated in Philadelphia in the late forties and a highly supportive press importantly complemented the redevelopment drive to effect the political and structural renewal the city so badly needed.[33] Nonetheless, whether represented by the middle-class voter or the affluent entrepreneur, the Philadelphia public embraced virtually all plans to combat urban blight.[34] Since Philadelphia has completed such an impressive number of redevelopment programmes, the strategy of the symbolic public message of blight is interpreted as having contributed significantly to whatever successes have been achieved.

On a much smaller scale, the Hyde Park-Kenwood programme of the 1950s provides another example of a positive consequence of a widely publicized pronouncement of blight. According to Berry and associates, from the moment the findings of a community study were revealed, the citizens of this Chicago district responded enthusiastically to city devised plans to combat the perceived commercial blight.[35] The public, including the business persons whose structures would be taken by the urban renewal projects, was buoyed by the very positive reaction of the Press. The district was successfully redeveloped, thanks in no small part to the early cooperation of the business community.[36] Although the business persons displaced by demolition were not properly compensated and in many cases faced liquidation, the eventual modern renewal of the commercial district was looked upon favourably by the remaining elements of the community.[37]

Customarily, State statutes require that an area be judged blighted before it can become eligible for redevelopment assistance.[38] The intent of the requirement is more to provide justification of public assistance than it is to inspire public enthusiasm for redevelopment projects, although the latter is unquestionably desirable. By way of example, in order to qualify for consideration as a Redevelopment Area in the State of California, an urban area must be deemed blighted on the basis of a Community Redevelopment Agency (CRA) study. In Los Angeles, these studies are undertaken at the request of the City Council members who represent the areas in question.[39]

The CRA is compelled to employ State criteria in appraising the condition of areas designated for study. These blight criteria comprise Sections 33030 through 33032 of the California Health and Safety Code.[40] The introductory paragraphs explain the purpose of the appraisal process.[41]

33030. Necessity of redevelopment

> It is found and declared that there exist in many communities blighted areas which constitute either physical, social or economic liabilities, requiring redevelopment in the interest of the health, safety, and general welfare of the people of such communities and of the State.

> A blighted area is one which is characterized by one or more of those conditions set forth in Section 33031 or 33032, causing a reduction of, or lack of, proper utilization of the area to such an extent that it constitutes a serious physical, social, or economic burden on the community which cannot reasonably be expected to be reversed or alleviated by private enterprise acting alone.

The remaining two sections of this part of the code list a very general set of conditions that may characterize a typical blighted area.[42] The flexibility of interpretation inherent in these non-specific criteria has been a source of great controversy in California. CRA critics contend that, given the broad appraisal latitude of the Health and Safety Code, practically any area could be adjudged "blighted".[43] The Los Angeles Community Redevelopment Agency prefers to think of the code criteria as conveniently comprehensive. Through such convenience, the CRA has been successful in persuading the Los Angeles City Council that fourteen areas of the city are sufficiently blighted to merit redevelopment programmes.[44]

Certainly, in those instances in which redevelopment projects have succeeded (at least in the opinion of the agencies), the strategy may be considered constructive, but in not all cases do Los Angeles or other California city redevelopment plans achieve fruition. Similarly, not all public pronouncements of blight in other states inspire sufficient private-sector confidence or participation to accomplish stated redevelopment goals. This is the negative aspect of public blight declarations.

The consideration city agencies must acknowledge is that the wide-spread broadcast that an area is blighted could discourage the spirit of cooperation or capital investment required of the private sector.[45] Just as the individually-achieved citizen realization that an area is blighted often prompts disinvestment, so too might a public declaration of blight deflect capital. This is particularly likely when the declaration is not accompanied by a solid, well-funded proposal to defray, at least partially, the expense of redevelopment or revitalization. Since a revitalization project customarily receives considerably less public-sector support in proportion to a redevelopment project, the chances of discouraging private participation in revitalization would appear to be even greater when a label as indicting as blight is disseminated.

In some cases, a public declaration of blight may also worsen or extend the negative condition besetting that urban quarter. Sociologists and psychologists employ a "Labeling Theory" for the process that can occur when a critical label is affixed.[46] The theory holds that a negative label can prolong or exacerbate the problem it identifies or classifies. In his article on labelling, sociologist Mordecai Rotenberg cities an example from medical science found in psychologist Ronald Laing's The Politics of Experience[47]

> the diagnostic labelling act sets in motion the vicious circle of self-fulfilling prophecy, as a result of which the patient finally internalizes the diagnostic stereotype and behaves accordingly.

Furthermore , the jaundiced image derived from a diagnostic label may not only promote the perseverance of the negative condition, but may also create problems where none had existed.

If we follow the lead of sociologist Sean Damer, we may apply the Labelling Theory to a geographic unit.[48] While the unit Damer studied was a large neighbourhood, his conclusion could find parallels in larger entities such as urban sections or districts. He learned that a negative diagnosis often becomes a pejorative label that helps to perpetuate negative conditions in an area and to hinder their removal.[49] Following that logic, we can see that the identification of an area as blighted may in itself become a blighting force.

In the past, when renewal or redevelopment plans accompanied a public message of blight, area deterioration was often accelerated and expanded. The implicit suggestion that buildings might be demolished drove out many old tenants and discouraged new ones. This frequently led to vandalism and abandonment of properties.[50] Even nearby streets that were not earmarked for redevelopment suffered.

This chain of events was especially damaging to building owners and tenants alike when the proposed renewal or redevelopment project either never materialized or dragged out over a long period of time. Considering the findings of Martin Anderson that redevelopment projects have taken an average of nearly twelve years from start to finish, it is not difficult to envision how investors could be alienated by a decade or two of deteriorating and abandoned structures or vacated parcels awaiting government-fostered redevelopment action.[51] In some cases, landlords had retained ownership of or invested in buildings purportedly located in sectors slated for demolition, anticipating profitable compensation at such time as the Government assumed ownership. When the actual taking was long delayed, the property had often decreased in value so severely that the eventual remuneration did not come close to an approximating the accumulated cost of the property. In those instances where the taking never came about the owners assumed even greater financial losses and the properties they deliberately neglected became even more blighted.[52]

It must be realized that in some cases business persons resist redevelopment and revitalization because they are protective of a blighted environment they find personally profitable. Some entrepreneurs capitalize on the deteriorated condition of districts either by renting facilities to marginal businesses, or to operations that are, generally, seen as socially undesirable, or by themselves operating such enterprises.[53] Some owners of blighted property might oppose a revitalization scheme, under the assumption that it might merely shore up the marginal businesses operating in the district. For those desirous of being bought out in a redevelopment land-taking process, the thought of minor improvements is dismissed as being too costly.

For the inhabitants of an area that the city has labelled blighted, an unwillingness to participate in or cooperate with a redevelopment or revitalization programme can be prompted by more than the fear of losing capital invested in a deteriorated sector. They may also fear the social as well as the financial costs of displacement. Unquestionably, all too many "successful" redevelopment programmes have removed deteriorated residential and commercial structures only to replace them with buildings the former occupants could not afford.[54] Even in those cases that merely involve the refurbishment of blighted structures, sometimes simple improvements increase the value (rent) of the space beyond the means of the leaser. To these people, the blight label is tantamount to an eviction notice.

## SUMMARY

This brief review of the concept of urban blight firmly establishes the complexity inherent in the term. Urban blight has been shown to be virtually impossible to define and to appraise in a universally-acceptable manner. Furthermore , the literature demonstrates that the public application of blight labels has promoted both successful and regrettable consequences.

Therefore, depending upon a broad range of circumstances, the decision on the part of a city agency to classify an area as blighted must not be undertaken lightly. Certainly, in some cases it could provide the inspiration required to arrest blight and revive the area. However, under other circumstances, the blight label could become a self-fulfilling prophecy that worsens the condition of the area or contributes to its complete destruction.

Experience demonstrates that a public blight declaration is most effective when it is rendered in conjunction with a realistic revitalization or redevelopment scheme. Such a programme would, of necessity, comprise a feasible, comprehensive plan in which private-sector participation would be assured. In many cases, this sort of private-sector involvement in revitalization or redevelopment projects is contingent upon strong public-sector leadership and financial assistance. Without a serious commitment from the parties capable of promoting and producing positive change, even the most accurately assessed blight verdict could result in a worsened situation.

FOOTNOTES

1. Mabel L. Walker, **Urban Blight and Slums: Economic and Legal Factors in Their Origin, Reclamation, and Prevention** (New York: Russell & Russell, 1938), p.4.
2. Ibid., pp.4-6; Jerome Rothenberg, Economic Evaluation of Urban Renewal: Conceptual Foundation of Benefit-Cost Analysis (Washington, D.C.: The Brookings Institution, 1967), p.35; "Blight, "**Webster's New Twentieth Century Dictionary of the English Language,** unabridged, second edition, William Collins and World Publishing Co., Inc., 1978, p. 195.
3. R. Krumm and R. J. Vaughan, **The Economics of Urban Blight.** Paper P-5712, Rand Corporation, Santa Monica, Ca., 1976; Walker, op. cit., p.5; Rothenberg, loc. cit.
4. Clarence Arthur Perry, **The Rebuilding of Blighted Areas: A Study of the Neighborhood Unit in Replanning and Plot Assemblage** (New York: Regional Planning Association, Inc., 1933); Edith Elmer Wood, **Slums and Blighted Areas in the United States,** U.S. Federal Emergency Administration of Public Works, Housing Division Bulletin No.1; Mabel L. Walker, **Urban Blight and Slums: Economic and Legal Factors in Their Origin, Reclamation, and Prevention** (New York: Russell & Russell, 1938).
5. Harry W. Richardson, **Urban Economics** (Hammondsworth, England: Penguin Books, Inc., 1971), p.133.
6. Fred E. Case, "Prediction of the Incidence of Urban Residential Blight, "**Papers and Proceedings of the Regional Science Association,** Vol. Eleven (1963), p.212.
7. Brian J. L. Berry (assisted by Robert J. Tennant, Barry J. Garner, and James W. Simmons), **Commercial Structure and Commercial Blight in the City of Chicago,** Department of Geography Research Paper No. 85, Chicago: University of Chicago, 1963, pp.179-81.

8. Ibid., pp. 179-203.
9. Allen A. Twitchell, "Measuring the Quality of Housing," in Coleman Woodbury (ed.), **Urban Redevelopment: Problems and Practices** (Chicago: University of Chicago Press, 1953), p.11 as cited in Scott Greer, **Urban Renewal and American Cities: The Dilemma of Democratic Intervention** (Indianapolis: The Bobbs-Merrill Company, Inc., 1965), p. 21.
10. David Lowenthal, "The Offended Eye: Toward an Excrescential Geography," in Pierce F. Lewis, David Lowenthal and Yi-Fu Tuan, eds., **Visual Blight in America**, Association of American Geographers, Commission on College Geography, Resource Paper 23, 1973, pp.29-32; Yi-Fu Tuan, "Visual Blight: Exercises in Interpretation," in Lewis, op. cit., pp.23-27; Pierce F. Lewis, "The Geographer as Landscape Critic," in Lewis, op. cit., pp. 1-8.
11. Interview, April 19, 1979, with Mr. David Landry, Coordinator of the Community Development Strategy Staff Liaison Team, Community Development Department, Long Beach, Ca.; Community Development Department, **A City of Long Beach Community Development Strategy: A Phase One Report of the Community Development Strategy Task Force**, Long Beach Community Development Department, October, 1978.
12. Landry, loc. cit.
13. Sample DART survey forms provided by Mr. David Landry of the Long Beach Community Development Department. They include the "Building Condition Code Guide," the "Landscape Condition Code Guide," and the "Ambiance Code Guide."
14. Kevin Lynch, **The Image of the City** (Cambridge: The M.I.T. Press, 1960), p. 131.
15. Greer, op. cit., p. 21.
16. George L. Peterson, "A Model of Preference: Quantitative Analysis of the Visual Appearance of Residential Neighborhoods", **Journal of Regional Science,** Vol.7 (Summer, 1967), pp.19-31; J.B. Lansing and R.W. Marans,"Evaluation of Neighborhood Quality," **Journal of American Institute of Planners,** Vol. 35 (May,1969), pp.195-99; Henry Sanoff and Man Sawhney, **Residential Livability: A Study of User Attitudes Toward Their Residential Environment** (Raleigh: Urban Affairs and Community Service Center, North Carolina State University, 1971); Yi-Fu Tuan, **Topophilia: A Study of Environmental Perception, Attitudes, and Values** (Englewood Cliffs, N.J.: Prentice-Hall, Inc., 1974), pp. 64-65; Douglas Pocock and Ray Hudson, **Images of the Urban Environment** (London and Basingstoke: The Macmillan Press Ltd., 1978), p.67; Jacquelin A. Burgess, "Stereotypes and Urban Images," **Area,** Vol. 6, No. 3 (1974), pp. 167-71; Jane Jacobs, **The Death and Life of Great American Cities** (New York: Vantage Books,1961), p.122; William H. Ittelson, "Environmental Perception and Urban Experience," Environment and Behavior, Vol.10 (June, 1978), pp.193-213.
17. Tuan (1974), loc. cit.
18. Pocock, loc. cit.
19. Lynch, op. cit., p.46; Peter Orleans, "Differential Cognition of Urban Residents: Effects of Social Scale on Mapping," in Roger M. Downs and David Stea (eds.), **Image and Environment: Cognitive Mapping and Spatial Behavior** (Chicago: Aldine Publishing Company,1973), pp.115-21.
20. Ittelson, op. cit. p. 197.
21. Herbert Gans, **The Urban Villagers: Group and Class in the Life of Italian-Americans** (New York: Free Press, 1962).
22. Herbert Gans, "The West End: An Urban Village," in Michael E. Eliot-Hurst (ed.), **I Came to the City** (Boston: Houghton-Mifflin, 1975), p.151; see also Gans, **The Urban Villagers,** op. cit., pp. 12, 149-62, 308-17.

23. Gans, **The Urban Villagers**, op.cit., pp.12-16, 45-119.
24. Peter K. Eisinger, "The Urban Crisis as a Failure of Community: Some Data," **Urban Affairs Quarterly**, Vol.9 (June, 1974), pp. 437-61.
25. Kenneth E. Boulding, **The Image** (Ann Arbor: The University of Michigan Press, 1956), p.165.
26. Ulric Neisser, "Visual Imagery as a Process and as Experience," in John S. Antrobus (ed.), **Cognition and Affect** (Boston: Little, Brown and Company, 1970), pp.159-78.
27. Boulding, op. cit., p.89.
28. Pocock, op. cit., pp.100,104,125,127; Harold Kaplan, **Urban Renewal Politics: Slum Clearance in Newark** (New York: Columbia University Press, 1963), p.163.
29. Kaplan, op. cit., pp.136-37; Boulding, op. cit., pp.90-91.
30. Jeanne R. Lowe, **Cities in a Race with Time** (New York: Random House,1967), pp.322-23; Conrad Weiler, **Philadelphia: Neighborhood, Authority, and the Urban Crisis** (New York: Praeger Publishers, 1974), pp.130-31; Kirk R. Petshek, **The Challenge of Urban Reform: Policies & Program in Philadelphia** (Philadelphia: Temple University Press, 1973), p.23.
31. Weiler, loc. cit.
32. Lowe, op. cit., pp.323-404; Weiler, op. cit., p.131; Leo Adde, **Nine Cities:The Anatomy of Downtown Renewal** (Washington, D.C.: The Urban Land Institute,1969), pp.15-42; for a well-illustrated description of many elements of Philadelphia redevelopment see Edmund N. Bacon, **Design of Cities** (New York: The Viking Press, 1974), pp. 264-307.
33. Petshek, op. cit., pp.26-255; interview, November 14, 1980, with Mr. Alois K. Strobel of the Community Planning Department of Philadelphia.
34. Lowe, loc. cit.
35. Brian J. L. Berry, Sandra J. Parsons, Rutherford H. Platt, **The Impact of Urban Renewal on Small Business: The Hyde Park-Kenwood Case** (Chicago: Center for Urban Studies, University of Chicago, 1968), pp. 12-15, 19-20, 25, 28-31.
36. Ibid., pp.18, 20, 30-31; Kaplan (op. cit., pp.32-33, 138, 140) frequently alludes to the contribution of the Press which enthusiastically supported redevelopment in Newark.
37. Berry, Parsons, and Rutherford, op. cit., pp. 28-34, 170-72.
38. According to Berry and Associates (ibid., pp. 26, 48) the statutes applied in the case of the Hyde Park-Kenwood redevelopment plan were the Illinois Blighted Areas Redevelopment Act of 1947 (Il. Rev. Stat Ch. 67°, 65 (j), 1947) and the Urban Community Conservation Act of 1953 (Il. Rev. Stat. Ch. 67°, 91.8-91.16, 1953).
39. Harvey S. Perloff, Tom Berg, Robert Fountain, David Vetter, and John Weld, **Modernizing the Central City: New Towns Intown ... and Beyond** (Cambridge, Ma.: Ballinger Publishing Company, 1975), p. 328; interview, May 7, 1980, with Mr. Robert Fazio, a planner with the Planning Department of the Los Angeles Community Redevelopment Agency.
40. Ibid.
41. **Deering's California Codes: Health and Safety Code, Annotated, of the State of California: 1979 Pocket Supplement (32000-38999)** (San Francisco: Bancroft-Whitney Co., 1979), p.19.
42. **Deering's California Codes: Health and Safety Code, Annotated, of the State of California (32000-38999)** (San Francisco: Bancroft-Whitney Co., 1975), p. 79.
43. Robert E. Sweet, " 'Blight' Area Designation Held Misused," **The Washington Post**, November 20, 1975, part B, p.15.

44. Fazio, loc. cit., **Facts and Figures**, prepared by the Community Redevelopment Agency of the City of Los Angeles, California, January, 1980.
45. Boulding, op. cit., p.91; Kaplan, op. cit., pp.136-37.
46. Mordechai Rotenberg, "Self-Labelling: A Missing Link in the 'Societal Reaction' Theory of Deviance," **The Sociological Review**, Vol. 22 (August, 1974), pp. 335-54; Sean Damer, "Wine Alley: The Sociology of a Dreadful Enclosure, "**The Sociological Review**, Vol. 22 (May, 1974), pp. 221-48.
47. Ronald D. Laing, **The Politics of Experience** (New York: Ballantine Books, 1967), as cited in Rotenberg, op. cit., p.336.
48. Damer, loc. cit.
49. Ibid., pp. 222-40.
50. George Sternlieb and Robert Burchell, **Residential Abandonment: The Tenement Landlord Revisited** (New Brunswick, N.J.: Center for Urban Policy Research, Rutgers University, 1973), p. 299; George W. Sternlieb, Robert W. Burchell, James A. Hughes and Franklin J. James, "Housing Abandonment in the Urban Core," **Journal of the American Institute of Planners**, Vol.40 (September, 1974), pp. 321-332.
51. Martin Anderson, **The Federal Bulldozer: A Critical Analysis of Urban Renewal, 1949-1962** (Cambridge: The M.I.T. Press, 1964), pp. 73-90; Berry, Parsons, and Platt, op. cit., pp.180- 81; Sternlieb (1973), op. cit., p.25; Rothenberg, op. cit., pp.216-20; Michael J. Dear, "Abandoned Housing," in John Adams (ed.), **Urban Policymaking and Metropolitan Dynamics: A Comparative Geographical Analysis** (Cambridge, Ma.: Ballinger Publishing Company, 1976), pp.59-99.
52. Sternlieb (1973), op. cit., pp.300-301.
53. Rothenberg, op. cit., pp.45-54.
54. Perloff, et al (1975), op. cit., pp.117-18, 135; Anderson, op. cit., pp.52-70; Rothenberg, op. cit., pp.147-51, 223-29; Herbert J. Gans, "The Failure of Urban Renewal," **Commentary**, Vol.39 (April, 1964), pp.29-37; Berry, Parsons, and Platt, op. cit., pp.32-35, 170-72, 181-87; Chester Hartman, "The Housing of Relocated Families," **Journal of the American Institute of Planners**, Vol.XXX (November,1964), p.271; Marc Fried, "Grieving for a Lost Home," in Leonard H. Duhl (ed.), **The Urban Condition: People and Policy in the Metropolis** (New York: Basic Books, Inc., Publishers, 1963), pp. 151-59, 167-70; Kaplan, loc. cit.; Herbert J. Gans, "The Failure of Urban Renewal: A Critique and Some Proposals," Commentary, Vol.39 (April, 1965), p.30.

THREE

Peter Marcuse

# THE DECLINE OF CITIES IN THE UNITED STATES
## Inevitable or Deliberate ?

To European eyes, John Kasarda's explanation of events in the United States must seem a strange explanation of a strange phenomenon, with even stranger policy recommendations attached. The abandonment of cities has not been a wide-spread occurrence in Europe since the unwilling departure of the Romans in the dark Ages. Yet, according to Kasarda, this is what is happening in the United States, it is inevitable, and government policy ought to swim with the tide and adapt to it rather than fight it. Strange: when one looks around Europe, vital cities seem to be thriving, the factors that lead to their prominence seem to be in full sway, and governments are everywhere concerned to foster city development and renewal and improve the quality of urban life. Even in those few cases where long-term regional changes pose a threat to specific cities (Essen or Dortmund in the Ruhr are examples), government policy is formally fully committed to maintaining the viability of these cities despite the changes in their roles.

Are things really so different in the United States? No, and yes. No, the underlying factors influencing city growth and/or decline are not different; yes, government policy is different indeed and produces differences in result. Certainly the explanatory factors to which Kasarda alludes are the same in Europe and the U.S. "Advances in transportation and communications technology," to which Kasarda attributes the new role of cities, are certainly similar, and in fact are often directly transferred from one country to another. The underlying forces producing these new roles are also similar: the "economic and social dynamics" of advanced industrialized private market economies are structurally the same. The development of the tertiary sector, the rising building costs and costs of land, the ecological problems, the changing costs of energy, are all essentially similar. The most direct and immediate influence on the shape and future of cities, what Kasarda calls "The sixth sense of profit of entrepreneurs," is the same in both countries.[1]

What is different in the role of government, the State? Curiously, Kasarda's paper reads as if government policy had always been oriented towards protecting or reinvigorating older cities, and needed to be changed to different direction. In fact, the truth is exactly the opposite. Government policies in the U.S. have historically fostered, and continue today intensively to foster, the decay and abandonment of older cities and the growth and prosperity of newer ones. These policies have not been the result of autonomous or mistaken decisions by a handful of political leaders or government administrators; they have rather been adopted to serve particular groups and interests in the United States which, because of a balance of interests and forces (political, economic, social) quite different from those in most European countries, have been able to use government in the service of their goals in a manner that has produced an urban landscape for many years already quite different from that in Europe.

The factors that have produced and continue today to produce these different results in the U.S. can be summarized as follows:

- (i) Government policy subsidizes, and thereby accelerates,the momentum of the movement of business activity generally;
- (ii) Government provides major tax incentives to investment in new plant and facilities in new locations;
- (iii) Government provides public infrastructure for newly moved or expanded businesses;
- (iv) Governments, largely local and State, provide special incentives to businesses that move through loans, tax concessions, provision of physical plant, even freedom from normal regulation as to environmental standards, occupational safety, etc., if the Reagan Administration has its way;
- (v) All of these incentives and benefits are provided without any attempt to control, guide, or even plan the most appropriate location of the activities being assisted;
- (vi) These government policies produce results in an unbalanced pattern throughout the nation; the problems these policies create have specific locational consequences:
- (vii) Where economic activity is declining, local governments are forced to pick up all of the social costs left behind by business movement in terms of unemployment, health,

delinquency, abandonment, etc.;

(viii) Local governments in areas of growing activity are not obligated in any way to transmit to areas of decline any of the public benefits of such growth, where indeed they have not already sacrificed such benefits to attract the growth in the first place;

Government policy thus contributes to the crisis of older cities in the U.S. in three ways:

1. It increases the pace of modernization and the consequent relocation of economic activity by subsidizing investment in new plant and equipment, whether or not socially needed and wherever located.
2. It does so through government expenditures (and the surrender of public claims against private resources), thus increasing the private sector's resources at the expense of the public sector.
3. It permits a locational maldistribution of costs and benefits so that public costs borne in one location can not be charged against potential public benefits accruing in another location.

The importance of these governmental activities should not be underestimated:

> The Federal Government affects the pattern of investment through tariffs, quotas, and marketing agreements; tax laws and rulings; loan guarantees and subsidies; public land management; publicly financed insurance. In 1980 alone, tax benefits to particular industries totalled \$ 70 billion; the Government issued \$ 221.6 billion in loan guarantees and \$ 60 billion in direct loans, and it had \$ 2 trillion worth of outstanding insurance. Taken together, these Government expenditures that act to promote certain industries or businesses amounted to 13.9 per cent of the GNP.[2]

The fact that these Governmental policies and governmental expenditures are undertaken following private and profit rather than socially oriented locational decisions makes government in the U.S. a major partner in producing the very urban problems Kasarda takes as inevitable. To give some details: Government policy through the tax laws encourages the replacement of old facilities by new. It provides investment tax credits, tax write-offs of old facilities, accelerated depreciation of new, and, locally, real estate tax abatements, low interest loans, and other major inducements to investment in new facilities.

Table 3.1 lists the provisions of the federal tax laws

(leaving out State and local tax concessions) that favour new construction and investment, and their costs.

This subsidy is more than twice the total budget of the United States Department of Housing and Urban Development for each year, and almost three times the total federal expenditure on community and regional development for the whole country. As in other cases, the Reagan Administration is ac

TABLE 3.1
**Tax Subsidies Promoting Mobility**
(in millions)

| | 1975 | 1977 | 1980 | 1982 |
|---|---|---|---|---|
| Exclusion of payments in aid of construction of water and sewage facilities | $ N.A. | $ 15 | $ 60 | $ 110 |
| Exclusion of interest on State and local industrial development bonds | 175 | 290 | 910 | 1,555 |
| Expansion of housing construction period interest and taxes | 1,510 | 625 | 695 | 775 |
| Excess first year depreciation | 275 | 185 | 185 | 205 |
| Depreciation on (new) rental housing in excess of straight line | 520 | 400 | 385 | 430 |
| Depreciation on other buildings in excess of straight line | 440 | 300 | 255 | 285 |
| Accelerated asset depreciation | 1,410 | 2,055 | 3,030 | 4,120 |
| Proposed constant rate depreciation* | | | | 9,035 |
| Deferral of capital gains on home sales | 805 | 890 | 1,010 | 1,220 |
| Investment credit | 5,810 | 10,955 | 18,250 | 20,765 |
| Credit for purchase of new home | 650 | 100 | | |
| Total | $11,595** | $15,815 | $24,780 | $38,500 |

* Proposed for 1982; would provide increase in depreciation rate by approximately 40% and provide other tax benefits for assets placed in service after Dec. 31, 1980.(Special Analysis, p. 232.)

** Does not include first item.

Source: Statistical Abstract of the United States, 1978, 1979; Special Analysis Budget of the United States Government, fiscal year 1982.

celerating the trend: the write-offs permitted for investment in plant are expected to increase by $ 9.7 billion in 1982, $ 18.3 billion in 1983, and $ 30.0 billion in 1984.

A single case is illustrative. Bethlehem Steel in 1977 closed one of its larger and older steel mills. It received $167 million in tax write-offs for the closed facilities, and $100 million in "other costs associated with the reduction of capacity," as a result of its change in the location of its activities. The resultant savings can finance a good bit of new investment. Without these write-offs—essentially a federal tax subsidy—the old facilities might still be in use today. In 1979, U.S. Steel, which shut down a number of its plants in 1979 (including some profitable ones—but more profits could be made elsewhere), had, for that year, as a result of the tax treatment of these shutdowns, "net profits which actually exceeded its gross profits."[3]

George Peterson, of the Urban Institute, perhaps the leading authority on the impact of taxation in this area, summarized: "The effect of subsidizing new investment (through the investment tax credit) has been to shorten the useful life of older capital.... In effect, the bias of the tax laws in favour of new construction becomes a bias in favour of suburban and fringe development and, indirectly, a bias against preservation of the economic role of older parts of the metropolis."[4]

State and local governments also offer a wide array of high-visibility inducements to business firms to get them to move to a particular location: tax abatements (see list of recipients in footnote 6 below) industrial park space, low interest loans, training programmes and manpower recruitment services, etc. Robert Goodman, in The Last Entrepreneur, describes many of these vividly: the competition for the Volkswagen assembly plant is a classic example.

These are generally offered in the name of competing with other localities for firms who will ultimately contribute more than the amount offered to the local tax base. Almost all studies have shown that the choice of destination is at most marginally influenced by such inducements.[5] Typically, a Library of Congress study of firms taking advantage of local tax abatements showed "such firms made their locational choices first, and then discovered and applied for the program." Even Business Week (June 21,1976) speaks of such local tax incentives as a "rising spiral of government subsidies as companies play off against city and State against State for the most advantageous terms." Thus, the net overall impact is to subsidize the costs of almost any private move with public funds.

If indeed, any one factor should be singled out as inducing the choice of locations for business firms, it would be the cost of labour. Kasarda refers obliquely to the impact of "trade union restrictions"; labour costs is a shorter way of saying the same thing. Firms will tend to move from high labour cost areas to low cost areas (internationally too, of course). In the United States, where regional variations are very significant, and the level of union organization is very different by area and bargaining is local much more than national, these factors contribute significantly to capital movement and thus the problem of older cities, with their generally better organized, with a more militant workforce. Differential labour laws in the different states play a major role in shaping these wage differentials.[6]

While government policies in the U.S. thus contribute dramatically to the relocation of economic activities, there is equal effort to influence that relocation within the framework of national policy, as there is in many European countries. The social waste and the net economic inefficiency resulting from the lack of planning and coordination are still within the capacity of the system to tolerate, with its reserves of wealth and political acquiescence. There have, indeed, been voices from within the establishment calling for a change of policy, for "national economic planning," and President Carter at least thought there was appeal in talking about a "National Urban Policy," even though the document of that name issued by his administration hardly took the idea seriously. Proposals included no nationally established regional policy; no uniform regional planning by any lower level of government; no plan for the location of productive facilities financed by or producing for the public sector; no set of locational permits required for new plants or offices; no national or State, and very rarely local, policies, let alone programs, dealing with desirable city size, suburban sprawl, metropolitan growth. The Reagan policies[7] move firmly even further away from the regulation of private business, even as governmental tax support for it grows; the exacerbation of the urban crisis by governmental action will clearly be heightened. The political pressures, economic constraints, and international circumstances that forced movement towards national planning in many Western European countries after World War II have not been felt as severely in the U.S.

The picture produced by adding these facts to the canvas are very different from that suggested by Kasarda's, and explain, as Kasarda's do not, why the U.S. situation appears so different from the European. It is, in fact, a matter of deliberate government policy, produced by a balance of forces different from that in Europe, that produces the different result. The "explanation" that urban decline is the inevitable result of inevitable technological, social, and economic developments becomes itself a factor in producing and legitimating the precise conditions it purports to explain.[8]

## FOOTNOTES

1. For a more detailed description of the differences in one important area of urban policy, housing, see Peter Marcuse, "The Determinants of State Housing Policies: The Cases of West Germany and the United States," in Susan and Norman Fainstein (eds.), **The State under Advanced Capitalism,** Sage Publications, Beverly Hills, forthcoming.
2. Robert B. Reich, Director, Policy Planning, United States Federal Trade Commission.
3. Harry Brill, "The Runaway Steel Industry," **The Nation,** Feb. 9. 1980.
4. Testimony, U.S. House of Representatives, Subcommittee on the City of the Committee on Banking and Currency, June 16, 1977.
5. See, for instance, William Schweke (ed.), **Plant Closings: Issues, Politics, and Legislation,** 1980, and Ed Kelly and Lee Webb (eds.), **Plant Closings, Resources for Public Officials, Trade Unionists, and Community Leaders,** 1979, both published by the Conference on Alternative State and Local Policies, Washington, D.C.
6. For a more detailed discussion, see Peter Marcuse, "The Targeted Crisis: On the Ideology of the Urban Fiscal Crisis and its Uses," **International Journal of Urban and Regional Research,** Vol. 5, No.3, September, 1981.
7. Kasarda is himself a respected adviser to the Reagan Administration.
8. The ideological, if not obscurantist, nature of such explanations is witnessed even by the language employed: the pattern of suburban sprawl and decimation of open and green space that government policy is now being called on to further is described, not as sprawl, but as a "multi-modal multiconnective ecological field of interdependent activity centres!"

FOUR

Lutz Holzner

# CULTURAL FOUNDATIONS FOR THE DECLINE OF AMERICAN CITIES

## INTRODUCTION

During the 1970's millions of Americans have moved from cities in the industrial Northeast and Midwest to the so-called sunbelt States in the South and Southwest of the country. The population migration has been accompanied by an equally hasty southward mobility of industrial, wholesale and retail firms and research and other service establishments. This already enormous relocation of people and capital is only the beginning. It can be expected that the North-South migration will swell during the current decade and might assume the character of an exodus. The dams are broken. Sunbelt cities small and large burst in their seams. They are now experiencing what thirty years earlier began so promisingly in the cities of the North: a seemingly boundless growth and prosperity fired by optimism and the belief in unlimited opportunities. The old Industrial Belt is now in the midst of what may be called a malaise. Many cities which the masses are leaving behind are facing financial bankruptcy and deteriorate rapidly. Factories close and unemployment is above the national average. Shops are empty, residential houses and apartments are all but impossible to sell above cost. The monstrously sprawled-out megalopoli of the 1950's and 1960's are not only stagnating but face outright economic and demographic decline.[1]

Once prosperous and booming cities such as Boston, New York, Detroit, or Chicago are caught in the demographic squeeze and can afford to maintain only intolerably minimal staffs on their police, fire fighter, and refuse collector operations. Whole school districts close early year after year or reduce services because the funds to pay for operating school buses, teacher salaries and the heating and maintenance of school buildings can no longer be sufficiently generated. Such

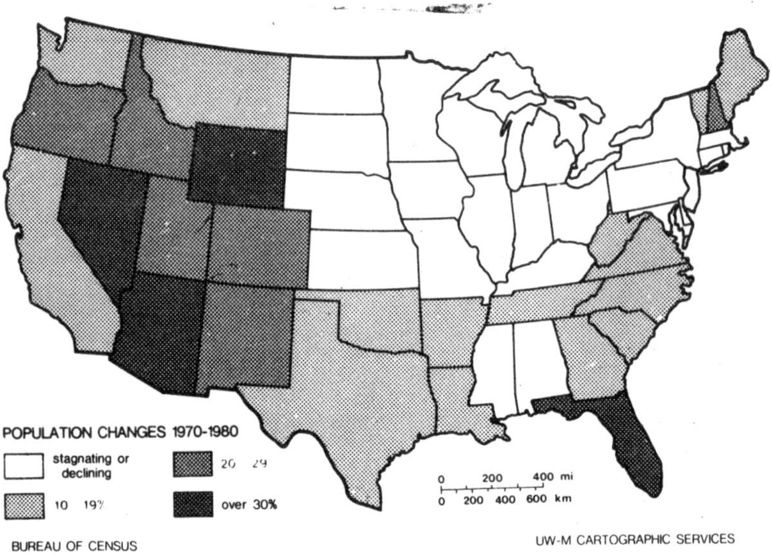


deteriorating conditions have in turn spurned yet further out-migration of people usually in the middle and upper income levels who scramble to leave the sinking ship. The alarming results of the 1980 census now made available and broadcast by the media have caused additional panic not to "miss the train". As happened before in American history, "the rush is on", and nothing presumably can stop it. Everyone appears concerned and the word is to 'get out of here'. Down South or out West is the place to be.

Compared with other countries or cultures such an event is almost without precedence. The disastrous decline of many cities in large areas within a short period of time not induced by war or natural catastrophes is indeed a rare phenomenon, even when viewed in the context of the entire human history. Periods of sudden urban decline as for instance in the ancient and medieval tropical and subtropical cultures of the Toltek, the Maya, or the Khmer have not yet been sufficiently explained, but might very well have been caused by natural disaster or rapid climatic change, civil war, or invasion. In the Northern United States, however, such processes are clearly not at work. What forces are to be blamed then? How should such a sudden massive relocation in the United States be explained? The answer is not easy, because in the United States itself these events seem not at all to be considered exceptional or extraordinary. A national emergency has not been declared, perhaps because the current recession in the country as a whole tends to camouflage the more fundamental roots of the malaise in the American Northeast and Midwest as just a temporary downtrend in the economic cycle. Are there more fundamental causes for the decline of the Northeast and Midwest? Indeed, is it not in keeping with the national character of Americans to abandon exploited urban areas where quick riches are no longer to be expected, just as cut-over forests or depleted strip-mining districts were left behind in earlier periods of American history? In the following, attempts will be made at some answers.

## NATIONAL CHARACTER AND CULTURAL FOUNDATION

A Presidential Commission drafting a "national agenda" for the coming decade was set to work in 1980 under President Carter yet and concluded (under President Reagan) that instead of trying to stem the apparently inevitable decline of older cities in the Northeast and Midwest, the Federal Government should rather encourage and aid people in their search for jobs and other economic opportunities in the sunbelt States of the South and Southwest. In its final report the 45-member panel, known as the President's Commission for a National Agenda for the Eighties, headed by William J. McGill, former president of prestigious Columbia University, seriously suggests that "contrary to conventional wisdom, cities are not permanent. Their strength is related to their ability to reflect change rather than to fend it off. Growth and decline are integral parts of the same dynamic process in urban life. When the Federal Government steps in to try to alter these dynamics, it generates a flood of demands that may sap the initiative of urban government via the expectation of continuing support."[2]

The Commission's complacent reaction to an almost catastrophic decline of cities in the Northeast and Midwest of the United States has not at all aroused an outcry of opposition in the country. On the contrary, many long established Federal subsidia and programmes for cities have been cut or entirely eliminated under the new Reagan Administration with the approval of the majority of Congress, affecting cities that right now would be in need of massive aid more than ever. Even the left-oriented media, otherwise vocal proponents of public programmes, have so far found no more than sorry notes on the sad state of the declining cities in the North. It appears that the majority of American voters is prepared to accept the inevitable as something not entirely out of the ordinary. A mass migration has begun, unleashed by mismanagement and failure, and it seems quite natural to accept that large areas of the country are being depopulated and emaciated while others are teaming with new arrivals. The cliche "of the American frontier comes to mind. Or is it a cliche"? The frontier spirit is not dead in America. It was always nothing out of the ordinary to leave one's home in search for better opportunities elsewhere when conditions seemed less rewarding, or turned somewhat difficult, or simply when the urge to move became too strong. In the early days farmers would move on when harvests failed, or locust plagues or droughts made life miserable, or gold discoveries promised quick riches elsewhere. During the last quarter of the twentieth century, whole urban areas are abandoned and left to marginal elements of society, the poor, the uneducated, the unskilled, and the minorities. To get rich quick, or to hope for a happier life someplace else, and, in the process, not to sink deep roots anywhere, are still driving forces of the American way of life. This is not new at all but appears like a red thread leading through the history of the United States. Any attempt to explain the present decline of American cities in the Northeast and Midwest would be futile if only present economic difficulties were to be considered without weighing concomitant long established culture-immanent values and behaviour patterns of American society as well. The decline of American cities in the old Industrial Belt seems pre-programmed through the national character and cultural foundation of American society.

## RESTLESSNESS, MOBILITY AND IMPROVISATION

"The United States are in a constant state of transition. Nothing is final, nothing established to last; a constant mania for change, a perennial quest for innovation seems to drive all classes of society." This statement appropriately describes one of the essential characteristics of American culture: its unique restlessness and mobility. In view of the massive exodus from Northeastern and Midwestern urban regions, these words could have been written today. They were uttered more than 130 years ago, however, by the German traveller Dr. A. R. Thummel.[3] He continues: "Institutions, which were in force for only fifty years, farm estates that had been under cultivation for only twenty, are considered worn out, and everybody is eager to replace them with different and presumably better ones. Every year thousands of people leave the older Eastern States and flock to new, less cultivated regions either in search for quicker profit, or simply in the hope for a life of innovation, adventure, and change.... It is natural that in such an atmosphere attachment to one's homeland (Heimat) and devotion to domesticity (Hauslichkeit) are rare phenomena indeed. The American is a migratory bird or better a nomad who is not tied to any particular place or residence but feels happy only when moving on. In his youth he leaves behind the land of his birth with indifference and the graves of his fathers with no concern. In his mature years he will, with similar equanimity sell the land he cultivated, together with the cradle of his children and the place of his suffering and joys, to settle anew a thousand miles away and to start a new career" (Thummel pp. 159/60, my translation). It would be difficult to describe the reasons behind the present people's migration in the United States in any better way today. Young people without work or threatened by the current economic decline of Northern cities, or simply in search for a new exciting life, leave everything behind and pursue their happiness on the other side of the continent, as far as possible from home. Old people, longing for sunshine and the easy life, burdened with ever climbing property taxes in the bankrupt cities of the North, sell their homes and start a new life in the Sunbelt. Life begins with sixty. Entrepreneurs are attracted by a better tax climate, less rigid unionization of the labour force, and the ensuing accumulation of capital in the South. Blue- and white-collar workers, craftsmen, teachers, retail and wholesale merchants alike follow the newly created jobs and the new markets in the Sunbelt.

Nearly half of all Americans moved during the last half of the 1970's. Of 202 million Americans five years and older, 91 million or 45.1 per cent moved to a new home sometime between 1975 and 1980. The highest mobility occurred naturally among people aged 25 to 29 with 77 per cent changing residences in this age bracket reflecting the establishment of new households by young adults who have just finished school, recently married, or entered the labour force. The tendency to move was also directly related to education, however, with 55 per cent of all people with four or more years of college moving during the same time periods, an indication that the exodus is not at all spurned by the desperate during a temporary decline of regional economic opportunities in the North. (Source: U.S. Bureau of Census, 1980).

During the ten years since 1970, New York and Chicago together lost over one million inhabitants, a population decline of 10.4 per cent in New York and 10.8 per cent in Chicago. Boston lost 12 per cent, Baltimore 13 per cent, Philadelphia 13.4 per cent. Even more drastic declines were recorded in Detroit (20.5%), Cleveland, Ohio (23.6%) and St. Louis, Missouri (27.2%). While central cities in the Northeast and Midwest lost most, the suburban communities in metropolitan countries lost population also or stagnated during the same time period. In the Sunbelt States, on the other hand, central cities, metropolitan suburbs and non-metropolitan counties gained substantially. Los Angeles city grew by 5.5 per cent alone, Dallas by 7.1 per cent, Tulsa, Oklahoma by 9.3 per cent, San Antonio, Texas by 20 per cent, San Diego, California by 25.5 per cent, Houston, Texas by 29.2 per cent, and Phoenix, Arizona even by 31 per cent. For the first time in U.S. history, more than half of the nation's population lives now in the South and West of the country. (Source: U.S. Bureau of Census, 1980).

Americans always seem intended to be prepared to move on, never really growing roots anywhere, so as to be ready to grab a perceived opportunity elsewhere. Under such circumstances, it cannot be expected that anybody would whole-heartedly make long-term and lasting investments which would tie one down permanently. Improvised or temporary arrangements are preferred and investments kept as low as possible so that, when the price is right or the call for moving on is heard, little would stand in the way. This might explain the typical shoddy improvisations in housing construction, business ventures, and urban planning. Tens of thousands of residential homes constructed during the 1950's, 1960's and 1970's in the sprawling metropolitan areas of the Northeast and Midwest, for example, were not connected to public water and sewer lines, but depend on individual wells and septic tanks. The resulting groundwater pollution in some Midwestern urban regions has progressed so far that health authorities have proclaimed a total construction stop. The City of Milwaukee lost a spectacular Federal Court Case six years ago, because large amounts of raw untreated sewerage flows into Lake Michigan through clear water channels at times of snow melt or heavy rain. The Federal Environmental Authorities stipulated that Milwaukee and its suburbs construct sufficient treatment plants and subterranean deep tunnel storage caverns at an estimated cost of between three and four billion (milliard) dollars. Initially, Federal subsidies were promised. Under President Reagan, however, most of these aids have been eliminated, but the court order remains. As a result, the new facilities are being constructed in a scaled-down and improvised version, costing the local tax payer dearly, but not solving the problems anyway.

To quote Dr. Thummel of 1848 again: "Public institutions or programmes, initially hailed as the ultimate of human wisdom, are considered outdated after only a few years and in need of profound reforms; new laws are called for and instituted, but quickly repealed in turn without allowing for sufficient time, to test their beneficial or detrimental effects" (Thummel p.160, my translation).

What cannot be achieved with minimal financial imput and personal sacrifice remains undone or is cheaply improvised.

Public projects above all are subject to the tax payer's consent. Since one day he will move again, why volunteer to increase the tax burden unnecessarily. The new homes and factories, and the myriads of shops and fast food shacks now being built in the warmer climates of the South and West are even more cheaply and scantily put together than their counterparts in the North had ever been. The American improvisation of temporary arrangements assumes a grotesque magnitude in the Sunbelt. While the average life expectancy of an ordinary one-family home in the North, for example, is believed to range around 35 and 40 years, that of a home in the South is maybe twenty.

More and more Americans in the South and West live in mobile homes, extreme expression of restlessness, mobility, and improvisation. During the 1970's, the number of mobile homes has increased to approximately 4 million all-year-round occupied units. The popularity of living in a home that, at least theoretically, is not stationary, not built of conventional material, without a firm foundation or basement, and not subject to property taxes, is not sufficiently explained by financial considerations alone. Robert M. Beckley holds four syndromes or "fantasies" responsible for the American love affair with the mobile home:

1. the cowboy syndrome or mobility as a generally admired and accepted value of American society;

2. the gypsy syndrome or restlessness as a long-established ethically condoned expression of the American way of life;

3. the technology syndrome: conventional house construction is rooted in the traditional crafts of the middle ages. With the technology of the 20th century, we can mass-produce more homes cheaper and move them about as well;

4. the suburb syndrome: I want a home that looks like a subur ban house, but is cheaper and costs no property tax, nor does it tie down the occupant in any other way.[4]

The unfinished appearance and improvised quality of American settlements, rural and urban alike, and the underlying restlessness and mobility of their inhabitants was noted by almost every European traveller of the 18th and 19th centuries.[5] In the days of the still on-going colonization and expansion of the frontier, little more could have been expected, if it had remained a passing phenomenon. But the same symptoms are prevailing now as ever in a society often described as "post-industrial" and mature. It appears that those early travellers levelled their observations and criticisms at more than a passing symptom of a young expanding society, but pointed towards a much more deeply ingrained cultural foundation of American society that is as valid today as it was in the days of the frontier experience. In his American Notes Charles Dickens, for example, observed a quality about the American landscape that he saw from the window of the train, which surprised and amused him. "All the buildings looked as if they had been built and painted that morning, and could be taken down on Monday with very little trouble."[6] The villages and towns of New England appeared to Dickens to consist of "cardboard" houses none of which seemed to be built to last. "Not only did the houses look impermanent; they looked unprivate ... those slightly built wooden dwellings ..."[7] Dickens wondered if Americans ever intended to settle down. "The suburbs", he wrote, "are, if possible, even more unsubstantial-looking than the city. The white wooden houses ... are sprinkled and dropped about in all directions, without seeming to have any root at all in the ground; ... I almost believed the whole affair could be taken up piecemeal like a child's toy and crammed into a little box" (Charles Dickens, American Notes, p.26). Russell Lynes believes that Charles Dickens saw "something more than white clapboards that gave America a here-today-gone-tomorrow look. It was more than just the newness of the houses and the fresh white paint ... It was something in the American character . . .a restlessness, an urge to move on, a sense of there being unlimited space to be used or wasted, an unwillingness, in spite of all protestations to the contrary, to put down permanent roots. The truth of the matter is that ours is a society as mobile as wheels, ambition, almost unlimited expanses of land, an itch to sample the grass in the next pasture can make us. To move is as natural to the American as maintaining roots is to the European" (Russel Lynes, p. 6).

The restlessness, mobility, and improvisation of Americans approached Dickens one day in a matter of grotesque symbolism on a street in Lebanon, a small town near St. Louis. He wrote: "I walked into the village where I met a dwelling house coming down-hill at a round trot, drawn by a score or more of oxen" (Charles Dickens, American Notes, p.182). Today, such moving still goes on a lot, only much faster, not only down a hill, but over many miles, on superhighways, at 55 miles per hour. The architect and editor of The Architectural Forum, Peter Blake, wrote in LIFE, Special Issue, "The U.S. City, Its Greatness is at Stake", in 1965: "Throwaway architecture is nothing new in America. It has existed almost from the day the continent was finally opened up. The traditional American city is casual about permanence. It is, and always has been, some kind of way station along the Open Road—that Open Road which has been the great, central theme of this country from the outset: a road, first for covered wagons, then for trains, next for cars, now for jets." One need add no more (LIFE, Vol. 59, No. 26, 1965, p.49).

## GREED AND PROFITEERING

In his recent book Contemporary Suburban America, Peter O. Muller discusses a series of powerful values and beliefs which are "ingrained in the American national character and native culture" and which are ultimately responsible for the phenomenon of the chaotically decentralized and excessively sprawling outer city (suburbia).[8] Brian Berry, paraphrazing the observations of the late-eighteenth-century French traveller Crèvecouer, had earlier catalogued these cultural traits of Americans: "Foremost ... was a love of newness. Second was the overwhelming desire to be near to nature. Freedom to move was essential if goals were to be realized, and individualism was basic to the self-made man's pursuit of his goals, yet violence was the accompaniment if not the condition of success--the competitive urge, the struggle to succeed, the fight to win. Finally, (there is) a great melting pot of peoples, and a manifest sense of destiny."[9]

Not mentioned, at least not directly, is another aspect of the American national character which, in all fairness, must be considered as at least as important, if not more profoundly responsible for the current mass migration, the hectic boom and burt of cities, and the general improvisation and shoddyness of so many American institutions, than the abovementioned values and beliefs of the American native culture. It is greed, avarice, or profiteering, an all-driving force of American society. In one of his famous memoirs, the French statesman and diplomat Charles Maurice de Talleyrand (1754-1838) considered the lumberjack a befitting symbol for the American spirit of combined greed, destruction, and carelessness: "The American woodcutter does not interest himself in anything; every sensible idea is remote from him .... The number of strokes of his axe required to fell a tree fills all his thoughts. He never planted; he knows not the pleasure of it. A tree of his own planting would be good for nothing in his estimation; for it would never, during his life, be large enough to fell. It is by destruction that he lives; he is a destroyer wherever he goes. Thus every place is equally good in his eyes; he has no attachment to the spot on which he has spent his labour; ... and if, in quitting the abode of many years, he does not by chance forget his axe, he leaves no regret behind him".[10]

Again, one might argue that such sentiments might be expected in a land that is to be newly settled and tamed. John Madson describing the American frontier society of the late 19th century writes: "A hard and pragmatic knowledge was needed ... with almost no margin for failure, there was little time or concern for anything that could not be applied directly to the land and to survival of the family. Gentle custom and effete courtesies were scarcely thought of.... It was a culture reduced to functional essentials. The prevailing tenor of the frontier was anti-intellectual".[11] But has such sentiment really changed in the America of post-industrial urban vintage? When in 1981 the British Prime Minister Margaret Thatcher, known for her conservative thrift, visited President Reagan, it became known that, just prior to her departure, government subsidies for the Royal Opera House had been increased by fifteen per cent to twenty million dollars a year. The entire federal subsidies for all opera companies in the United States in 1980 did not exceed five million dollars. In 1981, President Reagan succeeded in cutting 46 million dollars of federal aid for the arts in general including opera (Arts Endowment), a sum which incidentally is still below the expenses occurring annually in connection with U.S. military bands.

Most anything that does not yeild profit, or does not produce quick wealth, or cannot be used for practical purposes, is in low esteem. To gain, to profit, to get rich quick, greed, is the all-driving motor of the American. Thummel writes as early as 1848: "They seem to be rooted in the all-encompassing desire: to win, to get rich" (Thummel, p.27, my translation). Much earlier, in 1814, the Chevalier Felix de Beaujour published his observations of the United States in which he discusses at length the role of greed in American culture (Beaujour, see footnote 9): ..."Among the foreigners who have been accustomed to the good society of Europe, some consider (the American) coarse and unpolished, because he is devoid of softness in his manners, and delicacy in his sentiments; whilst others describe him as haughty and vain, because he esteems nothing but riches and ostentation. In general he pays little regard to merit when surrounded by indigence; and the first question that issues from his mouth, when a stranger is presented to him, is to ask what is his fortunes, as if to give to each a reception proportioned to his riches. Names and rank are no illusion to him, and he classes every man without distinction by the same scale, viz. by that of fortune (Beaujour p.144). The Chevalier further observes that..."the conversation (at parties) generally hinges on politics, or purchases which some propose and others accept; for the American never loses an opportunity of enriching himself. Gain is the subject of all his discourse, and the lever of all his actions; so that there is scarcely a civilized country in the world, in which there is less generosity of sentiment, less elevation of soul, and less of those soft and brilliant illusions which constitute charm or the consolation of life. There a man weighs everything, calculates all, and sacrifices all to his own interest. He lives only in himself, and for himself, and regards all disinterested acts as so many follies, condemning all talents that are purely agreeable...." (Beaujour p. 145).

It is no coincidence that the overwhelming majority of artists in the American art world was born and educated abroad, most notably in Europe including Russia. Unfortunately, the history of Europe has made it easy for America indeed to replenish her art world regularly without having to change her attitude towards nurturing and furthering "talents that are purely agreeable", who are not bent towards profit making. They came as refugees, in 1848, in the 1890's, 1918/19, 1938, 1945, 1956, 1968 practising their arts for arts sake, because their profession makes no man rich in the United States. Beaujour concludes with the harsh statement that... "virtue has always been considered as the principle, or the chief spring of all republics; but that of the American republic seems to be an unbounded love of money. This is the effect of the political equality that reigns there, and which leaves to the citizens no other distinction than that of riches, and invites them to fill their coffers by every means in their power. Everything among them favours this vile cupidity; their disdain for the agreeable arts, their taste for the comforts of life, their coarse intemperance, which deprive them of all love and activity for everything that is not personal; and in short, even their laws, which by their ambiguity, seem to be the secret accomplices of fraud and bad faith. With them, justice is the result of calculation, but never of sentiment...and in the greatest part of their commercial towns, bankruptcy, who would believe it, is the shortest as well as the surest road to arrive at fortune" (Beaujour p. 146). Thummel also sees no other basis for American society in 1848 than the passion to win, to get rich. "To that end", he writes, "the American is not always delicate. Because of this, the frequent open or covert frauds, the numerous bankruptcies...." (Thummel p.97, my translation). Both Beaujour's and Thummel's words could have been written today. Bankruptcies and fraud abound in the wake of the masses leaving for the Sunbelt. Nothing, it appears, has really changed, the practices are the same and so are the sentiments. It is not important, how one makes money, what counts is that one makes it, and lots of it. During the recent ABSCAM scandals it was not so much the Congressmen found guilty of accepting bribes who were considered the villains by the populace, but the FBI who had tempted them. Every man has his price.

The extreme desire for profiteering and winning, one of the highest values in American society, often prevents long-term and solid investments in business, factory, or home. To invest as little as possible, to profit as quickly and as much as possible, then to sell out, to escape, to move on, is the practice everywhere. It is not surprising then that millions are leaving the cities of the Midwest and Northeast without regret. There, the profits are made, the investments played out, the cities' economies ruined. It is time now to move to new ground and start the racket all over again. It is true that the United States are still large enough to allow such practice. The question is only for how long.

There is probably no other developed country in which miners have to work under similarly hazardous and skimpy safety devices as in the United States. The railroad network built as cheaply as possible and barely maintained has become so unsafe that the travel speed of freight trains never exceeds forty miles per hour. Between 700 and 1,000 trains derail every year often spilling flammable or toxic cargo and endangering whole communities. It is not surprising that residential houses, factories, warehouses and business buildings are being constructed so cheaply that they last only a few years. Cities in America are indeed not built to last. No wonder that they are being abandoned helter-skelter. The lumberjack will not forget his axe, but he will surely not leave regrets behind either. The forest is cut, the cities used up. So let's all move on, a popular theme in American literature and country music folklore.

In this connection it is understandable that manual production work in the fields, the mines, or in the factories is so very unattractive. Such work will never get a man to reach "the American dream", namely to get rich and thus obtain status in society. For a long time, it was the poor immigrants who constituted the willing worker armies to drive the American economy and productivity: the Irish, the Germans, the Poles, the Italians, later rural blacks from Southern States, then Puerto Ricans and Chikanos from Mexico and other Latin American countries. The business man, the entrepreneur, the speculator, all these truly Americanized profiteers, looked down upon the dirty, thrifty, hard-working people who lived in small houses or cheap overcrowded apartments, keeping a pig in the basement and growing kraut in the background, until they too, or their children, were affected by the American spirit of profiteering and smart greed to let others do the work.

American productivity has fallen, because more and more people prefer to cut in on the business world or push papers rather than produce material values (Fig. 4.2). The extreme development of the United States into the prototype of post-industrial society is not an accident but appears logical in a society which values quick riches above anything else. Today, only 23 per cent of the gainfully employed labour force is in manufacturing and fifteen per cent in the non-industrial productive sectors of economy such as construction, mining, and farming. 62 per cent, however, are in the non-productive white collar jobs. Everybody wants to get rich quick, open a business, sell something, cheat. There is nothing extra-ordinary to travel along a highway lined for 35 miles or more on both sides with rows and rows of business shacks and quick "eateries", as is the case near Fort Lauderdale, Florida, for example. Between 1973 and 1980 eleven million new jobs were created in the United States, about as many as all jobs in Canada put together. Over seventy per cent of these new jobs were in retail

**U.S. Labor Force by Percentage of Employment**

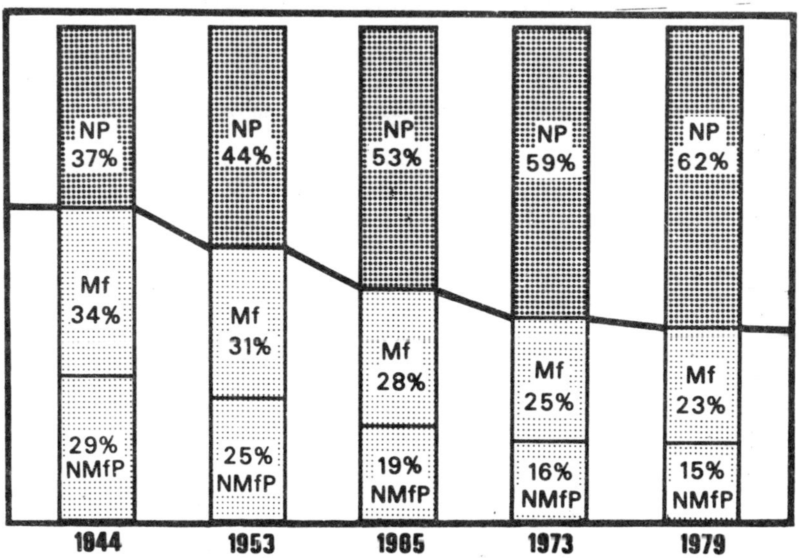


NP Non-Productive
Mf Manufacturing
NMfP Non-Manufacturing Productive

businesses and services. Just the increase in employment in the restaurant and fast food business alone was larger than the total combined employment in the automobile and steel industries. The three service sectors: restaurant and fast food, health services, and sales services (mailorder, janitorial) employ more people than all productive basic industries put together including construction, machines and tools, electric and electronic industries, motor vehicle industries, airplane and shipbuilding, the entire chemical sector of industry, and instruments. McDonalds employs more people today than U.S. Steel. Newsweek commentator George F. Will has wittily but correctly stated that "Golden arches, not blast furnaces, are becoming the symbols of American enterprise".

## VIOLENCE

In conclusion one more characteristic of American soceity ought to be mentioned briefly, which has always made life in American cities unpleasant: violence. There is no other country in the whole world, in which everyday life in cities is as dangerous as in the United States. In New York in 1980, for example, a total of 710,153 violent crimes were committed, including 1,814 murders, 100,500 violent street muggings and 210,703 house burglaries with use of violence against people. But New York does not even rank first in the murder rate in the country, i.e. murders per 100,000 population. This place is occupied by Detroit, followed by Dallas, Los Angeles, Washington, D.C., and Chicago, with Miami moving rapidly ahead.

Is this something new in America? Is the almost uncontrolled possession of firearms to be blamed for such unprecedented crime statistics? Or are there again more deeply rooted characteristics of American society that might cause violence to remain a prominent part of American culture even if the possession of firearms were to be limited? Why are firearms, particularly hand guns, not controlled? Why do American people privately own more hand-fire power than the entire Red Army and NATO put together? The great majority of American people from the hard hat worker to the President share the conviction that the right to bear arms is a constitutional guarantee and an inalienable right: symbol of extreme individual liberty and the right to pursue one's happiness and success with whatever means necessary. Is this then nothing less than the expression of a violent basis of a culture, a society which values success, particularly the financial success, so very highly? Is it surprising then that violence, even with the use of arms, has always been the natural accomplice of American everyday greed?

Violence has indeed a long tradition in America. It accompanied the frontier settlement of the West; its nonchalant acceptance by the American populace led to the almost complete genocidal extinction of the American Indian; it is the basis for the tastelessly brutal mass sport spectacle known as American football. Violence is also one of the everyday means to succeed in society. This is not only true for organized crime, for example the Mafia, which, according to official estimates, controlls between twenty and twenty five per cent of the entire Gross National Product, legally. It is also true for the ordinary citizen. One should not always visualize the American murderer as a brutal, mean looking character lurking in dark alleys. On the contrary, one should remember those "all-American" types who shot John Lennon, J. F. Kennedy, his brother Robert, and almost got Reagan as well. Not one professional gangster, just very ordinary, normal Americans. The only murderer with a record was James Earl Ray who killed Martin Luther King. A pretty young woman of Milwaukee shot her husband's ex-wife last summer never having met her before. The reason for this crime was that she wished to stop the alimony payments her husband had to make to his first wife. All this is not new in America. Many travellers of the 19th century made reports about excessive violence. The Englishman D. W. Mitchell, for example, wrote in his book Ten Years in the United States, published in 1862, that in any given year there were as many murders committed in the City of New York as in all England. Violent crime of all kind was so rampant "which made it common prudence to carry arms after ten o'clock at night. Respectable young men found self-defence clubs to practise gymnastics and the use of weapons, and to provide themselves with proper pistols, knives, etc". Mitchell concludes: "It was proved in a trial that leaden weights were manufactured for the purpose of sinking bodies in the water" (D. W. Mitchell, pp. 143-44).

FOOTNOTES

1. David C. Perry and Alfred J. Watkins, **The Rise of the Sunbelt Cities,** Sage Publications,1977.
2. President's Commission for a National Agenda for the Eighties, **A National Agenda for the Eighties,** 1981, The New American Library, Inc., New York.
3. Dr. A. R. Thummel, **Die Natur und das Leben in den Vereinigten Staaten von Nordamerika in ihren Licht - und Schattenseiten,** Erlangen, Palm' sche Verlagsbuchhandlung, 1848.
4. Robert M. Beckley, Urban Research Center Seminar, University of Wisconsin-Milwaukee, April 1, 1981 (unpublished).
5. Selected works by European travellers include: Heinrich Bornstein, **75**

**Jahre in der Alten und Neuen Welt,** 2 Vols., Leipzig, 1884; Michael (Misha) Hauser, Aus dem Wanderbuche eines osterreichischen Virtuosen,Leipzig, 1859; Joseph Salzbacher, **Meine Reise nach Nordamerika im Jahre 1842,** Wien 1845; Ferdinand Kurnberger, **Der Amerikamude,** Franfurt/Main 1855; T. S. Baker, **Lenau and Young Germany in America,** Philadelphia, 1907; Karl Knortz, **Deutsch in Amerika,** Leipzig, 1906; Traugott Brommes, **Hand-und Reisebuch fur Auswanderer und Reisende nach den Vereinigten Staaten von Nord Amerika,** Dr. Buttner, 9th ed., Bamberg, 1875; Friedrich von Raumer, **Amerika and the American People,** translated by W. W. Turner, New York, 1846; Prince Max von Neu Wied - Wied, **Journey through North America,** New York,1856; Paul Wilhelm Herzog (Duke) von Wurttemberg, **Journey in North America in the Years 1825-26** (rare books, AGS Collection, Milwaukee); Friedrich Ratzel, **Stadte und Kulturbilder aus Nordamerika.** Brockhaus, Leipzig,1875; Henry Tuckerman, America and Her Commentators, New York, 1864.

6. Charles Dickens, **American Notes and Pictures from Italy,** Oxford Univ. Press, London, 1957, p. 71.
7. Russel Lynes, **The Domesticated American,** Harper and Row, Rochester, New York, 1957, p. 5.
8. Peter O. Muller, **Contemporary Suburban America,** Prentice-Hall, Inc., Englewood Cliffs, N.J., 1981, p. 20:
9. Brian J. L. Berry, "The Decline of the Aging Metropolis: Cultural Bases and Social Process", in: George Sternlieb and James W. Hughes(eds.), **Postindustrial America: Metropolitan Decline and Inter-regional Shifts,** New Brunswick, N.J., Center for Urban Policy Research, Rutgers Univ., 1975, p.175.
10. Charles-Maurice de Talleyrand, "Memoirs Concerning the Commercial Relations of the United States with Great Britain, in: Le Chevalier Felix de Beaujour, **Sketch of the United States of North America at the Commencement of the Nineteenth Century From 1800 to 1810,** translated by W. Walter, Dondon, 1814, pp.147-49.
11. John Madson, "Grandfather Country", **Audubon,** Vol. 84, No.3, 1982, p. 56.

FIVE

N. N. Patricios

# CONSENSUAL AND CONFLICT PERSPECTIVES OF INNER CITY DECLINE AND REVITALIZATION

## INTRODUCTION

In this article I restrict my discussion to the issues of decline in predominantly residential areas (as against commercial or industrial areas) in British and North American cities. Decline can be defined as a process that may appear in certain residential areas and is distinguished physically by three progressively worsening forms: deterioration, various degrees of decay, and finally slums. We can apply the term blight to the first two stages of decline, which is the area of concern here. The areas are also distinguished by social and economic measures of deprivation. We need to be clear, however, about the meaning of urban blight as well as the terms urban renewal and revitalisation.

**Urban blight** is "merely a poetic metaphor indicating the decline of use and value in areas which were once high on these particular scales" (Greer, 1965, p. 155). Moreover blight is not so much a description of an undesirable change in the buildings, environment or activities of an area but it is a judgement of the degree of decline. That is, a weighting or an emphasis is given to particular characteristics or conditions of a residential area in the process of decline according to one's value position (Greer, 1965; Rothenberg, 1970; Patricios, 1973). That blight is relative in meaning is crucial as an area as judged by officials and planners to be depressed or declining can lead to the demolition of people's homes.

**Urban renewal** is the term most commonly used to describe the actions, such as redevelopment or rehabilitation, that are employed to deal with blighted areas. Due, however, to the connotation urban renewal has now of extensive demolition of buildings leaving large areas of vacant land or boarded-up buildings awaiting redevelopment, I prefer the term **revitalisation**—the process of infusing vitality into areas judged to be, in some way, substandard.

In the majority of situations the residential areas which are judged to be blighted are found in inner city, in and around the central core. Generally in these areas buildings are declinig into decay, environmental conditions are poor, and functional obsolescence is usually evident. From a socio-economic point of view there is in most cases evidence of an exodus from the inner city of the young, the energetic and the potential leaders to the outer city. Left behind, or "trapped", are an increasing proportion of the elderly and unskilled, the problem families, large families often at the poverty line, and young small families who cannot earn enough to buy a house outside the inner area (Hancock, 1976). In addition there may be the phenomenon of large minorities of immigrants who tend to move into the inner city to find an initial place in the employment market and to obtain low rent housing.

It should be recognised, as Gittus (1969) has argued, that there are two kinds of communities that may be found in the inner city. Firstly there is the residual area in which live a comparatively respectable and cohesive social community. Secondly there is the transitional area in which there is a concentration of a number of social problems—the deviants, the anti-social, the psychologically abnormal, the disabled and also a large number of those unable to escape from the cycle of poverty. The combination of physical decline of an area with problems of overcrowding, poverty, poor education, unemployment depict a situation of "multi-deprivation" in the inner cities (Hancock, 1976).

## Context

Of course the concern over the poor quality of urban life and the demand for improvements is not new. In 19th century manufacturing towns the degradation of the living, working and environmental conditions contributed to widespread social unrest (Lambert and Weir, 1975). The possibility that the discontent of the urban poor would turn to something more dangerous in the absence of improvements in health and housing made commentators anxious. They feared mob violence and the possible revolutionary consequences of appalling living conditions. Reactions by social idealists, philanthropic industrialists, and housing associations as well as the carrying out of community experiments had a marginal effect on the perceived problems (Cherry, 1976). Health legislation and local government reform were probably the most influential in eliminating the degradation of the inner areas of industrial cities (Wohl, 1977).

Today the need to tackle the problems of the inner city is still very much there. The physical, social and economic nature of the solutions, though, bear a strong resemblance to 19th century approaches. Physical determinism was very much in evidence during the 1950s and 1960s, the assumption being that a better physical environment will deal with the social problems and give people a better life. Contemporary approaches now have a social dimension, for example the Educational Priority Area Programme (begun in 1967 but now terminated), Community Development Projects, and the Ford Foundation's grey area project begun in the U.S. in 1960. An economic emphasis is reflected in the compaign against poverty in the inner city by the Urban Programme, started in 1968, to a certain extent by the Housing Act of 1969 which introduced GIAs, and by the Housing Act of 1974 which added the HAAs. In the U.S. this emphasis was quite clear in the Economic Opportunity Act of 1965 and the Housing and Community Development Act of 1974.

Furthermore there is also the "total" or "integrated" approach, for instance the Comprehensive Community Programme begun in 1974 and the DoE's Inner Area Studies and Area Management Trials, which seek to identify the range of economic, social and environmental problems. In the U.S. the Model Cities Program, which was started in 1966, was similarly broadly based in attempting to rebuild or restore entire sections of slum and blighted areas by the concentrated and coordinated use of all federal aids together with local, private and government sources.

All is not well, however, with the various approaches to urban renewal. There is increasing scepticism as to whether any of these programmes or projects aimed at revitalisation will have any significant impact on solving the inner city problem (Berry, 1973). In Britain the plight of the inner cities has grown immeasurably worse despite an era of "planning" (Wood, 1977), while departmental rivalry and the relatively inadequate allocation of resources are matters of serious concern (Hancock, 1976; Perry, 1976). Recent reports indicate that General Improvement Areas are having a limited success, that there are conflicts in objectives and that areas of stress are not benefitting as they should (Perry, 1976; Gibson and Langstaff, 1977). It is also reported that Housing Action Areas will not remedy the socio-economic problems of inner city residential areas (Lawless, 1977). According to a recent evaluation (CDP, 1977) the problems of "deprivation" are as acute as ever for those who live in them, and the prospects are bleak. The British government's poverty initiatives and general policies towards the poor could not be said to have had much impact on the problems facing the people who live in the older urban areas. Furthermore the programmes have always been small compared to the size of them. In the U.S. the Model Cities Program, despite its unquestionable aims, has turned "into a tussle over citizens' control" (Marris and Rein, 1974, p. 297), and commitment of resources in the war on poverty was so cautious as to be called trivial (Marris and Rein, 1974).

The questions I would like to raise in this context are what is our understanding of the nature of urban decline and the process of revitalisation? Is there something wrong with our theory? In attempting to answer these questions I proceed then to the second part of this article and consider consensual theory which is the prevailing and dominant one and which implicitly underlies our thinking on decline and revitalisation.

## CONSENSUAL THEORY

In the literature consensual theory is also known as functional theory, functionalism or structural-functionalism. I set out below, very briefly, the principles of the theory and then apply them to our area of concern—inner city residential decline and revitatlisation.

### Consequence and Cause

(i) The term functionalism has been applied by Wallace (1969) to a situation in which a single phenomenon is both a consequence and/or a cause of other phenomena. That is, functionalism means that something is perceived to be a function of and/or functional for other things. This is the scientific meaning of "function" and is not to be confused with the dictionary definition which refers to purpose. The theory, then, seeks to explain the social as being a consequence of the behaviour of at least one participant (whether an individual or a group) towards others, the consequences of effects, presumably being both necessary and beneficial to the society in question (Zeitlin, 1973).

### Consensus

(ii) A basic postulate of the theory is that in society there is a tendency to a consensus on values (van den Berghe, 1963). Value consensus can be considered the broad aims or principles which most members of a given social system consider desirable and agree upon and which underlie the whole social and cultural structure.

**Equilibrium**

(iii) The other basic postulate of the theory is that societies tend toward stability and integration (van den Berghe, 1963). It is assumed that the value system is the most important source of integration or dynamic equilibrium, that is, responses to outside changes tend to minimise the final amount of change within the social system. The dominant tendency is thus towards stability as maintained through mechanisms of adjustment and social control. Deviance is equated with non-conformity to institutionalised norms, the solution of which is adjustment.[1] Thus those activities that may transform or eliminate social stability are regarded as "dysfunctions" (Wallace, 1969) and the concern is, therefore, with those activities whose consequences can lead to the genesis and/or maintenance of the social structure.

**Decline and Revitalisation: A Consensual Perspective**

I now apply the three principles of consensual theory, those of consequence and cause, consensus, and equilibrium in describing an outline of the essentially economic model of residential decline and revitalisation (derived from Medhurst and Parry Lewis, 1969; Ahlbrandt and Brophy, 1975).

**Consequence and Cause Principle**

The single phenomenon of a lack of sufficient income forces households to spend a substantial percentage of their income on housing. The income itself, however, is often inadequate and precludes households from satisfactorily maintaining their property, or from paying rents high enough to enable landlords to afford a normal or adequate level of maintenance. The consequence of inadequate income subsequently results in dwellings deteriorating faster than would normally be the case and will contribute to the general decline of the area in which they are located.

While income is an important determinant of the direction of change social, physical and other factors as well as public and private actions also exert a significant influence. It is economic forces, however, which are seen as the phenomena which contribute to disinvestment in inner city residential areas and indirect costs such as dangers to health, environmental deterioration or falling values of neighbouring properties. Consequences such as the physical decay of houses, functional obsolescence, and various social characteristics may be caused independently of one another, or each may lead to the others.

### Consensus Principle

Consensus is reflected in a general agreement with the statement that older neighbourhoods need to be saved that "are in various stages of decline, and (in which) the homeowners are worried about increasing crime rates, poor schools, a physical shoddiness that is becoming obvious, and the future value of their homes. These neighbourhoods are not slums, but they will become slums unless preventive action is taken" (Ahlbrandt and Brophy, 1975, p.1).

### Equilibrium Principle

In order to stabilise an area, to regenerate a viable living environment and housing market, action in the form of revitalisation is taken to stem the decline. To maintain the urban system unsatisfactory housing is cleared and replaced in many cases by public housing while houses with sound structures are rehabilitated. If we conceptualise inner city residential decline as a continuum then at one end we have a healthy viable area, with incipient decline, clear decline, accelerated decline in between and at the other end abandonment. It is considered necessary, however, for public action to be taken before an area reaches the third stage of clear decline if stability is to be maintained.[2]

### Difficulties with the Consensus Perspective

There are a number of difficulties with this consensus perspective of inner city residential decline and revitalisation. These are discussed below.

### Consequence and Cause Difficulties

(i) The first difficulty with the consequence and cause principle is that decline as a form of urban change involves many factors with complex inter-relationships and it is exceedingly difficult to capture the contribution of a specific factor to the change that does occur (Harvey Cox, 1976). The basic concept of the essentially economic model of consensus theory in explaining consequence and cause in inner city residential areas is thus somewhat tenuous.

(ii) A second difficulty with this principle is that blight can actually be a consequence of a public authority's urban renewal programme. Large numbers of empty houses are boarded up to await demolition in anything from one to eight years' time (Rowland, 1973).

In 1968 as a result of a reshowing on television of "Cathy Come Home" a squatters' movement was born in London to occupy empty properties (many in areas earmarked for central area redevelopment). The immediate aim of the London Squatters Campaign was to rehouse families from hostels or slums in the empty houses by means of squatting (Bailey, 1973). Eventually the Ministry of Housing sent a circular to all local authorities urging them to use all properties in a reasonable repair and with a life of two years or over; it also urged them to allow housing associations to take over property with a life of less than two years.

In the case of Liverpool houses were demolished on such a vast scale over the years that in 1976 there were 450 hectares of **vacant** land, constituting 15 per cent of the city's inner area, of which only 62 hectares was included in any firm programme for development (Stones, 1977).

The existence of large tracts of vacant land, boarded up houses, abandoned buildings (primarily in some U.S. cities) and the actions of squatting and urban homesteading (Ahlbrandt and Brophy, 1975) were certainly not the intended consequences of a consensual perspective but are unforeseen effects.

(iii) A third difficulty with the consequence and cause principle is that rehabilitation is doubtful of success as a form of revitalisation in a weak housing market. It may not be appropriate in areas of high concentrations of low-income households because of their lack of income as well as the loss of investor confidence (Ahlbrandt and Brophy, 1975). As such the choice of a residential area for rehabilitation becomes crucial and would seem to be relevant in areas composed predominantly of homeowners in the middle income bracket.

## Consensus Difficulties

(i) Tho firct difficulty with the consensus principle is that "decency" of housing rests on value premises that vary widely among groups of different economic, ethnic, and socio-cultural backgrounds (Rothenberg, 1970). It has been found that areas which officials may perceive as severely blighted are wanted by low-income families who, given their poverty, see the low-quality as part of their optimal use of resources.

(ii) A further difficulty with the principle of consensus is that in the U.S. Community Action and Model Cities Programs generated conflict "from the disparity between their aims and resources" (Marris and Rein, 1974, p. 327).

In Britain the conflict in the allocation of resources for both expanding areas in the outer cities and the declining areas of inner cities has been pointed out by Cullingworth and Donnison (Harvey Cox, 1976). Furthermore lack of consensus on goals of renewal in the U.S. legislation led to the emphasis on city centre redevelopment and to the destruction of more low-income housing than was built (van Til and van Til, 1973). Also that there is such a thing as the "public interest" has not been substantiated (Davies, 1972; Patricios, 1976).

(iii) A third difficulty with consensus is that coordination on urban renewal activities is difficult and hence unlikely in the context of "a multiplicity of separate interest groups and organisations each having defined its own problem, each seeking different sets of goals, and each jealously guarding its own powers and prerogatives" (Muchnick, 1970, p.20). Not only have there been conflicts between residents and officials but between municipal departments and between departments and politicians. Studies of the politics of renewal (Rossi and Dentler, 1961; Meyerson and Banfield, 1964; Kaplan, 1963) reveal that the interests of different groups can result in conflict.

(iv) A fourth difficulty is exemplified by studies of the 1960-65 clearance scheme in Sunderland (Dennis, 1970). Of the residents covered by the scheme 43 per cent were opposed to demolition, and 23 per cent considered they would be very much worse off in a council estate as compared to their present area. Inhabitants opposed the official view that houses had to be demolished when they considered them satisfactory. Little effort has been made even in other projects to establish inhabitants' preferences and attitudes (Harvey Cox, 1976).

(v) A fifth and a major difficulty is that instead of concensus there is coercion. Compulsory powers are being used against supposed beneficiaries to coerce them into what they would not want to do. The **Evangelistic Bureaucrat** (Davies, 1972) is about such a situation that occurred in Rye Hill, Newcastle. It is likely that Davies' description of people as helpless victims of power wielding by politicians and professionals is more widely applicable. He labels planners "evangelistic" as having seen the light and being in possession of a wisdom, others must be taught the truth so that they too can be converted.

**Equilibrium Difficulties**

(i) The first difficulty with the principle of equilibrium is that stability is not being achieved when expensive housing is substituted for cheap houses, when the quantity of low-price housing is rapidly eroded, and when more houses are demolished than are erected (Rothenburg, 1970; Harvey Cox, 1976). Revitalisation may in fact disturb any equilibrium that may exist by reducing the stock of low-quality housing available to the poor and those who choose to live in the inner city by choice.

(ii) A second difficulty regarding equilibrium is that major and rapid change in redevelopment breeds insecurity as the fragile stability of their (the inhabitants') known environment is shattered with little guarantee that better conditions would emerge at the end of the upheaval (Cherry, 1976). In addition the displacement of large numbers of families and the breaking up of communities in urban renewal programmes have been its most glaring weaknesses (Palen, 1975) and have caused damage to the social fabric of cities.

(iii) The public housing redevelopment project of Pruitt-Igoe in St. Louis, which was completed in 1955, proceeded from an architectural award in 1958 along a profile of failure until finally dynamited by the Housing Authority in 1972. It was completely demolished in 1973 (Palen, 1975) and must have disrupted any equilibrium that city may have had.

(iv) The further difficulty is that life in the zone of transition of the inner city in which most declining residential areas are situated is a life of squalor, of underprivilege and of conflict and is a world far from the functionally integrated social system which some sociologists are fond of discussing (Rex, 1969).

## CONFLICT THEORY

With these difficulties of consensual theory in mind it would be useful to look for an alternative theory to apply to inner city residential decline and revitalisation. The other basic theory that contemporary sociologists (Coser, 1956; Dahrendorf, 1958: Rex, 1961; Simmie, 1974), geographers (Harvey, 1973; Smith, 1977) and increasingly planners (Patricios, 1979) draw upon is conflict theory. The essential difference is that consensual theory postulates consensus as the foundation of social order whereas conflict theory regards conflict as the essence of society (Strasser, 1976).

The argument against consensual theory is that its two basic postulates are untenable (van den Berghe, 1963). Firstly, instead of consensus on values society actually has groups with contradictions and conflicting values, political or religious ideologies and scientific or philosophical theories. Secondly, the maintenance of structural stability and functional efficiency of practically all living groups is based on the principle of authority. However, authority generates conflicts and tensions which can threaten the disruption of groups. Rex (1961) furthermore points out that activities can be judged necessary or unnecessary, functional or dysfunctional, according to which of a number of conflicting standpoints they are looked at. In other words an action may have a beneficial consequence to a group responsible for that action but may have a detrimental effect on another group. The same argument applies when explaining activities in terms of the "need" to maintain a social structure. The difficulty is defining whose need, which depends upon the interests, aspirations, or values of different individuals or groups. Rex (1961) thus calls into question the consensus and integrationist assumptions and concludes that consensual theory would appear to be making false claims. It appears valid only when we require "the roughest of proofs." (p. 76).

According to conflict theorists "society is nothing if not a plurality of groups, strata, organizations, and classes with their respective interests and values ... whose relationships are characterized by competition, conflict, and patterns and domination" (Zeitlin, 1973, p. 133). Thus while functionalism is basically concerned with the primacy of order and integration, conflict theory focuses on patterns of conflict between groups with opposed aims and perspectives as well as power and wealth differences. As Strasser (1976) describes it functionalists think in terms of the "whole" ignoring antagonisms and struggles between the "parts" whereas to the conflict theorist these struggles and their resolution are central.

## Principles of Conflict Theory

### Conflict

(i) The basic postulate of conflict theory is that society is to be studied as a more or less organised struggle between groups over valued goods and services, expressed in terms of material wealth, power or prestige (Wallace, 1969). The concern here is confined to the frictions between the rulers and the ruled in a given society, between authorities and the public—"them" and "us". Myrdal's (Rex, 1961, p.122) three assumptions concerning American society are worth noting:

(a) there are conflicts of "value-premises" or aspirations and aims between groups.

(b) these conflicts are sufficiently radical in scope to affect the structure of the society at almost any point at which we care to study it

(c) the actual course of events is likely to be determined by the power at the disposal of groups and that the balance of power might change so that particular value premises might gain in social significance.

The main lines of the first postulate of conflict theory then are that social systems may be thought of as involving conflict situations instead of being organised around a consensus of values, and thus the existence of a plural and not a unitary society.

**Unequal Power**

(ii) The second postulate (Myrdal's third point) is that in most cases the conflict situation will be marked by an unequal balance of power which may change from time to time. Conflict results in particular from unequal distribution of privileges and rights where they are considered non-legitimate, according to Coser (Strasser, 1976). Power is interpreted here in the sense of the ability to effect or resist change.

**Change**

(iii) The third principle is that change is a central feature of human societies. In contrast to consensual theory conflict theory incorporates change and gives it a major place in its structure. Coser (1956) argues that when a society has sufficient flexibility to tolerate and institutionalise conflict the purpose of conflict is frequently to revitalise existent norms or contribute to the emergence of new norms. Conflict resolution can thus be seen as a mechanism for improvement or a regenerative force by adjusting to new conditions. It is in regid systems, however, where conflicts are suppressed that their potential emergence would tend to disrupt the society (Strasser, 1976). The rigidities, according to Blau (1964), are due to vested interests and powers, organisational commitments, and traditional institutions which defy modification and adjustment.

In identifying the principles of conflict, unequal power, and change of conflict theory I am mindful of Rex's (1961) suggestion regarding this theory. He maintains that the notion of conflict is far more applicable to the analysis and understanding of the central problems of modern industrial societies than any other theory of society. Furthermore "there can no longer be any doubt that no real penetration into social reality is possible ... only when one has also taken into account those conceptions which the participants have of it, how they experience their tensions in this situation, and how they react to the tensions so conceived." (Mannheim, 1960, p. 40)

## Decline and Revitalisation: A Conflict Perspective

**Conflict Principle:** The focus in decline and revitalisation of inner city residential areas from the conflict perspective is essentially on the struggle between the low-income inhabitants and public authorities and institutions. In contrast to the consensual perspective the conflict perspective's emphasis is on people and not physical structures. Beyond the functionalists' explanation of the causes of social phenomena there is a need to analyse the aims, interests, values and aspirations of the different groups involved in any situation (Simmie, 1974).

The major area of conflict is between the views inner city inhabitants have of their area and what should be done and the views of administrators and financial institutions. Although officials may define an area as blighted or a "ghetto" overwhelming numbers of residents do not view their area in an unfavourable light (Palen, 1975) and for them it may provide a protective community and a valuable social world (Greer, 1965). Blighted areas are defined by authorities according to their values and there may not be a broad consensus on them. The bias is towards those who control power of approval and development with residents having little say in defining areas of blight. Furthermore the location and design of new housing may not suit displaced tenants or owner-occupiers and rents will usually be higher than those paid previously (Medhurst and Parry Lewis, 1969). Financial institutions, in particular, perceive inner city areas as ones of high risk and by "red-lining" districts they reduce the inflow of necessary private sector capital (Ahlbrandt and Brophy, 1975).

**Unequal Power Principle:** The principle of unequal power is revealed in studies of inner city areas that authorities regard as blighted and which then go through a revitalisation process (Harvey Cox, 1976). The studies point to the political and economic powerlessness of inhabitants to their situation and to the changes occurring around them. To quote just two examples: firstly in Liverpool there was little opposition to the massive clearance scheme as the inhabitants had a general feeling of powerlessness and inability to affect policy (Muchnick, 1970). They had no choice or control over the redevelopment policies that affected them so directly. Secondly the cohesive Italian community in Boston's West End were powerless against the bulldozers which forced them to relocate (Palen, 1975). The city, then, can be seen as an arena for contesting power and resource allocation (Lambert and Weir, 1975).

Economic powerlessness is reflected in the poverty of inner city residents, in their "relative lack of command over resources and access to opportunity" (Cullingworth, 1972, p.21). Inner city disadvantage is further compounded by disparities in social services provided by authorities relative to investment in the outer city (Cherry, 1976). In the U.S. the reaction against urban renewal which displaced the poor, the deprived and the disadvantaged gave rise in the 1960s to the "advocacy planning movement" (Davidoff, 1965; Peattie, 1968; Goodman, 1972).

**Change Principle:** The principle of change and thus process in the urban system is stressed in the conflict perspective in contrast to the emphasis in consensual theory on equilibrium and thus structure. The change is the exodus of capable households to the outer city leaving behind in the inner city the poor, the less skilled, the less well-educated, the unemployed suffering poor housing and housing stress (Hollamby, 1977). The recent Inner Area Studies in Britain (DoE, 1977) reveal the growing polarity between the inner and outer city with the increasing concentration of problems in the inner areas.

The primary challenge that has to be faced is how to deal with this change that is leading to concentrations of losers in the inner urban cores of American and British cities, of those trapped by poverty, bad education, bad housing, the "no-chance people" (Rowland, 1973, p. 12). The winners, the aspirants are those with the income and greatest capability, who have the greatest housing choices and mobility of location and who can in general look after themselves.

**A planning strategy:** What form, then, would a planning strategy (using the term planning in its broadest sense) take base on a conflict perspective of inner city residential decline and revitalisation? It would be founded on the principles of struggle and conflict between different groups, of unequal power and a focus on urban change (i.e. the dynamism of cities) in comparison to consensual theory principles of simple consequence and cause, consensus and the attempt to achieve equilibrium.

**Regulating conflict:** A cornerstone of a planning strategy founded on these principles is to resolve or manage conflict, firstly by articulating it and secondly by establishing mechanisms to deal specifically with conflict. This is supported by an important conclusion from a study on poverty and inequality "that common purpose can be better served by articulating conflict than by searching for consensus...and (by) a pattern of government where coordination comes from the continuous arbitration of conflicting interests...and where the interests represented are far wider than before" (Marris and Rein, 1974, p. 358). We should be very conscious of the danger of not resolving conflicts concerning living conditions (but which may be contained temporarily) that will eventually crystallize into violence (N.A.C. on Civil Disorders, 1968).

There are mechanisms for regulating conflict as in industry, for exmaple. Between employers' associations and trade unions there are channels for collective bargaining and arbitration. When deprived groups develop awareness of actually being negatively privileged hostile feelings can lead to increasing degrees of conflict depending on the presence of mechanisms for regulating conflict. The lack of any mechanism to recognize and cope with potential conflict can lead eventually to violence, as illustrated in the Watts riots where poor housing, inferior education, unemployment, etc., were symptoms of the problem (Strasser, 1976).

If conflict is not to be repressed there is a need to set up some form of mechanism to overcome the failure to communicate, to overcome dispute by continuous open debate. This could be in the form of, say, community councils, neighbourhood groups, super-agencies (Muchnick, 1970) which will represent the interest of both the inner city inhabitants and the larger political and social structure.

In the process of regulating conflict people's attitudes and values will change. It could be that policies aimed at dealing with attitudes about an inner city area, about the use of public and private funds, and about the need to support an area "may be a more preventative and more cost beneficial approach than treating an area's physical condition" (Ahlbrandt and Brophy, 1975, p. 49). Conflicts may be resolved through a variety of processes including conciliation, mediation and arbitration and various procedures (Patricios, 1979).

**Overcoming powerlessness:** A planning strategy which involves overcoming powerlessness would need to include some means of local area control and public participation, changes in resource allocation, and recognition of self-help and urban homesteading measures.

The setting up of some system of local area control (Rowland, 1973; Muchnick, 1970) would provide inner city inhabitants with a sense of responsibility, involvement and commitment—knowledge that they had a personal, social and economic stake would mean they would take better care of their dwellings and area as a whole. The devolution of some power and decision-making responsibilities for local programmes and services to local elected representatives would overcome the feelings of powerlessness and apathy. New forms of grass-roots organisation, or micro-political groups as Donnison (1973) calls them, would hopefully promote closer contact and ensure that better services, increased opportunities for people and greater access to resources will be obtained. Real participation would have to mean the power to influence policy decisions and programmes and is not to be confused with token participation in which people are only informed or consulted (Patricios,1972).

The devolution of power and decision-making responsibility for local programmes and services to local elected representatives would ensure involvement. Local inner area groups may, for example, decide on how resources are to be allocated in improving their environment, what local roads should be closed, the creation of small parks, the need for particular social and welfare facilities, and so on. If any redevelopment is necessary they could decide on the clearance and rehousing schedule thus evolving policy from a grass-roots level and not from a bureaucratic machine.

We should recognise, however, that public participation which has been strongly advocated over the last decade is beset with difficulties of realization. On the other hand it would be a serious mistake to conclude that it is a waste of time. What is required is a need for clarity of the concept of participation rather than its rejection (Harvey Cox, 1976). Means need to be found to overcome situations of stalemate between citizen groups and political elites (van Til and van Til, 1973) and to avoid the mistake of the Model Cities Program of bypassing local political machines (Palen, 1975).

The Royal Town Planning Institute (1977) has suggested that to reverse inner city decline it may be necessary to switch resources from housing to jobs. The argument is that by improving job opportunities and thus the incomes of inner city inhabitants they will have a better chance of improving their houses themselves. Alternatively financial mechanisms should be developed to enable them to have access to funds at a price they can afford. Central government guarantees to financial institutions would thus be essential. The case is for subsidising people instead of dwellings.

In certain areas, especially those of high unemployment, "self-help" projects can be viable. In the U.S. there is, for example, the Flanner House project in Indianapolis where a co-operative movement with grants and training built over 235 houses themselves (Rowland, 1973). In addition the Fifth City community run organisation in Chicago's west side ghetto is engaged in the largest rehabilitation project in the nation (Palen, 1975). Over 100 units of which only the shells of the old buildings remained have been rehabilitated. The community's pride and identity have been restored, it runs its own health clinic and pre-school establishment, it has constructed its own small shopping centre and has succeeded in rebuilding one of the city's most hopeless neighbourhoods. Urban homesteading also appears to be an answer to the problem of abandoned buildings (Ahlbrandt and Brophy, 1975). Homesteaders, people willing to move into units which are really a shell of a dwelling, and who do not have sufficient assets to obtain a house in the normal market, use a combination of cash investment and "sweat equity" to improve pockets of abandoned inner city areas.

**Focusing on change:** The principle of change in the conflict perspective forces us to focus on the increasing polarisation of the inner and outer parts of large cities and the accumulating concentration of deprivation in the inner city. The precise form of a theory of change remains uncertain at present but it seems we are moving away from the 1960's idea of change as physical —the decay and replacement of buildings (Solesbury, 1975). The tendency is, now, to see change as primarily economic or social with physical change as a secondary effect.

What does appear fairly certain is that increasing deprivation is caused by complex factors and that solving the housing, employment, education, etc., problems individually are not likely to succeed. What is required is "an effective, and coordinated, package of policies for tackling low income, poor employment opportunities and the inequities in the provision of housing" (Harvey Cox, 1976, p. 85) which takes into account the needs of the inhabitants and their preferences.

As Blair (1975) points out the change in urban systems which results in polarisation is to the detriment of those left behind and to the community as a whole in terms of social costs. To deal effectively with this type of change requires conscious basic changes in the political and economic institutions. In particular actions are required to overcome powerlessness of inner city communities and in resolving conflict as outlined in the two previous sections.

## CONCLUSION

In conclusion I would like to point out that there may be situations of urban decline where the principles of consensual theory, of consequence and cause, consensus and equilibrium are applicable. It would seem to me, however, that the conflict perspective would be applicable in most situations. The distinctions between the principles of consensus and conflict and between the perspectives as a whole point to the fact that the social world can only be viewed from a particular stance (Elkin, 1974) and that we must choose between them.

That being the case I would like to advocate a new approach to the decline and the revitalisation of the inner city with the following components:

(i) Clear recognition by all concerned that conflict between groups of people exists and that it must be articulated and resolved through mechanisms that involve negotiation, conciliation, arbitration, and so on, and not through coer cion.

(ii) The establishment of grass-roots organisations with adequate powers to make meaningful decisions and to allocate resources in local matters; substantial funding particularly for self-help schemes; also the introduction of measures by the public sector to provide investor confidence.

(iii) An understanding of the process of polarisation between the inner and outer city as a result of economic and social change and the need arising therefrom to assist the disadvantaged, as well as recognition that necessary changes in existing organisational structures will have to be made.

Finally the new approach would not so much attack the symptoms of decline but the disease itself, deal not so much with buildings but with people, and instead of emphasising redevelopment or rehabilitation it would focus on poverty and powerlessness. The hope is that a **humane** approach to planned change will produce a more liveable and acceptable environment for the inhabitants of the inner city. As the psychologist Erich Fromm put it:"... only when he (man) can build a world based on human solidarity and justice, only when he can feel rooted in the experience of universal brotherliness, will he have found a new human form of rootedness, will he have transformed his world into a truly human home." (Rowland, 1973, p. 147)

## NOTES

1. A theory of stable social systems has, however, difficulties in explaining change. While it is assumed that a social system adapts to such factors as technological developments, explanations of change in terms of random mutations and natural selection, or internal change in terms of "growing", are less than satisfactory (Rex, 1961).
2. Public authority action is not always required. Non-governmental approaches, such as the Neighborhood Housing Services Organisation in Pittsburg, can be a vehicle that brings citizens, government and financial institutions together in order to move "a declining neighborhood towards stabilization". (Ahlbrandt and Brophy, 1975, p.125).

## REFERENCES

Ahlbrandt, R. S. and Brophy, P. C. (1975) **Neighborhood Revitalization: Theory and Practice**; Farnborough, Hants.: Lexington Books.

Bailey, R. (1973) **The Squatters**; Harmondsworth, Middlesex: Penguin Books Ltd.

Berry, B. J. L. (1973) "Urban renewal", **Proceedings of the Urban and Regional Development Seminar** (1972), K. S. O. Beavon & T. J. D. Fair (eds.) Johannesburg: South African Geographical Society, pp. 79-105.

Berghe, P. van den (1963) "Dialectic and functionalism; toward a theoretic synthesis", **American Sociological Review**, 28, October, pp. 695-705.

Blair, T. (1975) "Cities for citizens", **Built Environment Quarterly**, 1 (3), December, pp. 212-214.

Blau, P. M. (1964) **Exchange and Power in Social Life**, New York: John Wiley.

Coser, L. A. (1956) **The Functions of Social Conflict**, London: Routledge & Kegan Paul.

Cherry, G. E. (1976) "Aspects of Urban Renewal", **Growth and Change in the Future City Region**, T. Hancock (ed.). Lon don: Leonard Hill, pp. 53-71.

Community Development Project (CDP) (1977) **Gilding the Ghetto. The State and Poverty Experiments.** London: CDP Inter-Project Editiorial Team.

Cullingworth, J. B. (1972) **Problems of an Urban Society**, Volume II. London: Allen & Unwin.

Dahrendorf, F. (1958) "Toward a theory of social conflict", **Journal of Conflict Resolution**, 11, June, pp. 170-183.

Davidoff, P. (1965) "Advocacy and pluralism in planning", **Journal of the American Institute of Planners**, 31, November, pp. 331-338.

Davies, J. G. (1972) **The Evangelistic Bureaucrat**, London: Tavistock Publications.

Dennis, N. (1970) **People and Planning**, London: Faber and Faber.

Department of The Environment (DoE) (1977) **Summaries of Consultants' Inner Area Study Reports** (Liverpool, Birmingham and Lambeth) London: H. M. S. O.

Donnison, D. V. and Eversley, D. (eds.) (1973) **London: Urban Patterns, Problems and Policies,** London: Heinemann.

Elkin, S. L. (1974) **Politics and Land Use Planning: The London Experience.** London: Syndics of the Cambridge University Press.

Gibson, M. and Langstaff, M. (1977) "Scope for Improvement? Policies and strategy in gradual renewal", **The Planner,** 63 (2), March, pp. 35-38.

Gittus, E. (1969) "Sociological aspects of urban decay", **Urban Decay: An Analysis and a Policy.** F. Medhurst and J. Parry Lewis (eds.), London: Macmillan, pp. 27-35.

Goodman, R. (1972) **After the Planners,** Harmondsworth: Penguin Books Ltd.

Greer, S. (1965) **Urban Renewal and American Cities: The Dilemma of Democratic Intervention,** Indianapolis: The Bobbs-Merrill Co., Inc.

Hancock, T. (1976) "The Inner City", **Growth and Change in the Future City Region,** T. Háncock (ed.), London: Leonard Hill, pp. 93-101.

Harvey, D. (1973) **Social Justice and the City,** London: Edward Arnold.

Harvey Cox, W. (1976) **Cities: the Public Dimension,** Harmondsworth, Middlesex: Penguin Books Ltd.

Hollamby, E. (1977) "Inner area study reports: practice review", **RTPI News,** June, p. 44.

Kaplan, H. (1963) **Urban Renewal Politics: Slum Clearance in Newark: New York:** Columbia University Press.

Lambert, C. and Weir, D. (eds.) (1975) **Cities in Modern Britain,** Glasgow: Fontana/Collins.

Lawless, P. (1977) "HAAs: powerful attack or financial fiasco?", **The Planner,** 63 (2), March, pp. 39-42.

Mannheim, K. (1960) **Ideology and Utopia,** London: Routledge and Kegan Paul.

Marris, P. and Rein, M. (1974) **Dilemmas of Social Reform: Poverty and Community Action in the United States,** Harmondsworth, Middlesex: Penguin Books (2nd edition. First published in 1967).

Medhurst, F. and Parry Lewis, J. (1969) **Urban Decay: An Analysis and a Policy,** London: Macmillan.

Meyerson, M. and Banfield, E. C. (1964) **Politics, Planning and the Public Interest,** New York: The Free Press.

Muchnick, D. M. (1970) **Urban Renewal in Liverpool: A Study of the Politics of Development,** Occasional paper on Social Administration No.33. London: G. Bell & Sons.

National Advisory Commission of Civil Disorders, U.S. (1968) **Report of the National Advisory Commission on Civil Disorders,** Washington, D.C.: Government Printing Office (also supplemental reports published for the Commission by Praeger, New York, 1968).

Palen, J. J. (1975) **The Urban World,** New York: McGraw Hill Book Co.

Patricios, N. N. (1972) "The quality of the built environment: the process of urban renewal", **South African Journal of Science,** 68 (2), February, pp. 47-52.

-- (1973) "A comparative evaluation of urban renewal and the need for a conceptual base", **Proceedings of the Urban and Regional Development Seminar (1972),** K. S. O. Beavon and T. J. D. Fair (eds.) Johannesburg: South African Geographical Society.

-- (1976) **Urban Planning: its Basic Aims,** Johannesburg: University of the Witwatersrand Press.

-- (1977) **An Agentive Perspective of Urban Planning,** Discussion Paper, UCLA, Los Angeles: School of Architecture and Urban Planning.

-- (1979) "An Agentive Perspective of Urban Planning." **Town Planning Review** 50 (1), January, pp.36-54.

Peattie, L. R. (1968) "Reflections on advocacy planning", **Journal of the**

**American Institute of Planners,** 34, March, pp. 80-88.

Perry, J. (1976) "Review of General Improvement Areas", J. T. Roberts, Farnborough, Saxon House, **The Planner,** 62 (7), November, p.219.

Rex, J. A. (1961) **Key Problems of Sociological Theory,** London: Routledge & Kegan Paul.

-- (1969) "The sociology of a zone of transition", **Readings in Urban Sociology,** R. E. Pahl (ed.), Oxford: Pergamon Press Ltd., pp. 211-231. (Reprinted. First edition 1968).

Rossi, P. H. and Dentler, R. A. (1961) **The Politics of Urban Renewal,** New York: The Free Press of Glencoe.

Rothenberg, J. (1970) **Economic Evaluation of Urban Renewal. Conceptual Foundations of Benefit-cost Analysis,** Washington D.C.:The Brookings Institution (Fourth printing. First published in 1967).

Rowland, J. (1973) **Community Decay,** Harmondsworth, Middlesex: Penguin Books.

Royal Town Planning Institute (1977) "Inner city areas: economic development before houses", **RTPI News,** May, p. 34.

Simmie, J. M. (1974) **Citizens in Conflict: The Sociology of Town Planning,** London: Hutchinson Educational Ltd.

Smith, D. M. (1977) **Human Geography: A Welfare Approach,** London: Edward Arnold.

Solesbury, W. (1975) "Programmes into policies", **Built Environment Quarterly** (Theme: Urban Renewal), 3 (1), March, pp. 47-50.

Stones, A. (1977) "Liverpool now: inner city wasteland", **Built Environment Quarterly,** 3(1), March, pp. 47-50.

Strasser, H. (1976) **The Normative Structure of Sociology. Conservative and Emancipatory Themes in Social Thought,** London: Routledge & Kegan Paul.

Til J. van and Til S. B. van (1973) "Citizen participation in social policy: the end of the cycle?" **Cities in Change: Studies on the Urban Condition,** J. Walton and D. E. Carns (eds.), Boston: Allyn & Bacon, Inc., pp. 398-409.

Wallace, W. L. (ed.) (1969) **Sociological Theory: An Introduction,** London: Heinemann.

Wohl, A. S. (1977) **The Eternal Slum: Housing and Social Policy in Victorian London,** London: Edward Arnold.

Wood, A. (1977) "Opinion: Inner areas—too many cooks?" **The Planner,** 63 (2), March. p. 34.

Zeitlin, I. M. (1973) **Rethinking Sociology. A Critique of Contemporary Theory,** Englewood Cliffs, New Jersey: Prentice Hall, Inc.

SIX

Eberhard von Einem

# COMPARING URBAN REVITALIZATION IN THE UNITED STATES AND WEST GERMANY

## INTRODUCTION

The revitalization of declining and deteriorated inner-city neighborhoods is a stated political goal in most of the western industrialized nations, as is the minimization of its social costs. A number of policies have been introduced in recent years in order to stimulate urban revitalisation. The United States, Canada, Great Britain, France, Italy, the Netherlands, Belgium, Austria, Switzerland, the Scandinavian countries, and West Germany have one way or the other passed or amended urban laws, established housing programs for rehabilitation and renovation and/or allowed for special tax deductions that are supposed to encourage private reinvestment in the existing housing stock. In addition, major determinants of the housing market have changed during the 1970s, resulting in what now seems to have become a widespread, although highly selective, cross-national phenomenon: Private-market renovation of old buildings, especially those with some kind of nostalgic architecture, in some close-to-the-business-district neighborhoods. In fact, private-market revitalisation is now underway in such diverse cities as New York, Washington, San Francisco, Boston, Montreal, London, Paris, Milano, Amsterdam, Brussels, Zurich, Copenhagen, Stockholm, Munich, Hamburg and others.

In this paper I will concentrate and examine urban revitalisation in two countries, the United States and West Germany. First, I will compare private-market revitalisation, including the demographic characteristics of the "renovators" and the factors influencing the level of private-market renovations. Second, I will discuss public policies employed in the two countries, that aim at stimulating rehabilitation and coping with displacement.

## PRIVATE-MARKET REVITALISATION

For decades metropolitan areas in the United States have been expanding through new constructions on the urban fringe. The white middle-class households tend to move out of the central cities in the course of their social upward mobility, leaving inner-city neighborhoods for those that could not afford new homes on larger lots and to the immigrating poor black and hispanic families. Through filtering down the older urban housing stock deteriorated. The dynamics of decline, which have been analysed as occurring in stages (Goetze, 1979, Downs, 1981), have dominated the patterns of urban change resulting in housing abandonment in the final stage.

West Germany's inner-city neighborhoods also experienced decline, although to a much lesser degree and caused in part by specific factors that result from the housing shortage in the years after World War II (about 5 million housing units). Housing that survived the war intact was urgently needed to provide shelter for millions of refugees and those without any home. Governments of all federal levels concentrated on the reconstruction of destroyed cities and on the construction of new additional housing through social housing programs, subsidies for homeowners and tax deductions for landlords. Rents in the existing housing sector were controlled.

Given the technical obsolescence of many of the 19th-century multi-family structures, given the overcrowding in the 1950s, given the strong demand, and given the limited revenues of the landlords, the older housing stock deteriorated. Furthermore filtering contributed to the decline of inner-city housing conditions in the 1960s and 1970s. Gradually the German middle-class families moved—similar to their American counterparts—to the suburbs in order to occupy newly built single-family homes (West Germany still has an extremely low rate of homeownership, 38 per cent), whereas four million "guest-workers" including their families—filled the then vacated inner-city neighborhoods. One major difference to American housing markets, however, persists: the market for substandard housing and social housing, that low- and moderate-income households could afford, never reached an equilibrium in the rental sector. With the exception of speculative purposes, there have never been permanent vacancies or even abandoned buildings in Germany's inner-city neighborhoods. Not only has the owner of an old apartment-building always been certain to find some renters, no matter how bad the physical conditions of his structure are. Foreign "guestworkers" also are often willing to pay higher rents in a housing market, that increasingly became a dual market, thus inducing further decline.

Despite these differences in both extent and dynamics of urban decline, private-market revitalisation emerged on both sides of the Atlantic parallel as a secondary trend. Even the timing seems to coincide. The first cases of private-market renovation have been observed in the early 1970s. In the second half of the 1970s the new trend became clearly visible.

Contrary to the traditional middle-class family's preference for a single-family home in a suburban setting, a growing number of households chooses to live in inner-city neighborhoods. Clay suggested to differenciate two distinct strategies of private market revitalisation, gentrification and incumbent upgrading, strategies which can be found in both the United States and West Germany (Clay, 1979).

The British term gentrification refers to renovation by newcomers. It is associated with an upward change of the social class composition of a given neighborhood through immigrating households with relatively higher incomes and social status, displacing households with relatively lower incomes and social status (London, 1980). Gentrification seems to be a small, but widespread phenomenon, often taking place only in a tiny segment of any neighborhood. In the United States gentrification occurs in many cases through recent buyers, renovating the building for their own occupancy. In West Germany gentrification occurs in many cases through landlords, modernizing low-rent appartments for new renters, that can afford higher rents. In both countries condominium conversion has been discovered as a profitable business, thus reducing the supply of low-rent appartments. Gentrification implies a filtering up process.

Incumbent upgrading can be defined as renovation by longtime residents seeking physical and social upgrading without moving . Downs terms it "upgrading in place" as contrasted to "upgrading through movement" (Downs, 1979), 465; 1981). Incumbent upgrading seems an even more widespread phenomenon, visible in increasing maintenance and modernization expenditures (Einem et al, 1981). Incumbent upgrading occurs in many cases in lower middle-class neighborhoods. Households that previously tended to leave central cities, changed their plans and chose to stay and to improve their own living environment through reinvestment. Rather than moving, these households adjust their own home to their improved social status.

Exact data quantifying the housing units that have undergone private-market renovation are not available. Thomas Black reports that every second American city with more than 50,000 inhabitants experiences some kind of renovation activities (Black, 1975; 1980). Clay found private-market revitalisation in all of America's 30 largest cities (Clay, 1980). In West Germany private-market revitalisation is underway in parts of major cities and even in some cases in middle- and small-sized cities (Einem et al, 1981). On the other hand, private-market revitalisation is a highly selective process, affecting only pockets within neighborhoods, that show the following characteristics:

- location: close to the central business district and/or access to local mass transit facilities.
- housing stock: basicly sound structures, preferably with historic architecture, such as stucco facades, victorians, etc. Some of West Germany's cities with medieval houses, for example, have found their heritage a new resource for revitalisation.
- infrastructure: amenities like parks, schools, universities, shopping facilities and pedestrian zones proved to be a stimulus.

The extent of private-market renovation can also be glimpsed in the changing structure of private homeowner's investment patterns. In the United States average maintenance expenditures of city homeowners have continued to increase overproportionally since 1973-74 as compared to those of suburban homeowners (James, 1980). In West Germany maintenance expenditures increased their share of the overall housing expenditures from 12 per cent in 1970 to 22 per cent in 1977 (DIW, 1978). Another 19 per cent (1977) of all outlays have been allocated for modernization. These figures indicate a shift of the private investor's strategies towards reinvestment, energy conservation and improving the existing housing stock.

There is little doubt, it is misleading to lable private-market revitalisation a "back-to-the-city-movement", as it has frequently been termed by the media (Gale, 1976; Long, 1980). In quantitative terms urban revitalisation represents neither in the United States nor in Germany a reversal of major demographic trends. In the United States and in Germany urban flight of the middle-class to the suburbs is still dominant, as indicated by the 1980 United States census of population which again shows severe population losses of all large cities in the northeast and central north. It is also demonstrated by Germany's annual demographic data, showing a persisting pattern: net-outmigration from inner-city neighborhoods. In fact, case studies reveal "what is commonly referred to as back to the city is fundamentally a resettlement in and a renewal of older neighborhoods mainly by middle-class people who are presently residents in the city in other neighborhoods as renters" (Clay, 1980, 14). James found that not more than 11 per cent of the newcomers in reviving neighborhoods actually come from suburbs. The majority of the renovators (70 per cent) are either long-time residents or come from other parts of the same city (James, 1977). Urban revitalisation appears to be a "stay-in-the-city" phenomenon (Cincin-Sain, 1979, 54).

In terms of their socio-economic characteristics, renovators moving into older inner-city neighborhoods can be described as being predominantly young, white households. In many cases they received at least a college education. Their income is above the national average. In addition these "young professionals" have few children, if any. An overproportional number is living in one-adult households, in other households both partners are working (Gale, 1979; 1980; Spain, 1980). Corresponding studies have not been undertaken in Germany so far. However, interviews with renovators, real estate brokers, and developers indicate similar characteristics for resettlers in Germany's inner-cities: These are predominantly young couples with or without children, often forming their first households. They have better than average education and income and they often consciously choose to live in an inner-city neighborhood, because of economic reasons combined with a preference for avoiding the social norms of a suburban environment.

Analyses of the factors causing private-market revitalisation in both the United States and West Germany reveal a number of striking similarities that may explain to some extent the coincidence of the current trend towards urban reinvestment.

Rising energy costs and commuting costs affecting both countries may have contributed to inner-city resettlement. At least one scholar, however, has argued, its impact so far may be considered only as being marginal (Rosenthal, 1979, 10).

Changing patterns of life-styles have been observed on both sides of the Atlanctic. Young professionals especially seem to be attracted by core neighborhoods, even mixed ethnic neighborhoods, promising close contacts to people of various backgrounds. Also older buildings seem to appeal to this group of people more than single family homes in monoton suburbs (Clay, 1979, 16).

Apart from conservation motives and the young professional's interests in counter-cultural life-styles, which in particular may have influenced the early resettlers (Gale, 1980, 105: "risk-oblivious" households), economic and demographic factors are the main driving forces behind private-market revitalisation (James, 1980).

On the one hand demand for housing continues to grow in both countries, despite falling population figures of the central cities. In the United States the post-war baby-boom generation entered the stage of household-formation (Goetze, 1979). In West Germany a parallel baby-boom reached maturity, creating new demand on housing markets. Furthermore housing consumption per household increased (Baldermann et al, 1979, 439). In addition household-sizes decreased in both countries with the drop in marriage rates, the sharp climb of divorces, the falling fertility rates and the climbing women employment rates (Masnick et al, 1980), thus increasing the overall numbers of households seeking shelter.

On the other hand supply of new housing units does not keep up with household formation. Both the United States and West Germany's housing industry experienced a parallel business cycle: an extraordinary production boom in the early 1970s and a severe recession in the production of both subsidized and non-subsidized new (rental) housing since 1974-5 (Sternlieb, Hughes, 1980; Der Wohnungsbau, annual reports). Given the reduced level of new construction in both countries, private investors (owner-occupants and developers) shifted their attention to the existing housing stock. Inflation is an additional factor. In the United States the average price for a new single home is now—1981—well over $80,000, as compared to $19,000 in 1963. Similar construction costs and land prices in West Germany have continued to rise at rates higher than the consumer-index.

To built a typical single-family home in Germany requires 8-9 net-incomes of an average household. In the United States housing costs traditionally have been equivalent to 2, 5-3 annual net-incomes (Koster, Metzler, 1979, 29), with a rising tendency, however. Compared to these prices inner-city housing remained to be relatively cheap in the United States as well as in Germany, thus encouraging potential homeowners to buy a used house in one of the older inner-city neighborhoods, instead of building a new house on the urban fringe. (In the United States housing prices in some of the declining urban areas have actually been falling in real terms, a phenomenon unknown to German inner-city housing so far.)

## PUBLIC POLICIES TOWARDS URBAN REVITALISATION

A number of public policies have either a direct or an indirect impact on urban revitalisation. Such policies range from housing and urban development to transportation, environmental protection, schools, crime prevention, and economic development. Federal, state and local governments subsidize and regulate urban evitalization and try to cope with its costs, namely displacement. This paragraph cannot present a full picture of public policies, instead it will attempt only to give an overview and to discuss briefly those policies that are directly aimed at influencing urban revitalisation.

The federal government in the United States offers several programs that can be used to promote urban revitalisation. Community Development Block Grants are the principal financial source to finance urban revitalisation policies. Under the CDBG program entitled cities are enabled to allocate federal funds according to local needs. It is the municipality rather than a federal agency that has to formulate and decide revitalisation strategies and to make available public funds for home improvements, energy conservation, rehabilitation, street improvements and social infrastructure within the framework of broad guidelines. In addition the federal government runs a low-interest loan program (Sec 312) and a rehabilitation program (Sec 8 substantial rehab), both however with limited funding, as well as a number of small experimental programs, such as the Urban Homesteading Demonstration Program and a program to subsidize Neighborhood Housing Services. Neighborhood Housing Services seem to be one of the most promising revitalisation strategies, because it is targeted specifically at incumbent upgrading through existing owners, thus avoiding displacement. Under the NHS concept a three-way partnership is formed among the citizen's neighborhood organization, local lending institutions and the municipality ensuring each other mutually to cooperate through planning, code enforcement, technical assistance and providing mortgages even in high-risk cases (Clay, 1979, 53; Kuttner, 1980).

Most important of all, however, is the impact of the U.S. Federal Tax Code. It allows investors to deduct mortgage interests and property taxes from their taxable income, thus providing an enormous incentive for investing in housing. As Rolf Goetze has analysed tax benefits helped to speed up private-market renovations, especially condominium conversion up to a point, that these incentives "seem to stimulate more demand, but not more supply" (Goetze, 1981, 44, 51).

In West Germany federal and state governments base their urban policies on a number of laws and small special-purpose categorical programs, each with its own conditions and strings attached, namely the Modernization Program, the Energy Conservation Program, the Urban Development Assistance Program, historical preservation programs, as well as several anti-recession programs channeled into inner-city neighborhoods. Also Social Housing Programs can be used for rehabilitation of older buildings for low- and moderate-income households (Einem, 1982). These funds go either directly to private investors or they are granted to the local governments in order to help them to realize their urban revitalisation goals. Case studies, however, have shown that the majority of the local governments receiving urban grants used the funds for commercial revitalisation primarily instead of residential revitalisation. The renewal and restructuring of downtown retail districts through reorganizing the traffic, parking facilities, pedestrian zones, new shopping centers, public facilities as well as moderate and high income residential uses is till perceived to be the most urgent revitalisation goal in the perspective of many mayors and city councilmen (Einem et al, 1981).

Finally, Germany's Federal Income Tax Law contributes to urban revitalisation. The law allows tax deductions for accelerated depreciation and for mortgage interest payments (owner-occupants are excluded) as well as special tax deductions of all modernization costs since 1977. In the United States these provisions have been criticized for causing overconsumption in urban areas with favourable locations and strong real estate markets, instead of stimulating carefully targetted urban revitalisation in urban areas most in need (Birlem et al, 1981).

Counteracting displacement caused by private reinvestment is an emerging policy issue in both the United States and West Germany.

In the United States the federal government tends to delegate the responsibility for anti-displacement policies to the local level. In fact, displacement seems a problem with a low political priority in Washington. The Department of Housing and Urban Development seems to consider the benefits of urban revitalisation-middle-class resettlement, physical improvement of the inner-city housing stock, and increased tax base outweighing the costs (Sumka, 1980; Cincin-Sain, 1979). On the local level several strategies have been proposed and tried. Washington D.C. enacted an anti-speculation ordinance. Cambridge, Mass., banned condominium conversion. An early warning system has been recommended as well as a "rehousing bank" to provide housing for relocated and evicted residents (Grier, Grier, 1980, 264). Rental assistance may help tenants to pay increased rents and a program for low interest loans may enable some households to buy their housing units in reviving neighborhoods (Houstoun, O'Connor, 1980).

In Germany the federal, state and local governments tended to ignore the problems of private-market displacement for a long time pointing on the one hand to the formal relocation procedure, that is part of the enacted requirements for urban renewal (similar to the old U.S. urban renewal relocation regulations) and pointing on the other to the existing federal rent laws. German rent laws established a loose version of rent control: Rent increases are limited to the level generally paid for housing of comparable size, comfort, and location. In addition federal rent laws restrict rent-increases in cases of modernization to 11 per cent annually of the actual expenditures (excluding maintenance costs).

It has not been until the recent housing riots that the federal government took private-market displacement seriously. In May 1981 the federal government imposed a statutory period of notice in cases of condominium conversion. In order to discourage potential buyers any new owner is prohibited to evict present tenants before a period of seven years has passed.

Given the federal government's jurisdiction over rent laws, some local governments searched for other resources to prevent speculative investments in inner-city neighborhoods. Legal tools, such as zoning ordinances, statutory use limitations and preservation ordinances have been used successfully in some cases (Steinbach, 1979).

Clearly, the policies, employed in both countries, fall short to prevent displacement. They may be appropriate to limit the negative impact of private-market and government induced reinvestment on existing residents in some cases. The overriding problem, however, is the growing housing shortage for low- and moderate-income households on the one hand and the overinvestment caused by tax provisions and benefitting primarily high-income households on the other. These problems have not been attacked yet and, given the limited financial resources of both the United States and West Germany, it is not likely that they will be attacked in coming years.

## REFERENCES

J. Baldermann et al, Bevolkerungs- und Siedlungsentwicklung, in: Stadtbauwelt No 61 (1979) : 439

Torsten Birlem, Ursula Klingmuller, Umfang und Auswirkungen der Wohnungs-

und Stadtebauforderung in West-Berlin Gesamtforderungsbudgetanalyse, Berlin (Istitut fur Stadt- forschung Berlin) Gutachten 1981.

J. Thomas Black, Private market renovation in central cities: A U.L.I. survey, in: Urban Land No 34 (November): 3-9, reprinted in: Shirley B. Laska, Daphne Spain (eds.), Back to the City, New York (Pergamon Press), 1980: 1975, 3-12.

Biliana, Cincin-Sain, The Costs and Benefits of Neighborhood Revitalisation, in: Donald Rosenthal (ed), Urban Revitalisation, Beverly Hills (Sage Publications) (1979):49-75.

Phillip Clay, Neighborhood Renewal, Lexington, Mass. (Lexington Books) (1979).

Phillip, Clay, The Rediscovery of City Neighborhoods: Reinvestment by Long-Time Residents and Newcomers, in: Shirley B. Laska, Daphne Spain (eds), Back to the City, New York (Pergamon Press) (1980): 13-26.

DIW Zur Entwicklung des Bauvolumens 1978-79, in: DIW-Wochenbericht 40-41 (1978):381-388.

Anthony, Downs, Key Relationships Between Urban Development and Neighborhood Change, in: Journal of the American Planning Association, Vol. 45 (1979):462-472.

Anthony, Downs, Understanding neighborhoods (Brookings Institution (forthcoming) (1981).

Eberhard, von Einem et al, Kommunale Stadterneuerungs-politik und Investitionsverhalten privater Eigentumer in Stadter-neuerungsgebieten, Bonn, Schriftenreihe des BMBau (forth- coming) (1981).

Eberhard, von Einem, National Urban Policy - The Case of West Germany, in: Journal of the American Planning Association, Vol. 48 (1982), January.

Dennis, Gale, The back-to-the-city-movement, or is it? A survey of recent homeowners in the Mount Pleasant neighborhood of Washington D.C., Washington D.C. (George Washington University, Department of Urban and Regional Planning, (1976).

Dennis, Gale, Middle-Class Resettlement in Older urban Neighborhoods: The Evidence and the Implications, in: Journal of the American Planning Association, Vol. 45 (1979): 293-304.

Dennis, Gale, Neighborhood Resettlement: Washington D.C., in: Shirley B. Laska, Daphne Spain (eds), Back to the City, New York (Pergamon Press) (1980) : 95-115.

Rolf, Goetze, Understanding neighborhood Change, Cambridge, Mass (Ballinger) (1979).

Rolf, Goetze, The Housing Bubble, in: Working Papers for a New Society, Vol. 7 (1981): 44-52.

George, Grier, Eunice Grier, Urban Displacement: A Reconoissance, in: Shirley B. Laska, Daphne Spain (eds), Back to the City, New York (Pergamon Press) 1980: 288- 301

Franklin, James, Back to the City:, An Appraisal of Housing Reinvestment and Population Change in Urban America, Washington (Urban Institut) (1977)

Franklin, James, The Revitalisation of Older Urban Housing and Neighborhoods, in: Arthur Solomon (ed), The Prospective City, Cambridge, Mass. (MIT Press): (1980) 130-160.

J. Koster, J. Metzler, Wohnungseigentumsquote, Bonn, Schrif- tenreihe des BMBau No 07.005 (1979).

Robert, Kuttner, Stone Soup: Why Neighborhood Housing Services Work, in: Working Papers for a New Society, Vol. 7, (1980) No. 4: 42-51.

Bruce, London, Gentrification as Urban Reinvasion: Some Preliminary Definitional and Theoretical Considerations, in: Shirley Laska, Daphne Spain (eds), Back to the City, New York (Pergamon Press) (1980): 77-92.

Larry, Long, Back to the Countryside and Back to the City in the Same

Decade, in: Shirley B. Laska, Daphne Spain (eds), **Back to the City**, New York (Pergamon Press): 61-76.

Donald, Rosenthal, Introduction, in: Donald Rosenthal (ed), **Urban Revitalisation**, Beverly Hills (Sage Publications) (1979).

George, Masnick et al, The Nation's Families: 1960-1980, Cam- bridge, Mass. (Joint Center for Urban Studies) (1980).

Daphne, Spain, Indicators of Urban Revitalisation: Racial and Socio-economic Changes in Central-City Housing, in: Shirley B. Laska, Daphne Spain (eds), **Back to the City**, New York (Pergamon Press): (1980) 27-41.

Hartmut Steinbach, **Umwandlung von Mietwohnungen zu Eigentum- swohnungen** in Wiesbadener Erneuerungsgebieten and Ansteigen der Mietpreise nach Modernisierungsma B-nahmen, Ms. (Stadt Wiesbaden) (1979).

George, Sternlieb, James Hughes (eds), **America's Housing, Prospects and Problems**, New Brunswick, N.J. (Center for Urban Policy Research) (1980).

Howard Sumka, Federal Antidisplacement Policy in a Context of Urban Decline, in: Shirley B. Laska, Daphne Spain (eds), **Back to the City**, New York (Pergamon Press): (1980), 269-287.

Der Wohnungsbau, annual reports, in: Bundesbaublatt (Published by the BMBau)

SEVEN

Andreas Falke

# COMMUNITY MOBILIZATION AS A STRATEGY FOR INNER-CITY REVITALIZATION THE RECENT U.S. EXPERIENCE

## THE DECLINE OF COMMUNITY MOBILIZATION: COMMUNITY DEVELOPMENT CORPORATIONS AND INNER-CITY REVITALIZATION[1]

The transformation of community organizations, representing the poorest areas of American cities, into Community Development Corporations in the aftermath of the War on Poverty is probably the clearest indication that community mobilization is not sufficient to revitalize the ghetto. Protest and confrontation tactics serve well to get the attention of the public: the media, the politicians, and an unresponsive bureaucracy, which never considered poor and minority residents as equal partners in clientele relationships. They serve well to pressure for a change in existing service delivery arrangements and city policies (code enforcement, police protection, garbage collection, school and educational services). Above all, they help to establish a base of legitimacy for the leaders and organizers, from which further activities can be undertaken (Lancourt, 1979, pp. 35-107).

Conflict and confrontation tactics prove to be of no avail, however, when CDCs are faced with demands to deliver their own set of services and developmental activities. They become problematic, because they are only intended to achieve immediate or short-term victories. This intention conflicts with the need to develop a community-based service delivery system and to undertake physical development projects, in particular housing projects, which require outside resources, long-term planning and execution. Revitalization efforts on such a level call for a sustained effort, while community mobilization is hard to sustain over a long period.

With the shift from "protest to program development" high

pressure tactics lose their utility (Lancourt, 1979, p. 162-66; Ahlbrandt, 1979, p. 207). What counts now is the development of staff capabilities and expertise in project planning and execution. An organization will henceforth concentrate all its energies on developing such capacities to the detriment of continued community participation. The operating mode of a CDC will therefore become bureaucratic, and decision-making will be centralized (Cohen, 1979, pp. 356-357; Goering, 1979, p. 512; Glaser, 1979, p.536).

The pursuit of protest strategies is further impeded by the need to obtain outside resources. For this purpose ties and working relationships with outside institutional actors (banks, developers, government agencies) have to be established. The permanent challenge of those actors through confrontation is prohibited. CDCs will rather adopt negotiated approaches. They put a premium on creating legitimacy as partners vis-a-vis established institutions.

Legitimacy, for instance, is necessary for being recognized by federal agencies as an eligible not-for-profit sponsor, for obtaining Sec. 8 subsidized housing allocations from their offices in a competitive process with professional developers, for engaging in joint ventures or for raising capital through project syndication. Faced with physical development tasks, CDCs come to view community mobilization as largely dysfunctional (Fish, 1973).

This trend will not be reversed with the growth of the various program components. Routine management and administrative problems increase, and will demand continuous attention. In particular, by going into housing development, a CDC will have to assume the role of a landlord. The landlord-tenant relationship introduces a more antagonistic element that does not allow for the comparatively smooth service-provider-service-recipient relationship that goes with social service programs. The leadership of a CDC has to become increasingly sensitive to maintenance and rent-collections problems, which under the adverse social and economic circumstances of poor areas are a fact of life. In this situation the use of mobilization is prohibitive. Mobilization will rather turn into disciplinary action (Lancourt, 1979, p. 179).

Since ideology and reality frequently do not coincide, i.e. CDCs keep thinking of themselves as advocacy entities despite changed practices, they are ill-equipped to deal with the fact that everyday operation is dominated by constant crisis-hopping. CDCs possess few internal coping mechanisms for administrative conflict. (Fish, 1973, p. 302).

One of the major crisis-generating factors is the lack or fluctuation of competent personnel. Under the stress of recurring crisis, job burn-out occurs. Leadership and competent staff resign to take more lucrative and stable jobs in the private and public sectors.

The recruitment of community resident is as much a risk as an opportunity to supply jobs, as community residents are subject to peer and kinship pressure, which distracts them from their job responsibilities. Poor neighborhoods are not a talent pool for staffing complex and bureaucratic community organizations.

As everyday pressures and operational shortcomings mount, a CDC is tempted to resort again to mobilization tactics in an attempt to project internal conflicts and shortcomings onto outside actors. In this departure from the path of institutional cooperation a CDC stands more to lose than to gain as its behavior will be considered erratic and lacking any justification.

A more likely approach to overcome internal shortcomings of its operation is for a CDC to react to operational crises by expanding its program activities without regard to its ability to shoulder additional functions. From a public relations point of view, such an approach is attractive for the leadership, but it is actually a short-term solution to long-term problems.

The operational problems and the reactions that follow point to the fact that CDCs are bound to reflect the adverse social and economic environment in which they have to work. CDCs cannot really isolate themselves from the precarious and volatile social situation of impoverished areas and the pressures emanating from them.

The question is not so much whether community mobilization remains part of the tactics of a CDC, as it is the question whether CDCs, as they develop from protest to program organizations, are effective tools of inner-city revitalization.

The achievements of CDCs can be summarized in four points: (1) CDCs have managed to reach into the most isolated and segregated poverty areas to provide a high and concentrated level of urgently needed services, infrastructural supports, and housing opportunities. (2) They have done this by creatively combining various program components to form a level of policy implementation that allows for a broader and more coordinated mix than most government run programs could ever achieve. In a way, CDCs serve as program catalysts that forge quite disparate components into a geographically targeted whole. (3) CDCs have used a very creative mix of financing tools, which went far beyond governmental assistance. A large portion of their budget comes from private sources, mostly foundations and churches. In seeking private financing, they have managed to leverage a much greater amount of resources for their constituency than any governmental agency would have been able to do. (4) With regard to housing, it must be noted that CDCs have been much more willing to build large family housing units than private developers.

However, the costs of maintaining such a high level of service delivery and project development is high. In no case have CDCs achieved self-sufficiency to operate their programs out of self-generated funds. They continue to be dependent on outside funding, either private or public, i.e. they are highly subsidized enterprises.

Considering the amount of resources that is necessary to maintain a CDC, it is questionable whether CDCs can be taken as readily applicable models for the revitalization of the poorest areas in American cities. Since public as well as private resources are scarce, there is usually only room for establishing one such model in an urban setting. This means that only one group among a set of potential candidates emerges as a full-fledged CDC. This happens by virtue of the fact of being singled out by government agencies and private donors under conducive circumstances like a charismatic leadership potential, effective public relations campaign, spectacular protest activity and sympathetic media coverage. If such stimuli are successful, a spectacular model is created, which has a good chance of receiving sufficient assistance to make it an on-going enterprise. However, since resources are scarce, the model is not replicable. Under this view CDCs are single tokens of fulfilling social responsibility toward the most distressed areas in the city (Goetze, 1979, pp. 123-134; Goering, 1979, p. 510).

The crucial question remains whether CDCs had a significant revitalizing impact on their communities. The argument developed above suggests that CDCs are likely to become captives of their environment, instead of active forces of change. Even very supportive observers have stated that most CDCs have not been able to reverse the continued social and physical deterioration of their areas. The loss of population and of housing has continued unabated (Lancourt, 1979, pp. 144-146; Fish,1973, pp. 310-312). My own observations in St. Louis confirm that the social and physical upgrading through the efforts of CDCs have been marginal. In effect those efforts rather serve to prolong the phase of deterioration and decline.[2]

Attempts to stem the outmigration of the upwardly mobile segment of the population or to retract the middle class have usually failed. Because of the isolation of those areas there has been an inability and—if opportunity was present—a reluctance or unwillingness to tie in to more conventional development. There has been little opportunity or initiative to create an economic mix. CDCs have rather tended to rely on nurturing a dependent population for the provision of services, housing and limited job opportunities. Thus, they have rather served to administer and perpetuate the social conditions that led to their creation. Far from being an agent of revitalization, they may rather be viewed as a fairly conspicuous, though in its applicability limited attempt to contain and ameliorate the social problems of the poorest neighborhoods.

Under the account given here, it is not surprising that policy makers have not promulgated CDCs as an instrument for inner-city revitalization. CDCs have become accepted partners in dealing with the most distressed areas, but not accepted models for inner-city revitalization.

## THE IMPACT OF PRIVATE REINVESTMENT

The recent experience with the revitalization of older city neighborhoods indicates that residential revitalization is basically a private investment phenomenon (James, 1980; Black, 1980). Although the role of governments in creating the necessary public improvements, in subsidizing risky projects and developments for low- and moderate-income residents, and in supporting the new investments through incentives and rhetoric is not discounted here, the incidence of residential revitalization is attributable to a renewed demand for inner-city housing, (Clay, 1979; Spain, 1980).

Since it is maintained here that much of the community-based organizational activity is related to this trend, its nature and its extent will be shortly discussed in order to more accurately place the organizational responses in their proper contexts.

The demographic, social, and economic factors behind the so-called "back to the city movement" which, as studies suggest, is rather a resettlement of existing households within the city than a return from the suburbs (James, 1980, S. 198; Clay, 1980,

S. 14), have been well analyzed. They include the baby-boom generation's entry into the housing market, as reflected in an expanded 25-35 age cohort, an increase in the number of households, their changing composition (increase in childless and single person households), increased female participation in the labor force, the spiralling costs of suburban housing, and rising energy and transportation costs. Equally, changes in life-styles and in cultural and aesthetic preferences have aided the new demand (Solomon, 1980; Alonso, 1980; Clay, 1980; Allen,1980).

In terms of socio-economic characteristics the new inmovers represent the younger, more affluent and educated households of high occupational status, with the childless young couple presenting the prototype (Spain, 1980; Goetze, 1980).

Some observers have spoken of a fundamental resettlement process of the inner city, in which higher status households systematically displace lower-income and minority households, a process commonly referred to as gentrification (London, 1980; Hartman, 1979). Under this view the prevalent community-based organisation response is organizational conflict between newcomers and oldtimers.

However, the extent of inner-city revitalization through gentrification is by no means clear, and the overall impact on the social fabric of American cities is little understood. In particular, it has been pointed out that the extent of gentrification depends on the regional and metropolitan growth context of a city. According to this view, only a few American cities like Washington, D.C., San Francisco, Seattle, and maybe Boston have experienced significant gentrification (Goetze, 1979, p. 65-67; Gale, 1980; Goldfield, 1980).

In most other cities, especially those in the Northeast and Northwest, gentrification has been quite restricted, affecting only one or two neighborhoods of relatively small size (Clay, 1979, p. 17; 1980, pp. 20-22). It has also been argued that there still exists substantial barriers to residential resettlement in terms of continued attractiveness of the suburbs. Most older cities still continue to lose the younger, higher income group. In those cities demand for inner-city housing as well as reinvestment in inner-city neighborhoods has been sluggish and by far overshadowed by a continued exodus of the middle-class population and increased neighborhood deterioration and disinvestment (Lowry, 1980; Ahlbrandt, Cunningham, 1979).

The overemphasis on gentrification and displacement masks the fact that the context of organizational activity on the neighborhood level is still declining. It also ignores that the influx of new residents on an old neighborhood brings the opportunity to replenish the lost population, and to create an economic and social mix (Sumka, 1980, p. 279-280). Finally, this perspective neglects totally the phenomenon of incumbent upgrading, and how it interacts with the reinvestment (Clay, 1979, pp. 35-45).

The renewed demand for inner-city housing can have two results for the organizational life on the neighborhood level: (1) The influx of higher status residents can lead to the formation of organizations that vigorously defend the interest of the newcomers in a physically and aesthetically upgraded, and socially homogenized neighborhood at the expense of existing lower-status residents. Organizational community polarization may be the outcome. (2) The reinvestment may give a new impetus to the neighborhood by stimulating confidence and incumbent upgrading on the part of existing residents. The influx of new households may not polarize the community, but rather replenish the pool of articulate leaders, and enhance the organizational activity.

Recently the organizational conflict between young affluent restorationists and low-income existing residents has found a lot of attention by the media as well as by scholarly research. Some writers have suggested that the context of analysis of community-based organizational activity should be gentrification and displacement (Van Til, 1980; Auger, 1979; Levy, 1980). While the seriousness of the problems caused by gentrification, like displacement and disruption of old social networks, is not denied, and locally sensitive policy responses are strongly urged (Sumka, 1980, pp. 280-285; Goetze, 1979, p. 26), it does not seem appropriate to take gentrification as the major issue around which organizational activity is structured. The incidence of such conflicts is quite limited. Frequently they are blown out of proportion by ideological arguments and media attention (Van Til, 1980, p. 449).

In my analysis of such conflicts in St. Louis, I found that they are usually sparked off in areas where gentrification has not caught on or is rather slow. They are fuelled by the unrealistic expectations of the restorationists as well as the organizational self-maintenance needs of the representatives of low-income residents. Such conflict, far from producing any results for either group, can totally paralyse an area, as the city administration sees itself unable to mediate and withdraws all funds until an agreement has been reached (Auger, 1979).

Rather than holding that the major organizational activity pivots around social conflicts over gentrification, it is argued here that the most significant and widespread organization activity is to be found in those large "grey areas" that have experienced decline but still possess enough resources in terms of sound housing stock, a large percentage of homeownership and functioning social and institutional networks (Alonso, 1980, p. 46; Houstoun, O'Connor, 1980, pp. 291-92; Ahlbrandt, 1979, p. 22). These "grey areas" are mostly the older working class, lower middle class areas of cities.

## NEIGHBORHOOD-BASED REVITALIZATION IN "GREY AREAS"[3]

Although neighborhood groups in "grey areas" have not undertaken conspicuous projects nor sparked heated social conflicts, these groups have produced the most promising revitalization efforts. Their importance springs from the fact that those areas comprise large parts of older American cities and that they must be considered the key for the long-term stabilization of the major residential sections of American cities (Clay, 1979, p. 47). These areas also seem to be those where reinvestment can contribute to achieving an economic and social mix, and where the danger to existing social arrangements is small.

Although the social and institutional networks are still intact, these areas needed the impact of new investment and the influx of residents to trigger new organizational activity or redirect existing ones. It was not so much decline as such that led to the change, but the example that something could be done about it. Private reinvestment was essential for the reinvigoration of neighborhood groups in "grey areas". In addition, the availability of discretionary city funds for neighborhood development through federal grants stabilized this trend (Dommel et al., 1980, pp. 105-107).

The basic function of neighborhood organization in those areas is internal: to rebuild confidence in the neighborhood by reversing the image of decline (Goetze, 1979, pp. 99). One of the major strategies is to stimulate existing homeowners to upgrade their properties (incumbent upgrading or upgrading in place). This presents an effort to attempt stabilization with existing resources. It has the advantage of inducing those households to stay that might have otherwise planned to move (Downs, 1979, p. 466-67; Ahlbrandt, 1979, p. 141; Clay, 1979, pp. 35-45).

Despite the emphasis on incumbent upgrading newcomers are welcome, particularly if they fit into the existing neighborhood ethos. They are seen as an essential resource to keep the upgrading process going (Clay, 1979, p. 41).

Mobilization occurs. It is not primarily directed at government agencies, but is an appeal to mobilize resources internally. It rather relies on existing institutions (churches, businesses, clubs) than on outside organizers.

These neighborhood groups remain sensitive to the social consequences of the upgrading process. They try to develop strategies to cushion the impact of those who are endangered by upgrading: elderly homeowners who are unable to pay increased property taxes, or cannot maintain their property anymore, renters who are in danger of being displaced or are unable to pay rents that are increased as a result of the upgrading process.

Furthermore the upgrading process entails dealing with crucial outside actors, like banks, city agencies, small developers, speculators, whose involvement is either sought, or who become interested in the neighborhood by themselves. The neighborhood group also registers a need for technical assistance.

In short, it becomes necessary to develop strategies for guiding and supporting the upgrading process, for controlling the market forces behind it, for alleviating the social consequences, and for spelling out negotiated approaches about the involvement of outside actors.

All these tasks require expertise. Neighborhood groups which are run on volunteer basis will therefore be prone to undergo professionalization and develop small staff capabilities. This may take the form of a paid executive director or the creation of a housing corporation. Funding comes from churches, local business and CDBG funds.

It is only at this point that effective mediating strategies can be implemented: that banks can be approached to stimulate lending activity, that the city can be pressured to make the necessary improvements, that the various resources to alleviate the negative social impacts can be obtained (Sec. 8 subsidized housing allocations, low interest loans). Only now can a neighborhood group deal on a more equal footing with developers, and can take effective actions against absentee landlords and speculators.

The program activities range from neighborhood planning (preparing housing inventories and housing plans), technical assistance (rehab consulting, contractor selection) to housing and rental referral. Particular emphasis is placed on helping the elderly and moderate income residents. These efforts include weatherization programs, assistance in obtaining low interest home improvement loans, and development of subsidized housing for residents that are being displaced. The development of subsidized housing is seen exclusively as a buffer against displacement as it affects neighborhood residents, not as a contribution to solving the city-wide housing problems or to racially integrate neighborhoods. Although these neighborhoods are not exclusionary and may contain a substantial number of minority residents (15-20 per cent) they do not pursue active integration strategies. The program also includes assistance with the transfer of property from elderly homeowners to interested buyers who plan to live in the neighborhood. Neighborhood groups assume Realtor functions, to assure a fair market price for sellers and keep speculators out (Clay, 1979, p. 49).

The major role of the professional arm of those neighborhood groups will remain to encourage reinvestment and rehabilitation by incumbents as well as outsiders. Marketing and promotional campaigns are a part of this effort. The rationale behind the activities described above is to get the best of both worlds, i.e. to maximize investment, but minimize social costs. The groups want to take advantage of market forces and control them at the same time. The approach of such neighborhood groups rests on the conception of a socially balanced revitalization process. The approach seems attractive, because it makes use of market forces instead of excessive governmental assistance, it mobilizes existing energies and involves outsiders, but also stresses controlled, fine-tuned programs to cushion social impacts.

The question remains though, what the chances of success of such approaches are and what factors might endanger them. One threat to social balance is certainly that the membership of these groups is primarily made up of homeowners. Renters and low-income residents are under-represented (Ahlbrandt, 1979, p. 173; Cohen, 1979, p. 353). I have observed that it is frequently up to the staff to take the interests of the unrepresented segment of the neighborhood into account.

On the other hand, the professional staff capacity might in itself be a threat to the integrity of the neighborhood group. Its development entails that the majority of the decisions are made by the staff. Community input recedes accordingly. The staff is likely to be tied into extensive networks with institutional actors (banks, developers), which because of their stronger bargaining position can exert a much stronger influence on the staff than the membership.

One can also occasionally observe a marked tendency of the staff to become project entrepreneurs. If a neighborhood group undertakes housing development, the staff might become totally absorbed by this task, and promote it as a goal in itself with an eye on the proceeds of development activities in terms of developer's and syndication fees. If neighborhood opinion is not consulted anymore, the staff might become so isolated as to risk conflict or expulsion.

Caution about the success of the programs of such groups is also necessary because the areas referred to here have not been subject to heated market demand. If this should change, the goals of reinvestment without excessive social costs will not be accomplished. It is possible that a group becomes the victim of its own program. Constant monitoring of market forces as well as of organizational strategy seems required.

However, the change in the structure of more traditional neighborhood organization that has occurred with the addition of a professional staff component is a positive step in that neighborhood groups now have the expertise and the programming and planning capacities that enable them to pursue more sophisticated strategies, and be stronger partners in interactions with established institutions.

The crucial outcome for policy makers is that there exists now an institutionalized level in the neighborhood for defining the most pressing needs and setting priorities on the basis of informed strategies as well as acquiantance with the ethos of a neighborhood. This level can serve as an early warning system and information transmission system (Down, 1979, p. 469; Levy, 1980, p. 303).

In terms of policy implementation and program development, this level can serve as an area in which the different participants of the revitalization effort can be brought together to stimulate coordinate activities.

This level seems to complement activities of the more traditional city planners who are tied in the bureaucratic regulations and power structures, by adding the entrepreneurial status of the staff of neighborhood groups to seek for creative solutions below the level of pure administrative policies.

In St. Louis I have found that groups operating in the "grey areas" under the set-up described here have been quite successful. Although much work remains to be done, and long-term evaluation would be needed, there is sufficient evidence that they have contributed substantially to stabilizing neighborhoods above the level of previous decline.

## CONCLUSION

Perhaps the most significant change of community-based organization activity noted in this paper is that more traditional neighborhood groups in so-called "grey areas" have developed under the impact of renewed demand for inner-city housing, sophisticated and professional programming and planning capacities, a step that Community Development Corporations have taken much earlier, though under different circumstances and with different results. One conclusion is that in the seventies organizational activity is characterized across the board by a higher degree of institutionalization and sophistication, and a lesser degree of confrontation and protest tactics.

CDCs have failed to have a signifcant impact to bring about socially balanced revitalization. Neighborhood groups in declining working class/lower middle-class areas, which pursue a professionally supported strategy, seem to stand a much better chance to bring about revitalization, while maintaining a social and economic mix.

Little has been said here about the role of policy makers and planners. One conclusion seems obvious: planners and policy makers will find and have found a systematized relationship quite attractive, if a city-wide development policy is based on organizational capacity (Downs, 1979, p. 469; Cohen, 1979). These groups offer definite advantages: they have articulated and well-defined goals. The professionalization might be quite appealing to planners, since it fits into their bureaucratic ethos. They stress internal resource mobilization, and do not require excessive amounts of governmental assistance. They are able to manage social conflict from within.

However, planners cannot count on such organizations to arise in the area described here. Although the new demand for inner-city housing and functioning social and institutional fabric seem to provide the general context for the existence of such organizations, and city agencies might themselves undertake steps to stimulate organizational development, there are too many contingent factors involved. So far we do not have a systematic knowledge about the circumstances under which neighbórhood groups arise, nor how long will they be around.

## FOOTNOTES

1. The arguments presented here reflect, to a large extent, on-going research on community organizations in St. Louis, Mo., which is part of a larger research project on neighborhood groups in large American cities, carried out at the political science department of the University of Goettingen (W. Germany) under the direction of Prof. Peter Loesche, funded by the Volkswagenwerk Foundation. For a much more detailed illustration of theses presented here, I have to refer the reader to our forthcoming report. Many insights in this first section are derived from an analysis of the Jeff-Vander-Lou Organization in St. Louis. A summary of their activities and history can be found in: National Commission on Neighborhoods (1980).
2. The Woodlawn Organization in Chicago lost 34 per cent of its population and 24 per cent of its housing stock between 1960 and 1970 (Fish, 1973, p. 312). According to 1980 census data JVL in St. Louis lost over 30 per cent of its population and 20 per cent of its housing stock.
3. Although drawing on the general literature, this section relies heavily on an analysis of two neighborhoods in St. Louis, the Shaw neighborhood and the Garden Tower East area. For a complete description of organizations and activities the reader is referred to Community Program Development Corporation, **Shaw Neighborhood Improvement Program,** ST. Louis: Community Development Agency, 1981; and De Sales Community Housing Corporation, **Garden Tower East Neighborhood Development Plan,** St. Louis: Community Development Agency, 1980.

## REFERENCES

Ahlbrandt, Roger, James Cunningham, **A New Public Policy for Neighbourhood Preservation.** Ballinger, Cambridge, (1979).

Allen, Irving, "The Ideology of Dense Neighborhood Development, Cultural Diversity and Transcendent Community Experience". **Urban Affairs Quarterly,** 15, (1980), 409-428.

Auger, Deborah, A. "The Politics of Revitalization in Gentrifying Neighborhoods: The Case of Boston's South End." Stegmann (1979) 515-522.

Black, Thomas J. "The Changing Economic Role of Central Cities and Suburbs". (Ed. Arthur P. Solomon). **The Prospective City.** pp. 80-123, MIT, Cambridge.

Clay, Philip. **Neighborhood Renewal,** Lexington Books, Lexington, (1979).

Clay, Philip. "The Rediscovery of City Neighborhoods: Reinvestment by Long-Time Residents and Newcomers", in Laska/Spain (1980), 13-25.

Cohen, Rick, "Neighborhood Planning and Political Capacity", **Urban Affairs Quarterly,** 14, (1979) 337-362.

Downs, Anthony, "The Relationship Between Urban Development and Neighborhood Change," in Stegmann (1979) 462-472.

Dommel, Paul R. et al. **Targeting Community Development.** Government Printing Office, Washington, D.C. (1980).

Gale, Dennis "Neighborhood Resettlement: Washington, D.C." in Laska/Spain (1980) 95-115.

Gasser, William "The Southeast Land Bank" in Stegmann (1979), 532-537.

Goering, John M. "The National Neighborhood Movement: A Preliminary Analysis and Critique", in Stegmann (1979) 506-514.

Goetze, Rolf **Understanding Neighborhood Change.** Ballinger, Cambridge (1979).

Goldfield, David R. "Private Neighborhood Redevelopment and Displacement: The Case of Washington, D.C." **Urban Affairs Quarterly** 15 (1980) 453-468.

Fish, John H. **Black Power/White Control.** Princeton University Press, Princet n (1973).

Hartmann, Chester, "Comment." (1979) 488-491.

Lancourt, Joan E. **Confront or Concede. The Alinsky Citizen-Action Organizations.** Lexington Books, Lexington (1979).

James, Franklin J. "The Revitalization of Older Urban Housing and Neighborhoods." (Ed. Arthur P. Solomon) **The Prospective City,** 130-160, MIT, Cambridge (1980).

Laska, Shirley, Daphne Spain (eds.) **Back to the City.** Pergamon, New York (1980).

Levy, Paul R. "Local Strategies for Countering Displacement." in Laska/Spain (1980) 302-317.

London, Burce, "Gentrification as Urban Reinvasion: Some Preliminary Definitional and Theoretical Consideration." in Laska/Spain (1980) 77-92.

Lowry, Ira S. "The Dismal Future of Central Cities." (Ed. Arthur P. Solomon), **The Prospective City,** 161-203, MIT, Cambridge (1980).

National Commission on Neighborhoods. **People, Building Neighborhoods,** Case Study Appendix Vol. II., Government Printing Office, Washington, D.C. (1980).

Spain, Daphne. "Indicators of Urban Revitalization. Racial and Socio-economic Changes in Central-City Housing." in Laska/Spain (1980), 27-41.

Solomon, Arthur P. "The Emerging Metropolis." (Ed. Arthur P. Solomon). **The Prospective City.** MIT, Cambridge (1980).

Stegmann, Michael A., Ed., **Neighborhood Revitalization,** (Special Supplement to the **Journal of the American Planning Association**), 45.

Sumka, Howard J. "Federal Anti-Displacement Policy in a Context of Urban Decline," in Laska/Spain (1980) 269-287.

Van Til, Jon. "Citizen Participation in Neighborhood Transformation: A Social Movement Perspective", **Urban Affairs Quarterly** 15 (1980), 439-452.

EIGHT

Michael P. Smith and B. Guy Peters

# THE USES OF NEIGHBORHOOD REVITALIZATION

## The Consensual Models of Neighborhood Development

Three basically consensual models of neighborhood development are found in the literature. These three models are: a) the neighborhood as a social community; b) the neighborhood as a refuge, and c) the neighborhood as a means of social control. Let us briefly consider each of these themes in turn.

## The Neighborhood as a Social Community

Robert Park (1915) defined the neighborhood as "a locality with sentiments, traditions, and a history of its own." His research pioneered a tradition of sociological research doumenting degree of internal social organization, the nature and quality of social interaction arising from propinquity and shared fate, and the relative vitality of the social networks found in urban neighborhoods.

From this perspective, the neighborhood is viewed as a primary form of social organisation. The model of the neighborhood as community stresses the extent to which urban neighborhoods continue to provide working class and minority group subcultures material and cultural resources. Mutual aid networks and a sense of belonging to a historically rooted place have all been found to characterize particular urban neighborhoods (Smith: 1979, Ch. 5). Some urban policy analysts have designed neighborhood revitalizations capable of sustaining these important indigenous socio-cultural resources in the face of threats from the larger social-economic structure. The goal of such analysts is to construct a stable social order of mutually tolerant communities within society.

## The Neighborhood as a Refuge

In two of his works, Families Against the City (1970) and The Uses of Disorder (1970) Richard Sennett captures the ways in which middle-class residents have used urban and suburban neighborhoods to escape the stresses of life in the marketplace and the strain produced by the heterogeneity, diversity, and disorder of urban life. In Sennett's view, this use of the neighborhood as a refuge is psychologically harmful to those who seek escape from urban social conflict. This is because it forces the family to perform many functions once performed by neighborhood institutions that have disappeared from many urban neighborhoods. The decline of diverse public places conducive to social interaction among sociologically different classes and subcultures has, in Sennett's view, impoverished city life. Individuals who do not learn how to deal with diversity, but seek only escape into the primary relationships of the self-sufficient nuclear family, will eventually be forced by circumstances to confront conflicting values and interests. In his view, people who lack experience with such conflicts are likely to respond violently to situations of social crisis. If neighborhoods can be designed to recreate exposure to heterogeneity, people are capable of learning by experience to peacefully accept diversity and change. Thus, what some have depicted as a brief for urban disorder is, in fact, an argument on behalf of neighborhood-based politics of mutual learning, adjustment to change, and tolerance. Sennett advocates the creation of "survival communities"—neighborhoods in which social conflicts are channeled into larger institutions (e.g. a revitalalized urban machine) as a way of avoiding mutual self-destruction.

Interestingly, this theme of the neighborhood as refuge has been turned around by some policy analysts whose primary concern is the preservation of the self-sufficient nuclear family that Sennett sees as a barrier to psychological growth. In the face of rising divorce rates, youth crime and violence, these policy analysts regard a stable nuclear family structure as the linchpin of a stable social order. From this latter perspective, the neighborhood must be made a safe and secure enclave, indeed a refuge conducive to healthful child-rearing practices. This reasoning often underlines public policies designed to maintain the very ethnic and class homogeneous neighborhood life that Sennett sees as so threatening to the social fabric.

## The Neighborhood as Means of Social Control

A related model of neighborhood development is frequently enunciated by functional analysts of urban sociology. The neighborhood is often depicted as a stable anchor in the face of rapid change that threatens to undermine old values and ways of life. Those who would use the neighborhood as a means of social control would use both formal and informal neighborhood structures to reinforce the values and norms prevalent in the neighborhoods. More conservative proponents of "community control" (see, for example, Fein: 1971) envisage this process as providing neighborhood-base subcultures as means to reinforce prevailing values and behaviorial norms locally and to regulate anti-social behavior patterns (i.e. to control "deviance"). Thus, the neighborhood becomes a bundle of mutually reinforcing agencies of socialization. Communal values are maintained in the face of an assumed breakdown of norms ("anomie") and of erosion of traditional attachments engendered by capitalism, post-industrialism, demographic mobility, or other similar macro-social phenomena.

## Conflictual Models of Neighborhood Development

Contrasted to these three consensual models of neighborhood development are three more complex models that stress the desirability of competition or conflict either within or among neighborhoods, or between neighborhoods and larger political economic structures. Each of these conflict models has a more conservative and a more radical variant. The three conflict-oriented models include: 1) the neighborhood as a bundle of public goods for collective consumption; 2) the neighborhood as a political unit; and, 3) the neighborhood as real estate. Let us now consider each of these developmental models in some detail.

## Neighborhoods as Units of Service Delivery

Since Tiebout's (1956) classic statement of the issue, a growing body of urban researchers have contributed to what has come to be known as the "polycentric public choice" perspective on neighborhood development. This perspective has neo-conservative implications. The neighborhood is viewed as one metropolitan area as a whole is depicted as one vast market where "citizen consumers" can exercise choice among different levels and types of public service provision in urban neighborhoods and suburban communities that comprise the metropolis. Devotees of polycentric public choice are not concerned with equity issues of unequal provision of public services across different neighborhoods. Indeed, they encourage the widest variety (and by implication the widest inequality) among public services. This allows citizen-consumers dissatisfied with the particular mix of services provided in their current locale to vote with their feet for a different service mix. The fact that some jurisdictions can afford more, others less, public services, is seen as compatible with the most effective provision of public services in the metropolitan area. The availability of fewer, and hence cheaper, public services is envisaged as an option that should be preserved. This allows some citizen consumers to protect more of their disposable income for private consumption. Proponents of this approach to neighborhood development favour competition among neighborhoods for residents as a means to improve service quality and expand choice. In this conceptual framework the neighborhood can, and would be, no more than a lucus of limited liability and temporary attachment. More enduring ties based on tradition, friendship, or simply familiarity would only impede the smooth operation of the mark-based service delivery system.

The radical variant of the concept of the neighborhood as a locus of social service delivery is best represented in the work of the neo-Marxist urbanist Manuel Castells (1977; 1978) who depicts the neighborhood as the primary point of contact between state policy and social class. He views urban social services as designed to legitimize the capitalist state and reproduce the existing social order. These services, including housing, education, health, and recreation are collectively consumed in class-specific neighborhoods. Their purpose is to reproduce labor power and placate working class minorities while insulating the major beneficiaries of capital accumulation from possible political resistance by labor "in the community" (i.e. in working class and low-income neighborhoods). Thus, the national and local welfare state seeks to achieve the social stability necessary to the capital accumulation process by expanding social welfare activities. But this expends surplus capital that might otherwise be devoted to new production, circulation and accumulation. This contributes, in turn, to economic recessions and state revenue shortfalls.

In Castells' view, the local administration of the welfare state inevitably becomes highly politicized. Even without the larger contradiction of the fiscal crisis, the major areas of collective consumption—health, housing, and schools—are directly linked to people's everyday lives. Thus, neighborhood-based controversies over the delivery of these services are well suited to class mobilization. In short, because neighborhoods are the primary point of contact between the state and citizens, the neighborhood becomes the most fruitful arena for mobilizing class-based movements expressing discontent over the quality, distribution, and control of urban public services. Furthermore, metropolitan areas of advanced capitalist societies have been built and rebuilt primarily to speed the circulation of capital. Thus, urban policy problems such as housing and transportation are problematic for neighborhoods. When the quest for neighborhood stability or community-based land uses impedes speedy circulation, class conflict is a likely result. Yet, for Castells the target of this conflict remains the state rather than private capital. Interestingly, therefore, the capitalist state acquires a legitimation deficit that rightfully belongs to the main beneficiaries of accumulation. Ironically, Castells fails to consider the possibility that, at least in the short run, this delegitimation of government exacerbates the adverse consequences of the fiscal crisis. That is, the delegitimized state makes it easier for public opinion to accept the kind of retrenchment policies now being practised by conservative political parties and governments in the name of long-term investment and productivity.

**The Neighborhood as a Political Unit**

At least since the time of the settlement house movement and Perry's neighborhood plan, urban neighborhoods have been viewed as prime jurisdictions for the devolution of political authority. In 1918, for instance, in The New State, Mary Parker Follett depicted the neighborhood as a mobilizer of citizen involvement in public affairs and a unit of policy making capable of linking people's everyday concerns to national political life. In the late 1960's and early 1970's a spate of policy analysts sought to resolve the social conflicts and contradictions of that era by rediscovering the neighborhood as a political unit. Among the most influential of these was Milton Kotler's (1969) succinct plea for the creation of general-purpose neighborhood governments. According to Kotler, the collective or community interests of urban neighborhood residents had gradually been displaced from the political agenda; city-wide commercial and financial interests had come to dominate urban political life. This displacement was facilitated by the electoral "reforms" that replaced ward-based local elections to city councils elected at large. Ward Aldermen functioned as neighborhood representatives, whereas at-large councilmen served the interests of those with sufficient resources to influence city-wide elections.

Kotler was an early advocate of community development corporations (CDC's). He viewed CDC's not only as economic organizations but as political pressure groups. Economically, the CDC would attract outside capital to the neighborhood. Politically, it could use tactics ranging from coalition formation to "resistance" to achieve an eventual transfer of political authority to neighborhood governments.

In Kotler's view the neighborhood government would become the basic political unit of a dynamic participatory democratic society. By participating directly in a contentious political arena where general-purpose public policies were shaped, residents would become active citizens. In chracteristically Rousseauian fashion, Kotler's imagery envisages the gradual political emancipation of neighborhood residents.

Other, similarly optimistic consequences were anticipated by many early 1970's advocates of community control. Among the most common of these were expectations of: a) improved administrative efficiency, equity, and responsiveness of social welfare mobilization, by relatively powerless groups (Altshuler: 1970; Lipsky: 1973); and paradoxically, b) the redressing of a deficit of legitimacy by the state (Lipsky: 1973; Strange: 1973; Fein: 1972). The missing assumption underlying the apparent contradiction between more demands and more legitimacy is the belief, no longer so prevalent, that agencies of the state both can and will respond effectively to the increased demands placed upon the state.

Curiously, then, because they lacked a class-based analysis of urban politics and policy, both the devotees of public choice discussed earlier and the advocates and neighborhood government expected that mere decentralization would gradually reduce the degree of political alienation in the metropolis. In the former case, increased citizen-consumer choice would eventually lead citizens to migrate to their most preferred locale. Having done so, they should be satisfied with urban service delivery. In the latter case, political learning and increased confidence in themselves as citizens and in the accessible neighborhood political process would increase citizen satisfaction with the policy-making process and its outcomes. In both instances, the legitimation deficit produced by operations of the welfare state is overcome.

How do these analysts respond to those who offer a class-conscious criticism of metropolitan decentralization, pointing out the class character of residential segregation and the unequal resource base. Their answer to a class-conscious criticism of their ideas is the so-called "federated city." It is argued that if certain functions, including revenue raising were reserved for a metropolitan-wide political jurisdiction, while basic issues of human service delivery were left to neighborhood jurisdictions, the issue of unequal resources would be resolved.

But this conceptualization begs the question of what sort of political process would resolve the basic issue of the distribution revenue. To propose the federated city as a solution to this question is simply to avoid dealing with the harsh realities of structural inequality in schooling, labor market access, dual housing markets, and access to the means of social mobility. Why, after all, will those affluent neighborhood residents who have secured their own enclave, support the allocation of resources from their own taxes to provide a starting point for neighborhood government in working class and lower class neighborhoods? Why will they be any more willing to pay for services that go directly to less fortunate people and places? Why, in short, should we expect greater harmony, citizen satisfaction, and legitimation rather than greater class conflict, political aliention, and delegitimation?

These criticisms do not apply to more recent radical analyses of neighborhood political development (c.f. Smith: 1979, Chs. 5,6; Mollenkopf, 1981). Accepting the necessity, even the desirability of social conflict as a mean to include neighborhood values and issues into politics, Smith and Mollenkopf see the arena of community politics as one that systematically pits neighborhood-oriented policies against market-oriented policies. An analysis of the urban political conflicts of the 1970's reveals the class character of neighborhood revitalization programs, the name of protecting the disadvantaged from the adverse impacts of large-scale land clearance and displacement. These programs stressed housing rehabilitation and neighborhood "preservation" that reinforce market trends and thus serve the interests of the professional class against working class and minority residents (Mollenkopf: 1981, 35-36). In their view, the problem is not one that can be resolved by political decentralization alone. Without dynamic, neighborhood-based political organizations capable of forging wider political coalitions, even the limited gains achieved by New Deal and Great Society Welfare state policies will continue to erode. As Smith (1979: Ch 6.) points out, even if neighborhood-based political movements were to achieve neighborhood government, the need for an outside "push factor" to hold the decentralized jurisdictions accountable for the impacts of their policies on the neighborhood would remain, precisely because of the symbolically placating effect of the existence of neighborhood governments, the need for conflict-oriented community politics might be even greater. From this perspective, neighborhood political movements must be forged into organizational weapons capable of pressing agencies of the state at all levels as well as the private actors (e.g. banks and insurance companies) who have been most instrumental in shaping the market-oriented urban policies that have adversely affected the social networks, housing, and job opportunities of working class and minority group community life. Unless neighborhood political development encompasses the creation and maintenance of new coalitions at the local and national level, public initiative will continue to be a handmaiden of private market power. What would be the political agenda of such coalitions? In Mollenkopf's words, such coalitions "must control the margins of the housing and labour markets and prevent 'who can pay the most' or 'who has the right connections' from determining all the outcomes. Community-oriented local government could help to carve out a place in the city's economy and in its neighborhoods for those who have been excluded from market power and who currently suffer the consequences." (1981:35)

### The Neighborhood as Real Estate

The perspective of the neighborhood as real estate also has a conservative and a radical variant. The conservative variant envisages "gentrification" as the most expeditious means to revitalize both urban neighborhoods and declining central cities. The lower or moderte income neighborhood is seen as a repository of real estate that has lost its economic value and must be upgraded. The decaying central city is seen as an "Indian reservation," for managing the needs of a low-income surplus population but lacking the tax base to do so. As with many other previous urban policies designed to attract middle class taxpayers back to the central city, proponents of gentrification justify dislocation of this surplus population as a form of help. Arguing that the plight of the urban poor must be rectified eventually, proponents of gentrification contend if cities are once again made liveable for the middle class by gentrified enclaves, the tax base needed to service the surplus population will be restored. To serve their long-run interests, the urban poor are expected to suffer temporary dislocation. (For an excellent empirical study that documents the preferences of gentrifiers for the life-style of the "defended enclave", see Tobin and Judd: 1981). If housing reinvestment can improve the city tax base and industrial reinvestment can improve job prospects, the plight of this urban underlcass can be redressed.

Because of the current importance of the gentrification issue, we will return to it to illustrate another key difficulty in the literature on neighborhood development—the extent to which individual level variables (choice) or macro-level variables (structure) offer the more fruitful explanation of the gentrification phenomenon. Before doing so, however, we briefly explicate the final model of neighborhood development considered in this paper: the radical variant of the "neighborhood as real estate."

Radical political economists of urban land use like Harvey (1973) and Molocht (1979) assume that the dynamic process of capital accumulation determines the shape, rise and fall, and reconstruction of urban neighborhoods. These neo-Marxist scholars view the neighborhood as the most likely future arena of class conflict. Indeed, with the rise of the service economy and the decline of factory labor, the neighborhood has displaced the workplace as the principle arena of class struggle. Although factories have become fewer and more dispersed, neighborhoods remain concentrated centers where the working class interacts about common problems, become conscious of their exploitation, and mobilize to resist the incursions of those whose activities are antagonistic to their class interests.

In the main, the factions of capital that dominate urban development are subsumed under the label "rentier interests." These interets seek to convert urban land to more intense use. In addition to controlling access to the places where production takes place (e.g. land for industrial development), this "rentier class influences access to the means of reproduction (i.e. neighborhood-based housing). The basic interest of finance capital in central cities for more intense land uses (e.g. multi-story condominia in place of single-family housing) pits them inevitably against the class interest of "labor in the community" which seeks to use urban space for its own cultural and social uses; that is to say, for the reproduction of its own life-style. Radical critics who view the neighborhood in this way point to abundant examples of this phenomenon such as the recent destruction of a parish church and the dispersal of ethnic enclave in the area of Detroit known as "Poletown" to make way for an automobile factory. As Smith (1980) has summarized this perspective:

> The urban neighborhood thus is viewed in three distinct ways. First, it is a stake in the sometimes competitive, sometimes collusive process of capital accumulation by various sectors of the overall capitalistic class. Second, it is the location of certain forms of ... (social, cultural and material uses of space) by the working class, broadly defined. Third, resulting from those, it is a constantly shifting arena for class conflict over incompatible neighborhood land uses. (Therefore) ... neighborhood stability is deemed the rare exception, neighborhood turnover and transformation the structured resultant of the capital accumulation process. Far from offering a secure haven for orderly social life, even relatively stable neighborhoods are seen as a problematic context for survival in a constantly shifting network of exchange and competition among rival in-

terests and institutions.

## POLICY IMPLICATIONS

These alternative conceptions of neighborhoods have a number of implications for the policy choices made by government, and the mechanisms chosen to deliver policies once made. The manner in which a decision-maker perceives neighborhoods will determine to some degree his or her willingness to decentralize decision-making. Further, the perception which the decision-maker holds will also determine the goals for neighborhood development which he or she will attempt to implement. The above six models at once service as a guide for action and a set of goals toward which government and urban residents should be striving.

The choice between the consensual and the conflictive perspectives on neighborhood development provides a guide for action. Those who would desire a more stable and socially controlled society might advocate the neighborhood as opposed to the larger urban setting as the appropriate locus of activity. President Reagan's urban policy has stressed the importance of restoring neighborhood vitality to restore both social control over real or potential criminals in the society, and the perception of cities as a good place to live. In such a view, the neighborhood would provide mechanism for middle and upper class people to return to American cities. This has obvious implications for the gentrification movement, which would be seen as a means of restoring the urban tax base and the vitality of cities, rather than as exploitative.

Related to the perception of the neighborhood as a mechanism for social control is the use of the neighborhood as a means for delivering services. The use of "neighborhood Crime Watches" in American cities are perhaps the best developed mechanisms of this type. If the community is perceived as homogeneous and stable, then services of this type may have an opportunity to succeed. But in a conflictual setting they are unlikely to be accepted even if proposed. The development of neighborhood-based services of this type have obvious cost-saving attributes for hard-pressed urban governments, but also provide the additional benefits of community involvement.

Growing from the more direct utilization of the neighborhood as a mechanism for service delivery is the question of how to use the neighborhood as a locus of service delivery. Any number of such schemes have been advanced, from "little city halls" to more radical and complete decentralization to functioning neighborhood governments. As in the Tiebout model, these are intended to allow for greater choice for citizens, there remains as an obstacle to more complete decentralization the problem of fisal equalization in urban areas. For a system of decentralization to be effective, there must be some means of distributing the total revenue available to the city in an equitable fashion among the decentralized neighborhood governments. Thus, the best operating model of decentralization might be fiscal consolidation coupled with decentralization of service delivery. But this would assume a relatively consensual setting across the urban area, although the pressures to have neighborhood service delivery might indicate that such consensus did not exist. Thus, paradoxically, the conditions which might create pressures for decentralization of public services might be closely related to the conditions which would prevent them from ever working effectively.

Related to the question of decentralization of services are issues about the efficiency and effectiveness service delivery by different size governments. (Newton, 1978). As well as the political and participatory benefits which may accrue from the decentralization of services, "real" economic gains may be obtained. Some policies are arguably better delivered to smaller areas than to larger ones. Studies of policing have argued that smaller cities are more efficient, the same logic may apply to the delivery of fire services as well (Ostrom and Park, 1977). Perhaps the most radical idea would be to completely decentralize governmental services from the multi-purpose city government to a set of single-purpose governments each having an appropriate sized catchment area for its services.

The conception of the city as such a loose coalition would fundamentally alter the concept of the city and the urban area which exists in most modern societies. Much of the writing on urban government, at least in the United States, has stressed the importance of including the entire metropolitan area in the catchment area for public services. The neighborhood concept, on the other hand, would seek to insulate smaller areas within the city from the city as a whole, perhaps even to as great an extent as suburban communities are currently insulated. In such a conception, the city would become subsidiary to the neighborhood, and the metropolitan area would become little more than geographical concept.

The political and symbolic justifications of a neighborhood based service delivery system must also be taken into account. Citizens are presumed to be able to participate more effectively in a smaller setting, and the issues should be more comprehensible to citizens. Further, citizens may perceive a greater stake in their neighborhood than in the city as a whole, although the declining rates of participation in politics as one moves from national to subnational levels tend to belie that assumption. And the symbolic element of "our" services, and the proximity of services and decision-making to citizens may sustain a rapidly declining sense of trust of citizens in their government. Control over public services, as with the New York City schools, is an important symbolic element which may have very real consequences both for the effectiveness of programs and for the relationship of citizens to government.

In summary, the structure of cities is to some degree the structure of neighborhoods, and to understand the dynamics of change in those cities it is necessary to understand the meaning of the neighborhood to its residents and to the wider community. Neighborhoods serve a variety of purposes for their residents and may serve other purposes for the city, and, as there are increasing pressures to change cities through neighborhood revitalization, it is necessary to understand how the neighborhood fits into the larger community. This paper has been one effort in that direction, but we must conclude with the usual pleas for improved conceptualization and empirical research.

## REFERENCES

Altshuler, Alan, **Community Control.** New York: Pegasus (1970).

Castells, Manuel, **The Urban Question.** Cambridge: MIT Press (1977).

Castells, Manuel, **City, Class, Power.** London: Macmillan (1978).

Fein, Leonard J., **The Ecology of the Public Schools: An Inquiry into Community Control.** New York: Pegasus, 1971.

Follett, Mary Parker. **The New State.** New York: Longman Green (1918).

Fried, Marc and Gleicher, Peggy, "Some Sources of Residential Satisfaction in an Urban Slum," **Journal of the American Institute of Planners** 27 (November, 1961) xpp. 305-315.

Gans, Herbert, The Urban Villagers. New York: Free Press (1962).

Gering, John "Introduction to Marx and the City: A Symposium," Comparative Urban Research. 6 (2,3) (1978) 5-8.

Guterbock, Thomas, "The Political Economy of Urban Revitalization: Competing Theories, "**Urban Affairs Quarterly** (June, 1980) pp. 429-438.

Harry, David, Social Justice and the City. Baltimore: Johns Hopkins (1973).

Kohwe, Milton, Neighborhood Government: The Local Foundations of Political Life. Indianapolis: Bobbs-Merrill (1969).

Lipsky, Michael, "Street Level Bureaucracy and the Analysis of Urban Reform," in George Frederickson, ed., Neighborhood Control in the 1970's. New York: Chandler (1973) pp. 103-115.

Mollenkopf, John, "Neighborhood Political Development, the Politics of Urban Growth," **International Journal of Urban & Regional Research,** (1981) pp. 15-39.

Molocht, Harvey, "Capital and Neighborhood in the United States," **Urban Affairs Quarterly,** (1979) pp. 289-312.

Newton, Kenneth, "Is Small so Beautiful; Is Big So Ugly?" Studies in Public Policy No. 18 (Glasgow: Centre for the Study of Public Policy, University of Strathclyde) (1978).

Ostrom, Vincent, C. Tiebout and R. Warren, "The Organization of Government in Metropolitan Areas, "**American Political Science Review** 55 (December, 1961) pp. 831-842.

Park, Robert, "The City: Suggestions for the Investigation of Human Behavior in the City Environment," **American Journal of Sociology** 20 (March, 1915) pp. 577-611.

Sennett, Richard, Families Against the City. Cambridge: Harvard University Press (1970).

Sennett, Richard, The Uses of Disorder. New York: Vintage (1970).

Smith, Michael P., The City and Social Theory. New York: St. Martin's (1979).

Smith, Michael P., "Critical Theory & Urban Political Theory, "Comparative Urban Research. 7, 37 (1980) pp. 5-23.

Strange, John, "Local Strategies for Attaining Neighborhood Control," in George Frederickson, ed., **Neighborhood Control in the 1970's.** New York: Chandler (1973) pp. 167-178.

Tiebout, C., "A Pure Theory of Local Expenditures," **Journal of Political Economy** 64 (October, 1956) pp. 416-424.

Tobin, Gary A. and Judd, Dennis R., "Moving the Suburbs to the City: Neighborhood Revitalization and the 'Amenities Bundle'," (unpublished manuscript) (1981).

NINE

S. Gregory Lipton

# THE FUTURE CENTRAL CITY
## Gentrified or Abandoned ?

### INTRODUCTION

Demographers, urban researchers and the United States Bureau of the Census have reported on the movement of people from the center of U.S. cities to the suburbs. Neither the majority of blacks nor whites want to live in large cities according to statistics published in the 1978 HUD Survey on the Quality of Community Life prepared by Louis Harris and Associates.[1] At the same time that the cities are losing population, a conflicting trend of middle class people moving to the central city neighborhoods can be observed.[2] The middle class fix up the housing, increase demand for housing and force up housing prices. This has resulted in conflict between the middle class with high incomes and the indigenous poor populations.

Often the indigenous poor population is composed of racial minorities and the middle class population is usually white. The result has been a racial conflict that can be seen in areas such as Boston's South End and San Francisco's Mission District. The phenomenon of white resettlement in inner-city neighborhoods has been frequently discussed and is an issue of concern with both the government and the banking industry. The Housing and Community Development Act of 1974 stipulates that the millions given to cities should be of benefit to the poor who are often minorities. The banking industry is concerned about protecting its investment in inner-city neighborhoods and about not being accused of displacing minorities.[3]

Thus, we have two opposing trends reported, white and middle class resettlement of inner-city neighborhoods and middle class movement to the suburbs resulting in central city abandonment. This article argues that both of these phenomena can and are taking place simultaneously. They are responses to the changing role of the central city. A brief review of theory relevant to these trends precedes an empirical analysis of the changing central city.

## THEORY OF CENTRAL CITY REVIVAL

A theory of central city middle class resettlement based on expanding job opportunities in the Central Business District (CBD) has been previously articulated and will briefly be summarized.[4] According to the theory, ever increasing commuting distances to the CBD would increase the attractiveness of central city neighborhoods to those commuters who work in the CBD. Demographic changes such as fewer children per household and two adults in the labor force per household would also reduce the locational advantage of living in suburbia compared with living in the city. Expanded white collar jobs in the CBD will increase the likelihood of CBD revival.

Others have pointed out that the cost of new construction and land at the urban fringe has increased much more rapidly than the cost of central city properties.[5] Coupled with the rising interest in "historic" preservation, this has made many of the central city properties a good investment. Also, there has been a greater acceptance of condominium and cooperative ownership for multi-family housing which offers the tax advantages and equity appreciation for multi-family dwellings that was previously associated with single-family housing. This has helped breathe new life into some inner-city properties and into the middle class demand for those properties.

## THEORY OF DISPLACEMENT

Many have pointed out that the revival in demand has had deleterious effects on those who were previously living in the inner city. Case studies on Washington, D.C., Boston, New Orleans, Philadelphia, and San Francisco have documented that, in specific neighborhoods, a major problem of displacement exists.[6] The term "gentrification" has been borrowed from the British to describe the displacement of the poor by the gentry or upper-income groups.

A number of studies, however, have been undertaken to examine groups of cities rather than specific neighborhoods. These studies tend to say that gentrification is less of a problem. It has been shown that during the period from 1967-1971, 45,000 whites moved into central city housing previously occupied by blacks.[7] However, the same study indicated that

2,04,000 blacks moved into central city housing previously occupied by whites. Thus, if gentrification has a racial component, it was not significant at a national level during this period.

It is possible that gentrification did not begin until after 1971 but this possibility will be disputed later. Other research undertaken by the Urban Institute indicates that there were some small signs of resettlement of cities by the middle class, but that it was generally the exception rather than the norm.[8] This study used city-wide data and is subject to the potential problem of using the wrong level of data aggregation. For example, it is possible that some neighborhoods are experiencing an influx in middle income households while others are experiencing an exodus. The city-wide data would mask the countervailing trends.

In a survey of 105 neighborhoods that "have experienced some degree of private inner-city rehabilitation," it was found that gentrification did not take place in all cases.[9] However gentrification was more likely to occur within five miles of the central business district. This would give support to the theory that gentrification is limited to specific neighborhoods, at least at the present time.

## THEORY OF ABANDONMENT AND DECAY

Sternlieb and Hughes (1977) have pointed out that manufacturing jobs have been leaving the northeast and north-central regions.[10] The loss of manufacturing jobs in central cities is even more acute as those industries that do expand or locate in these regions take advantage of cheaper land at the urban fringe. This land is often made accessible because of the federal highway program.

Sternlieb and Burchell (1973) established the connection between abandonment and the decrease in the number of manufacturing and other jobs in Newark, New Jersey.[11] The loss of jobs is directly tied to the number of households looking for housing in the area. While not all workers who lose jobs relocate, many do, and there is an eventual adjustment in the housing market. Even if people choose not to relocate there is likely to be a drop in income and the ability to afford or maintain quality housing. Eventually the housing stock will fall into disrepair unless economic conditions change.

In summary, and at the risk of oversimplification, one would predict a reduction in housing demands and abandonment in central cities if the number of jobs in central cities decreased. A prediction of an increase in high quality, high priced housing would be in order if the number of white-collar high paying jobs increased in the CBD. Given both occurrences, gentrification could take place because there would be neighborhoods that (1) were not yet abandoned and were experiencing demand by the middle class or (2) were desired by the remaining blue collar population as well as by the middle class.

The remainder of this article will explore the changes in central cities since 1970. Since gentrification may have a racial dimension, migration by race will be discussed. In addition, change in the occupations of residents of central cities will be examined. The number of dwelling units and tenure of the occupants is presented to shed light on changes in the housing stock. The analysis proceeds from highly aggregated data (all central cities) to city level and census tract level aggregations. This will allow the reader to make his/her own judgment of the seriousness of the countervailing trends discussed above. The different levels of data aggregation are necessary for a complete picture.

TABLE 9.1

**Central City Mobility Status by Race: March 1970 to March 1973**
(Numbers in Thousands)

| Mobility Status | Total | White | Black |
|---|---|---|---|
| Same House in C.C. | 37,136 | 28,359 | 8,166 |
| Moved Within Same C.C. | 11,894 | 8,456 | 3,184 |
| Moved C.C. to Another C.C. | 1,856 | 1,513 | 285 |
| Total Movers Staying in C.C. | 13,750 | 9,969 | 3,469 |
| **Moved From C.C.** | | | |
| Within Same SMSA | 14,377 | 3,868 | 401 |
| To Other SMSA | 2,644 | 2,453 | 153 |
| To Outside SMSA | 2,078 | 1,943 | 126 |
| Total Moved From C.C. | 9,099 | 8,264 | 680 |
| **Moved to C.C.** | | | |
| From Same SMSA | 2,299 | 1,870 | 382 |
| From Other SMSA | 1,232 | 1,111 | 109 |
| From Outside SMSA | 1,547 | 1,292 | 225 |
| From Abroad | 1,012 | NA | 96 |
| Total Moved to C.C. | 6,090 | 4,272.* | 812 |
| Total Movers | 28,942 | 22,506.* | 4,961 |
| Net (-Loss/+Gain) | -5,181 | -3,922.* | +132 |

Source: Prepared From U.S. Census Bureau, Current Population Reports, Series P-20, No. 262, 1974.

*Excluding from abroad

## NATIONAL VIEW: CHANGES IN POPULATION, HOUSEHOLDS, AND EMPLOYMENT

Tables 9.1 and 9.2 provide migration figures for all United States central cities for two-three-year periods beginning in 1970 and 1975. During both periods there was a significant loss in central city population through migration. After this observation has been made, comparisons of the tables lead to conclusions that may be biased by one's own perceptions. Those who support the view that central cities are reviving—the optimists—can gain comfort by the fact that there was an increase in the number of people who moved and chose to stay in the same central city or who moved to another central city. In the period from 1970 to 1973, 997 million whites moved within central cities. The figure increased to 10.65 million for the period 1975 to 1978. The optimists will also point to the in

TABLE 9.2

**Central City Mobility Status by Race (for Population 3 Years and Over): March 1975 to March 1978**
(Numbers in Thousands)

| **Mobility Status** | **Total** | **White** | **Black** | **Spanish** |
|---|---|---|---|---|
| Same House in C.C. | 35,514 | 26,801 | 7,990 | 2,988 |
| Moved Within Same C.C | 12,848 | 8,888 | 3,688 | 1,672 |
| Moved C.C. to Another C.C. | 2,331 | 1,762 | 524 | 200 |
| Total Movers Staying in C.C. | 15,179 | 10,650 | 4,212 | 1,872 |
| **Moved From C.C.** | | | | |
| Within Same SMSA | 4,640 | 3,966 | 546 | 406 |
| To Other SMSA | 2,838 | 2,518 | 233 | 176 |
| To Outside SMSA | 2,437 | 2,185 | 207 | 89 |
| Total Moved from C.C. | 9,915 | 8,669 | 986 | 671 |
| **Moved to C.C.** | | | | |
| From Same SMSA | 2,231 | 1,931 | 261 | 154 |
| From Other SMSA | 1,449 | 1,253 | 147 | 92 |
| From Outside SMSA | 1,607 | 1,386 | 191 | 102 |
| From Abroad | 1,066 | 767 | 71 | 275 |
| Total Moved to C.C. | 6,353 | 5,337 | 670 | 623 |
| Total Movers | 31,447 | 24,656 | 5,868 | 3,166 |
| Net (-Loss/+Gain) | -3,562 | -3,332 (-2,565)* | -316 | -48 |

Source: Prepared From U.S. Census Bureau, Current Population Reports, Series P-20, No.331,197.

* Excluding From Abroad

crease in numbers of whites moving to central cities (presumably upper income whites.)[12] This number increased from 4.3 million to 5.3 million (excluding those from abroad) for the two periods studied.

Those who fear displacement will point to the net loss in minority populations through migration. Others, however, would more like interpret this as indicating expanded housing opportunities outside the traditional ghettos.

When looking at displacement, one must not only look at the number of people looking for housing in a particular location but at the number of housing units demanded. Table 3 shows the impact of migration on the potential demand for housing units for the period 1975 to 1977. Migration resulted in the reduction of over a million families and 400,000 unrelated individuals. Given that there was not a commensurate increase in household formation from among those who stayed in the city, there should have been a shrinkage in demand for central city housing of at least one million housing units. As Table 9.3 also indicates, the amount of money available to spend on housing and other goods in central cities decreased because of migration. Thus, with a reduction in demand, abandonment and increased vacancies or demolition of housing should have taken place. Indeed, that has happened.

Further evidence of a decrease in the number of people living in cetral cities is provided by Table 9.4. Between 1970 and 1977 there was a decrease of 3,49,000 people who were employed and also resided in central cities. Closer examination of the table indicates that a shift was taking place in the occupational categories of city dwellers which supports the hypothesis that gentrification is occurring. Three occupational categories show an increase in the number of city dwellers as employed. Two of these categories, "Professional, Technical and Kindred" and "Managers and Administrators", which can be considered high income white-collar professions, increased by over 700 thousand (12 per cent) since 1970.

The occupational categories that increased should be of no surprise to those who have witnessed the construction of office buildings in CBDs. Vacancy rates for office space have also been decreasing.[13] Table 9.5 shows the increase in office space in the CBD of specific cities (1970-1975) as well as estimates in the increase in the number of jobs and vacancy rates. Unlike the other tables, Table 9.5 presents information for specific cities. It indicates that cities are not alike; clearly some cities have had a much greater increase in office space in the CBD

TABLE 9.3

**Mobility and Resulting Change in Income of Central City Residence: March 1975 to March 1977***

| Mobility Status | Family | | | Unrelated Individuals | | |
|---|---|---|---|---|---|---|
| | Number (Thous-ands | Income Mean ($) | Income Total (billion $) | Number thous-ands | Income Mean ($) | Income Total (billion $) |
| **Moved From C.C.** | | | | | | |
| Within Same SMSA | 975 | 16,449 | 16.03 | 498 | 8,754 | 4.36 |
| To other SMSA | 547 | 17,157 | 9.38 | 289 | 7,445 | 2.13 |
| To outside SMSA's | 481 | 13,714 | 6.60 | 207 | 7,223 | 1.50 |
| **Moved to C.C.** | | | | | | |
| From same SMSA | 464 | 16,145 | 7.49 | 423 | 8,639 | 3.65 |
| from other SMSA | 266 | 15,530 | 4.13 | 234 | 7,201 | 1.69 |
| From outside SMSA's | 255 | 12,331 | 3.14 | 283 | 6,416 | 1.82 |
| Change (-Loss/+Gain) | -1,018 | | -17.25 | -434 | | -.83 |

Source: Prepared from U.S. Bureau of Census, Social and Economic Characteristics of Metropolitan and Non-Metropolitan Population, 1977 and 1970. Special Studies P.23, No. 75, 1978.

* Does not include movers to or from abroad.

**Occupation ot Employed Persons 16 Years Old ana Over for Central City Residence: 1970 and 1977**
(Numbers in Thousands)

| | Percent* 1970 | 1977 | No. Employed 1970 | 1977 | Change in No. Employed |
|---|---|---|---|---|---|
| Professional, Technical and Kindred | 15.2 | 15.8 | 3792 | 3890 | 98 |
| Managers and Administrators | 7.6 | 10.5 | 1908 | 2593 | 685 |
| Sales Workers | 7.4 | 6.4 | 1840 | 1577 | -263 |
| Clerical | 21.4 | 20.9 | 5335 | 5131 | -204 |
| Crafts and Kindred | 12.0 | 11.1 | 2993 | 2719 | -274 |
| Operatives, except transport | 12.9 | 10.8 | 3212 | 2653 | -559 |
| Transport Equipment Operatives | 3.8 | 3.7 | 960 | 913 | -47 |
| Laborers except farm | 4.5 | 4.3 | 1116 | 1051 | -65 |
| Farm Laborers & Supervisors | 0.3 | 0.2 | 65 | 39 | -26 |
| Farmers and Farm Managers | 0.1 | 0.1 | 27 | 16 | -11 |
| Service Workers, except private households | 13.1 | 14.9 | 3256 | 3659 | 403 |
| Private household workers | 1.8 | 1.4 | 439 | 353 | -86 |
| Total | 100.1% | 100.1% | 24943 | 24594 | -349 |

Prepared from U.S. Census Bureau, Social and Economic Characteristics of the Metropolitan and Non-metropolitan Population 1977 and 1970. Special Studies, p. 23, No. 75, 1978. The number of 1970 service workers as well as the percentages are in error in the Census Report. Adjustments have been made here.

* Does not add up to 100 per cent because of rounding error.

than others. If the theory that the desirability of central city residential property is a function of CBD office space and jobs is correct, those cities with little increase in office space should not be cities where gentrification is occurring. This is in fact the case if the location of case studies describing gentrification is a valid indicator of the severity of the problem in a city.

Information on the number of housing units and housing tenure by central city is presented in Table 9.6 for those cities in the earlier sample for which the Annual Housing Survey published appropriate data. In most cities, the number of housing units decreased between 1970 and the year the survey was taken. The major exceptions are in SMSAs that have two central cities (Los Angeles-Long Beach, Seattle-Everett) or in

TABLE 9.5

**Change in Office Space and Employment in Central Business Districts Gross Office Space[1] (Million sq ft.)**

| | 1970 | 1975 | Change | Change[2] in number of workers | Vacancy[3] Rate 1977 |
|---|---|---|---|---|---|
| Atlanta | 17.0 | 21.0 | 4.0 | 16,000 | 4.9 |
| Baltimore | 8.4 | 10.2 | 1.8 | 7,200 | 5.2 |
| Boston | 34.0 | 45.0 | 11.0 | 44,000 | 10.3 |
| Chicago | 63.0 | 84.0 | 21.0 | 84,000 | 5.1 |
| Cleveland | 11.0 | 15.0 | 4.0 | 16,000 | 2.1 |
| Dallas | 21.0 | 24.0 | 3.0 | 12,000 | 7.8 |
| Detroit | 18.0 | 22.0 | 4.0 | 16,000 | 12.0 |
| Houston | 25.0 | 37.0 | 12.0 | 48,000 | 1.5 |
| Los Angeles | 33.0 | 42.0 | 9.0 | 36,000 | 6.6 |
| Milwaukee | 9.4 | 11.0 | 1.6 | 6,400 | 12.9 |
| Minneapolis and St.Paul | 10.0 | 13.0 | 3.0 | 12,000 | 4.5 |
| New York | 240.0 | 290.0 | 50.0 | 200,000 | 4.1 |
| Newark | 14.0 | 14.0 | 0.0 | 0 | N.A |
| Philadelphia | 34.0 | 43.0 | 9.0 | 36,000 | 6.9 |
| Pittsburgh | 22.0 | 26.0 | 4.0 | 16,000 | 12.0 |
| St. Louis | 17.0 | 20.0 | 3.0 | 12,000 | 7.0 |
| San Francisco | 26.0 | 37.0 | 11.0 | 44,000 | 7.5 |
| Seattle | 8.6 | 12.5 | 3.9 | 15,600 | 6.6 |
| Washington, D.C. | 54.0 | 71.0 | 17.0 | 68,000 | 3.1 |

Source: 1. Armstrong, Regina, 1977. National Trends in Office Construction, Employment and Headquarter Location in U.S. Metropolitan Areas, New York, N.Y. Regional Plan Association.

2. The Building Owners and Managers Association estimate that the average sq. ft. per worker is 205 while Armstrong's estimates are 230 sq. ft. To be conservative and take into consideration vacancies, 250 sq. ft. per worker was used.

3. Zisler, Randall and Cole. Dustin A (1978). 1978 Downtown and Suburban Office Building Experience Exchange Report (Washington D.C. Building Owners and Managers Association International).

SMSAs with vacant land within the central city boundary (Houston). The data indicated that demolition (or more likely, conversion) is taking place. Even though the number of housing units has decreased, vacancies have generally increased, indicating a generally weak housing market for the central city as a whole at the time of the survey.

TABLE 9.6

**Change in Number and Tenure of Housing Units for Central Cities**
(in Thousands)

| Central City | Year-Round Housing Units | | (Owner) Occupied | | (Renter) Occupied | | Vacant | |
|---|---|---|---|---|---|---|---|---|
| | 1970 | 1974-6[1] | 1970 | 1974-6[1] | 1970 | 1974-6[1] | 1970 | 1974-6[1] |
| Atlanta[5] | 171 | 169 | 67 | 61 | 96 | 87 | 9 | 21 |
| Baltimore[6] | 305 | 288 | 289 | 269 | 161 | 147 | 16 | 19 |
| Boston[4] | 232 | 225 | 59 | 57 | 158 | 143 | 15 | 25 |
| Chicago[5] | 1207 | 1144 | 396 | 403 | 740 | 667 | 70 | 74 |
| Cleveland[6] | 264 | 251 | 115 | 108 | 134 | 123 | 16 | 20 |
| Detroit[4] | 529 | 508 | 299 | 281 | 199 | 184 | 31 | 43 |
| Houston[6] | 428 | 508 | 207 | 210 | 186 | 253 | 34 | 45 |
| Los Angeles[4]* | 1227 | 1277 | 482 | 486 | 688 | 703 | 57 | 89 |
| New York[6] | 2924 | 2845 | 669 | 704 | 2168 | 1959 | 81 | 178 |
| Philadelphia[5] | 674 | 652 | 642 | 606 | 259 | 237 | 31 | 45 |
| St. Louis[6] | 238 | 207 | 87 | 83 | 128 | 101 | 23 | 22 |
| San Francisco[5]* Oakland | 457 | 463 | 156 | 153 | 278 | 268 | 23 | 42 |
| Seattle[6]* Everett | 242 | 237 | 123 | 119 | 102 | 104 | 17 | 14 |
| Washington, D.C.[4] | 278 | 272 | 74 | 78 | 189 | 180 | 16 | 15 |

Source: Constructed from U.S. Census Bureau, Current Housing Reports: Housing Characteristics for selected Metropolitan Areas, 1974-1976.

* Central Cities combined.

1. Annual Housing Survey does not survey each city yearly. Numbers after the city name indicate year census taken during the 70's.

The vacancy rate in New York City increased from 2.8 to 6.8 per cent even though the number of housing units decreased by 2.7 per cent. Yet there are waiting lists to get an apartment in Manhattan, while a few blocks away there is abandonment. Possibly, Manhattan is a separate market within New York City.

When change in tenure by race is examined (Table 9.7), it becomes apparent that ownership by whites has decreased in the older northeastern cities, with the exception of New York City. Concurrently, black homeownership has increased. Again, a contradiction seems to exist. Blacks are owning and renting more central city housing at the same time that displacement is being alleged.

## View from the Census Tract

The contradictions are more evident as the level of analysis shifts to the census tract. Unfortunately, census tract data is limited to the decennial census. Even though this limits the analysis to 1960-1970 data, evidence of changes in the location of socio-economic groups in cities is apparent. An analysis of racial changes is reported below.

Table 9.8 shows the changes in racial composition of census tracts within two miles of the CBD for 20 major cities from 1960 to 1970. The overwhelming pattern is of a loss of white population and an increase in black population. However, each city had at least a few census tracts that had an increase in white population near the CBD. Except for those cities that experienced rapid growth in the 1960s (Los Angeles, Dallas and Houston), those cities with the greatest increase in the number of census tracts showing an increase in white population were also the cities where displacement was an issue in the mid-1970s (New York, Philadelphia, San Francisco, and Washington, D.C.).

The realignment of population by race is best observed by looking at a map. Two maps, one of Washington, D.C., and the other of Boston, graphically depict the changes (see Figures 9.1 and 9.2). Horizontal lines indicate that the non-white population is increasing, while vertical lines indicate that the white population is increasing. In both cities there are census tracts with only one race having an increase in population while the other has a decrease, tracts where both groups have increasing population, and tracts where both groups have declining population. The 1980 Census will shed more light on the magnitude of the realignment.

TABLE 9.7

**Change in Tenure by Race in Central Cities**
(in Thousands)

| | Owner-Occupied-Units | | | | Renter-Occupied-Units | | | |
|---|---|---|---|---|---|---|---|---|
| | White | | Black | | White | | Black | |
| Central City | 1970 | 1974-6 | 1970 | 1974-6 | 1970 | 1974-6 | 1970 | 1974-6 |
| Atlanta[5] | 40.0 | 29.9 | 26.6 | 31.4 | 50.9 | 36.0 | 44.4 | 50.2 |
| Baltimore[6] | 93.7 | 82.0 | 34.2 | 39.6 | 79.5 | 61.9 | 79.8 | 82.2 |
| Boston[4] | 53.1 | 49.3 | 5.5 | 6.8 | 129.6 | 111.8 | 26.2 | 26.9 |
| Chicago[5] | 319.3 | 290.8 | 74.2 | 107.3 | 489.7 | 407.2 | 239.0 | 245.5 |
| Cleveland[6] | 81.8 | 73.1 | 32.4 | 34.7 | 79.0 | 66.6 | 53.9 | 55.5 |
| Detroit[4] | 198.8 | 161.0 | 98.7 | 118.4 | 102.9 | 79.3 | 94.4 | 101.9 |
| Houston[6] | 165.9 | 158.8 | 40.2 | 48.9 | 134.9 | 186.1 | 34.1 | 45.2 |
| Los Angeles[5]* Long Beach | 410.0 | 408.8 | 55.9 | 66.4 | 538.6 | 546.4 | 120.7 | 119.7 |
| New York[6] | 580.1 | 581.5 | 83.5 | 111.2 | 1690.2 | 1395.9 | 439.2 | 449.6 |
| Philadelphia[5] | 289.6 | 261.9 | 92.5 | 104.0 | 153.3 | 132.8 | 102.7 | 99.6 |
| St. Louis[6] | 64.2 | 56.8 | 22.8 | 26.2 | 77.2 | 58.4 | 50.3 | 42.2 |
| San Francisco[5]* Oakland | 118.7 | 106.7 | 23.8 | 28.8 | 204.6 | 178.0 | 48.3 | 58.8 |
| Seattle[6]* Everett | 112.6 | 106.7 | 6.1 | 7.0 | 90.9 | 88.6 | 6.5 | 9.2 |
| Washington, D.C.[4] | 28.5 | 27.4 | 44.9 | 49.3 | 67.4 | 55.8 | 118.9 | 119.9 |

Source: Constructed from U.S. Census Bureau, Current Housing Reports: Housing Characteristics for Selected Metropolitan Areas, 1974-1976.

* Central Cities of two SMSA's combined.

1. Annual Housing Survey does not survey each city yearly. Numbers after the city name indicate year census taken during the 70's.

TABLE 9.8

**Number of Census Tracts Within Two Miles of the CBD Showing Increases in Number of Whites and Non-whites for Twenty U.S. Cities During the 1960s**

| City | White Increase | Non-White Increase | No. of Tracts |
|---|---|---|---|
| Atlanta | 9 | 34 | 71 |
| Baltimore | 3 | 31 | 54 |
| Boston | 4 | 18 | 23 |
| Chicago | 6 | 33 | 63 |
| Cleveland | 7 | 38 | 80 |
| Dallas | 15 | 28 | 42 |
| Detroit | 5 | 11 | 46 |
| Houston | 14 | 22 | 38 |
| Los Angeles | 37 | 52 | 91 |
| Milwaukee | 6 | 60 | 82 |
| Minneapolis | 11 | 54 | 70 |
| New York | 37 | 112 | 136 |
| Newark | 11 | 45 | 61 |
| Philadelphia | 18 | 48 | 107 |
| Pittsburgh | 10 | 43 | 80 |
| St. Louis | 4 | 15 | 28 |
| St. Paul | 7 | 30 | 33 |
| San Francisco | 16 | 63 | 77 |
| Seattle | 3 | 23 | 36 |
| Washington, D.C. | 15 | 26 | 66 |

Source: Compiled from 1960 and 1970 Census of Population and Housing.

## CONCLUSIONS

As early as 1970, signs of a shifting of location by whites and non-whites in central cities are apparent from the maps. The pattern of out-migration has continued since 1970, although at a slower rate. Migration figures since 1970 also indicate that in any three-year period approximately 45 per cent of the residents in central cities are living in housing units that are different from the units they occupied three years earlier. This pattern, coupled with the increase in new office space in the CBD and the higher occupational status of the residents in the central cities, indicates that some neighborhoods are experiencing increased demand and that displacement of the indigenous poor is likely to take place. The increase in black homeownership may indicate that middle income blacks are becoming part of the gentry pushing up housing costs and displacing lower income households.

However, the razing of residential structures will continue if the decrease in blue-collar jobs in central cities continues. The number of households and housing units in central cities

Figure 1

Racial Change in Census Tracts Within 2 Miles of the CBD - Washington, 1960 - 1970

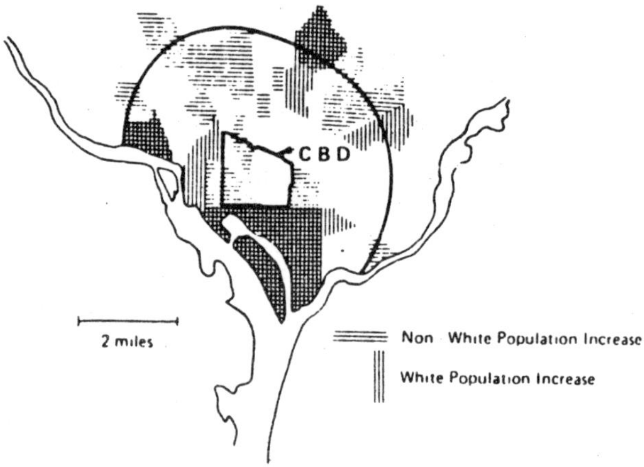


Figure 2

Racial Change in Census Tracts Within 2 Miles of the CBD - Boston, 1960 - 1970

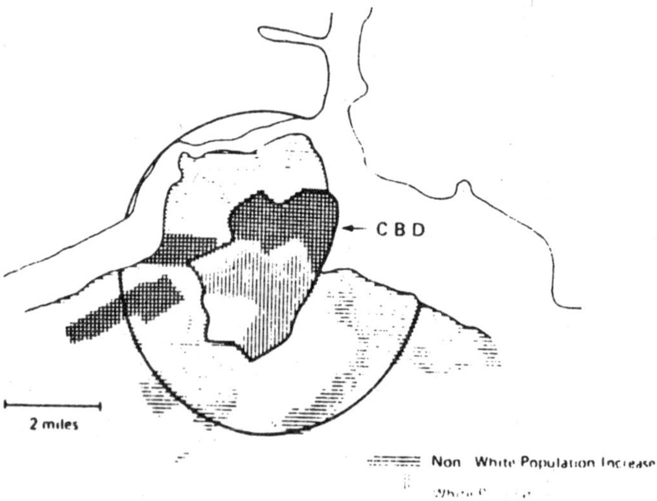

dropped in all the older eastern cities between 1970 and the last reported annual housing survey even though some new housing has been built in these cities.

The urban scene thus has highly localized submarkets. The magnitude of the displacement problem is quite acute in a few cities but the data do not indicate that it is as yet a national problem. However, central city locations near the CBD and other white-collar employment centers (such as universities) are likely to become the homes of middle income households.[14] The reason for this is not so much that millions of the gentry will look to these areas (though many will); the reason is more complex.

Part of the reason is that the location of new blue-collar jobs has shifted out of the central city and, in some cities, the white-collar high income jobs are being located near the CBD. Thus, as previously stated, commuting costs and preferences may bring about a shift in the location of the two work forces. Just as important, however, is that as the market for central city properties softens, much of the older housing stock is being razed. This in itself will limit low income housing opportunities. The replacement cost of this razed housing is likely to be greater than the cost of older housing in the early 1950 suburban tract developments.

Central city governments may resist building large numbers of low income housing units and prefer to entice high income tax payers to locate in the cities. Federally sponsored housing dispersal programs will encourage the location of lower income households in suburbia. The older suburbs may find an aging population that can no longer support the schools with dollars or children, and a declining ability to attract young middle income households that have children. If this happens, these suburbs are likely to undergo a change in their clientele.

One can easily postulate another scenario of continued increase in overall housing demand, high interest rates and increased cost of building materials, land and labor resulting in the cost of housing rising faster than incomes and inflation. This scenario leaves those in the lower end of the income scale worse off than the one previously discussed. The amount of deteriorated housing that will be razed in the central cities will decrease, but the cost of rehabilitating that housing will increase, thereby putting it out of reach of these groups. Demands in the inner suburbs will increase and close off this option for the poor. Moreover, the housing options in all locations will decrease as the current owners of land reap increased profits, thereby continuing displacement. The question is, where will the low income people go? Overcrowding and competition for housing will increase in those areas currently occupied by the poor. This situation has already been reported by the Washington, D.C., Press.

Although cries of gentrification will be heard loudly, an optimist would prefer to believe that a balance will take place. This can happen in a number of ways. First, demand for housing in central cities by high income individuals will not be great enough to push out lower income populations. Another option would be for lower income residents to buy housing before the price of housing adjusts to the decrease in the number of available units and the increase in high income demand. This strategy has the added benefit of reducing the rate of demolition and preserving the housing stock. It is a strategy that is being used by St. Ambrose Housing Aid Center in Baltimore, Maryland. St. Ambrose has succeeded in buying housing before prices increase, rehabilitating the house (rather than historically preserving it) and then selling the house to people on welfare.[15] Whether these new homeowners will prefer to sell their property when the value increases is not known. People in Alexandria, Virginia, resisted limiting their ability to resell their houses at speculative profits.[16] However, some homeowners may be forced to sell if increased property values result in property taxes beyond their means.

All three of these scenarios will be seen in the future. Individual cities may have submarkets that will result in all three scenarios taking place concurrently as their economic base changes. In this period of disequilibrium, local and regional planners can do much to foster racially and economically integrated cities, if not integrated neighborhoods, as a result of these changes. Planners, in conjunction with local groups, could emulate the work of St. Ambrose Housing Aid Center. This would require that the housing be bought at a reasonable price before it is beyond repair or, conversely, before the neighbourhood is "rediscovered." It may also require innovative ownership patterns such as cooperatives that guard against future gentrification. The planners will, however, have to closely monitor the local job and housing markets.

When housing in some neighborhoods becomes extremely low priced, abandonment and demolition can occur quickly. Coversely, an increase in housing prices can accelerate quickly as gentrification begins. Fortunately, neither gentrification nor abandonment has yet to become the dominant pattern in central cities.

## REFERENCES


1. Louis Harris and Associates, 1978 HUD Survey on the Quality of Life (Washington, D.C.: Office of Policy Development and Research, HUD), 1978.
2. S. Gregory Lipton, "Evidence of Central City Revival", Journal of the American Institute of Planners, April, 1977.
3. Thomas C. Westropp, New Approaches to Urban Housing (Chicago, Illinois: United States League of Savings Associations, 1977).
4. Lipton, Revival.
5. J. Thomas Black, "Private-Market Housing Renovation in Central Cities. A ULI Survey", Urban Land, 1975.
6. Dennis F. Gale, The Back to the City Movement ... or is it? Washington, D.C., Department of Urban and Regional Planning, George Washington University, 1977. Frank Smith, Rip-Off and Reinvestment: A Report on Speculation and Evictions in Washington, D.C. (Washington, D.C. Public Resource Center), 1977. Robert Fichter, Young Professionals and City Neighborhoods (Boston, Mass: Parkman Center for Urban Affairs, 1977). Shirley Laska and Daphine Spain, Inner-City Renovation: What Can We Expect. Annual Meeting of the Southern Sociological Society, 1978. Paul R. Levy, Queen Village: The Eclipse of Community (Philadelphia, Pennsylvania Institute for the Study of Civic Values, 1978). Jerry Hagstrom, Strategies Toward Racial and Economic Diversity. Presented at the Back to the Cities Conference. Hartford Conn., 1978.
7. Larry H. Long and Daphine Spain, Racial Succession in Individual Units, Current Population Reports, Special Studies Series P-23. No. 71, U.S. Bureau of the Census, 1978.
8. Franklin J. James, Private Reinvestment in Older Housing and Neighborhoods: Recent Trends and Forces, Washington, D.C., Urban Institute, 1977.
9. Phillip Clay, "Neighborhood Revitalization and Community Development" in Centre for Community Economic Development Newsletter, Cambridge, Mass., August-October, 1978, 1.
10. George Sternlieb and James W. Hughes, "New Regional and Metropolitan Realities of America", Journal of the American Institute of Planners, 1977.
11. George Sternlieb and Robert W. Burchell, Resident Abandonment: The Tenant Landlord Revisited. (Cambridge, Mass: MIT Press, 1973).
12. Conrad Weiler, "Achieving Social and Economic Diversity in Inner City Neighborhoods Through Increased Demand for City Housing by Middle Income Persons", presented at the Back to the City Conference, Hartford Conn., 1977.
13. Randell Zisler and Dustin A. Cole, 1978 Downtown and Suburban Office Building Experience Exchange Report, (Washington, D.C. Building Owners and Managers Association International, 1978).
14. Clay, Revitalization.
15. Vincente Quale discussed his program at the Back to the Cities Conference in Hartford, Conn. (1977). For more information, contact the St. Ambrose Housing Aid center in Baltimore, Maryland.
16. Hammer, Silver, George Associates, Final NEA Study Report to the City of Alexandria, Virginia (Washington, D.C., 1976).

TEN

Kevin C. Kearns

# INTRAURBAN SQUATTING IN LONDON*

Squatting is most commonly associated with developing countries in which rural-to-urban migration has led to the creation of shanty town-type settlements on the urban periphery. Intraurban squatting in Western industrialized nations differs in form and function from its Third World counterparts[1]. Renovation and reutilization of inner-urban buildings is a variant type of squatting symptomatic of urban maladies in many large Western cities; it is found in "most European countries".[2] Squatting has flourished in Britain, where London's squatter population has reached 30,000. Squatting has come to be regarded as a "significant factor in housing provision."[3]

Squatting is now well advanced in Great Britain, Italy, Spain, France, Denmark and the Netherlands and it is increasing in Sweden and West Germany. Close communication links have been established over the past five years among various European squatter communities, particularly British, Dutch, and Italian. Squatting has spread from London to other large cities in Britain and the total population is estimated at more than 50,000. In the Netherlands squatting commenced in 1968 and by 1975 there were squatters in "almost every town and city" in the country. In Italy, where squatting tends to be more poli-

---

*The field research for this study was conducted in London during the summer of 1978. The author would like to express his gratitude to the following persons for their kind assistance in the preparation of this paper: Piers Corbyn, London Squatters Union; Diana Shelley, Advisory Service for Squatters; Jim Wintour, Shelter; and Stephen Platt, Squatters Self-Help Housing Resource Library. I am especially indebted to members of the Huntley Street Squatters Community for their confidence and cooperation.

ticised, there are now squatting organizations in all the larger cities. Squatters in Amsterdam, who number at least 8,000, are especially well organized. The largest and best known squatter community in Europe is "Christiania" in Copenhagen, with over 1,000 members.

The squatting movement in Britain has progressed more rapidly primarily because the conditions which breed squatting are amplified. London squatters also benefited initially from the liberality of British trespass law. In 1977 a new Criminal Trespass Law was passed bringing British leglslation more closely in line with that of other European countries, but with no measurable effect on squatting. It is important to note that squatting is conducted in European countries with greatly differing legal, social, and political systems, testimony to its potential for transference.

### Squatting in London

Most large British cities suffer a housing shortage but London is measurably worse. Thirtyfive per cent of the city's households live at a density of more than 1.5 persons per room, compared with 16.1 per cent elsewhere in Britain. Only four per cent of the country's households have to share their home; the figure in the capital is twenty per cent.[4] Many of the more than 10,00,000 empty government-owned houses in London remain unoccupied for five to ten years, yet there are 1,90,000 homeless families on housing council waiting list.[5] Another 51,000 privately held properties are unoccupied, one-fifth of which have been vacant for at least two years.[6] The homeless reside in "temporary" government shelters or with relatives or friends under stressful, often intolerable, conditions.[7]

In London abandonment has claimed not only dilapidated property but also structurally sound and habitable dwellings. Grandiose government redevelopment schemes have meant depopulation of entire neighborhoods. Budgetary problems, construction delays, and mismanagement of housing stock, particularly nineteenth-century buildings, have left abandoned properties in desuetude for years.

Developments in the private rental sector have exacerbated housing stress. Increasingly poor returns on rented accommodations have reduced incentives for land to rent; it is often more profitable to vacate buildings for re-development or to seek land speculation profit. Government improvement grants provide the impetus for "gentrification" whereby owners upgrade property from densely populated, relatively cheap, flats to owner-occupied or more expensive rental accommodations. Between 1961 and 1971 London's rental sector declined by twenty-four per cent, resulting in the gradual exclusion of lower-income groups, childless couples, single adults, and young people from affordable housing.[8]

Contraction of the private rental sector forced the government to assume a greater role in housing. One-quarter of London's population is now government-housed. But an inequitable housing allocation system places differential constraints on needy groups. Borough authorities forge their own housing policies and most accept only families on waiting lists. Childless couples, when approved, are always accorded lowest priority. Young persons and single adults are the most victimized. Most housing councils refuse to even accept an application from anyone under age thirty.[9]

Squatting began in London in 1968 with a series of calculated token squats to appraise public attitudes and test legal strategy. Authorities unsuccessfully attempted illegal evictions.[10] From inception, the news media played a vital role in squatting campaigns by marshalling public sympathy behind squatters. In 1969 housing councils started relinquishing short-life, empty properties to squatters on an authorised basis. Between 1969 and 1972 squatting was orderly and regulated, restricted exclusively to families. Family squatting groups propagated, developing their own waiting lists. In 1972 the character of squatting changed dramatically because of a marked upsurge in young and single squatters, the outbreak of unauthorised, spontaneous squatting, and the incursion of some public permanent-stock housing and private properties.[11] Between 1972 and 1975 squatting proliferated both socially and spatially throughout London; the population increased from 1,500 to nearly 25,000.

Most squatters come from the privately rented sector, casualities of rising rates, deteriorating conditions, congestion and landlord harassment. Unaffordable rental fees is the principal stimulus. The second largest group comprises those previously living with relatives or friends under strained conditions. In 1976 there were an estimated 8,000 young people "sleeping rough" in the city.[12]

## DEMOGRAPHIC PROFILE

Squatters are a composite of diverse social, occupational, educational, and political types. The shared experience of housing stress is their common bond. Indeed, they commonly form "unholy alliances" integrating disparate types which "would never come together in any other way.[13] Nonetheless, there are some identifiable characteristics.

London squatters strongly reflect those groups most excluded from the rental sector. They are characteristically young, about ninety per cent between ages twenty and thirty-five; few are over fortyfive. Two-thirds are single and about sixty per cent are male. About seventyfive per cent are native to the United Kingdom; the remaining quarter originate mostly from Ireland, the Caribbean, Africa, and Asia. New immigrants rarely squat, fearing violation of the law and deportation. Approximately half the eligible population is fully employed and a fifth are recipients of some form of unemployment benefits. The remaining one-third comprises chiefly students and part-time or self-employed persons. Many communities include a number of professionals, usually teachers and social workers.[14] Very few squatters are political radicals or "social drop-outs."

## SQUATTING AS A FORM OF HOUSING TENURE

Squatting has become a viable, alternative form of tenure which, though extralegal, has achieved a de facto status in London's housing sector. Like other tenure forms it has certain economic and social advantages.

### Selection and Occupation

Most "squattable" dwellings are detected by means of the squatters "bush telegraph," a highly effective oral information channel, or through the assistance of an extensive network of squatters advisory organizations.[15] Squatters oridinarily research property ownership and redevelopment plans prior to occupation.[16] Public property is much preferred to private holdings since eviction procedures must be routed through the bureaucratic labyrinth, ensuring delays often lasting years., Private owners often resort to illegal, forceable eviction. Also, most squatters have a strong psychological and moral hesitation about invasion of private property. The act of squatters usually assumes the form of clandestine nocturnal entry. Daylight occupation is best accomplished by squatters posing as workmen or as legal agents.[17] Once ensconced, squatters may not be legally evicted without court possession orders. Gas and electricity companies are compelled by law to provide service to all "occupiers," but many squatters simply devise alternatives to standard utilities.[18] Unauthorized squatters live in "legal limbo" under the omnipresent threat of eviction. Still, many prefer the uncertainties of squatting to the inherent problems and insecurities of tenancy.

**Economic Aspects of Squatting**

The most apparent benefit is that squatters avoid rental or mortgage payments, incurring only repair costs of their own choosing and utility fees, often shared. Most squats are in ill-repair from neglect or vandalism but potentially quite habitable. Authorities contend that it is not economically feasible to rehabilitate such properties for short-term occupancy, though most could be restored to acceptable shape for $4,000 to $5,000.[19] Squatters renovate housing for a fraction of this amount and in far less time with voluntary labour, mutual aid, shared tools and expertise, unorthodox and second-hand materials, innovation, and determination. They are uninhibited and imaginative in shaping their physical environment. Structural modifications such as removal of walls between rooms or flats, or construction of extensions, are casually made to meet specific space requirements.[20]

Turner and others have hypothesized that, because of their rights of autonomy, many Latin American squatters are actually "better housed in absolute terms" (meaning self-expression and personal fulfilment) than the materially wealthier urban poor in North America.[21] This supposition may be applied to London squatters who enjoy a measure of dweller control and self-management denied the majority of regularized British tenants; they, too, may be better housed in the absolute sense. This contention is supported by the fact that most squatters at the communities I visited exhibited a strong sense of accomplishment and pride in home possession, preferring the retention of dweller control over their squat to acceptance of rehousing in council tenant estates.

## TYPOLOGY OF SQUATTER SETTLEMENTS

Most public property in London belongs to either borough housing councils or the Greater London Council (G.L.C), an autonomous authority with housing stock distributed throughout the city. Public real estate is also held by assorted government agencies, health departments, railroad companies, and educational institutions. Government housing stock is classified as "short-life," scheduled for demolition or renovation, or "permanent pool," suitable for tenancy. Most squats are the council-owned short-life type. An estimated 1,700 borough council properties in Inner London are occupied by about 20,000 squatters, or about seventy per cent of the population.[22] Approximately 5,000 more reside in 1,500 G.L.C. buildings. Ninetyfive per cent of this stock is short-life. Probably no more than three per cent of the squatter population reside in private property.

In terms of legal status, squats are "authorized" or "unauthorized".[23] Unauthorized squats have no official sanction and are usually the most fragile, impermanent type (Fig. 10.1). Authorized squats are those licensed by owners permitting squatters to remain in occupation until the property is required.[24] Licensing is a form of legitimization which grants security from sudden eviction. It also places squatting in a quasilegal framework with some semblance of containment and regulation by authorities and allows for a more equitable distribution of squattable properties. Licensed squats symbolize a "halfway house" between trespasser status and official tenancy. Authorization is based on a "no rent, no repairs" condition which frees owners from any responsibility. A nominal "licence fee" ($2 and $5 average) is usually assessed.

Licensing of squats has accelerated markedly over the last few years. In London's local authority housing sector rents now fail to cover even half the total costs, requiring massive government subsidies. Conversely, squatters assume full responsibility for repairs, maintenance, supervision, and management at no cost to authorities. Hence, in many Inner London boroughs squatters have proven a more profitable proposition than rent-paying tenants.[25] All boroughs now license squats largely on the basis of cost-efficiency. Of the 1,700 council-owned properties, 750 have been licensed, and about forty per cent of all squats in London are now authorised.[26]

Squats may evolve from unauthorized to licensed status and eventually may become registered housing cooperatives. Ten squatter communities, including several of the largest, are presently in this transitional process (Fig. 10.2).[27] Housing cooperatives can apply for govenment subsidies to lease or purchase their property. This legitimizes the community and confers permanent tenure rights similar to those achieved by Third World squatters residing in legalized settlements. Borough councils increasingly support the concept of transforming squatter communities into housing cooperatives since it is an efficient and effective solution to the housing problem.

The fortynine squatter communities I identified ranged in size from about 25 to nearly 400 members. Geographical foundations are important for communal development. Entire blocks provide the ideal territorial base. Occupation of both street sides enforces physical cohesion. Where this is not possible, adjacent flats within the same block are best. Separated dwelling units impede social integration. Squatters develop a strong sense of place and territorial identification and most adopt place names for their communities, such as "Huntley Street," "Villa

Fig. 10.1 : Unauthorized individual squat fortified against eviction threat by housing authorities.

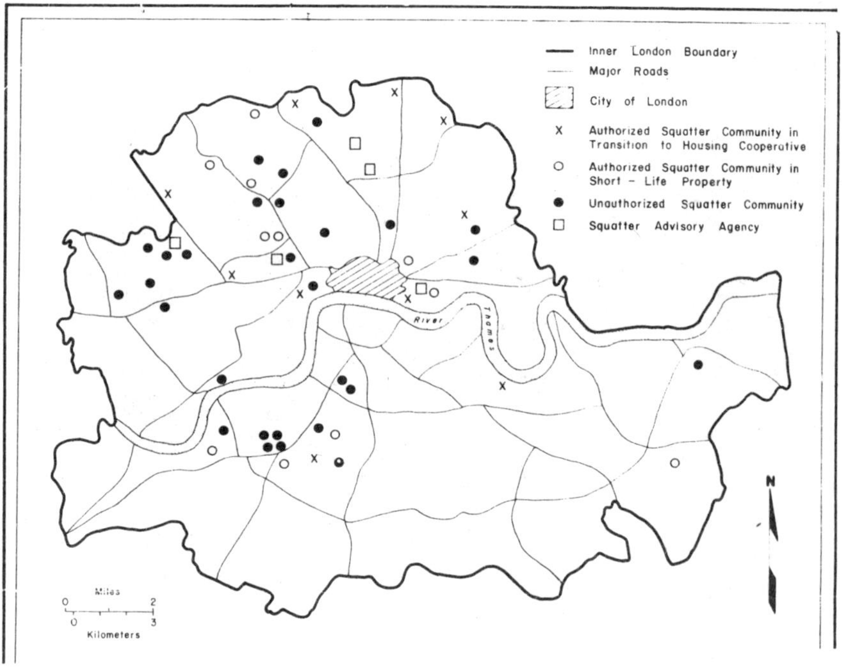


Fig. 10.2 : Squatter communities and major squatter advisory organizations in boroughs of Inner London.

Road," "St. Agnes Place," and "Tolmer's Square." They forge a sense of community and perceived territoriality becomes an integral factor in group solidarity, as evidenced by exhortations to defend "our street" or "our block" (Fig. 10.3) Few squats have been preplanned as communes promising a utopian life-style and these social experiments have been ephemeral.

## FACTORS IN GEOGRAPHICAL LOCATION

Squatting coincides with major redevelopment districts and other inner city zones of transition. Almost all squatted areas are characterized by some form of economic, demographic, or structural upheaval (Fig. 10.4). Most are lower-income, working-class neighbourhoods, many with some immigrant population. The disinvestment of privae capital from these districts has led to the wholesale purchase of deteriorating buildings by the government. For example, Camden's housing council annually acquires as many as 400 such properties for its designated "general improvement areas."

Fig. 10.3 : Authorized "Villa Road" squatters community. One hundred and forty squatters fully renovated the entire block of unoccupied, council-owned flats and emblazoned the end wall with "cosmic" mural.

Fig. 10.4 : Striking contrast between semirenovated squatter community on left and fully modernized, middle-income rental property on right. This is a typical "transitional zone" in terms of economic, demographic, and structural change.

Squatting occurs in all twelve Inner City boroughs, though relative rates vary (Fig. 10.5). In Islington, Camden, and Tower Hamlets the correlation between housing stress and squatting is especially pronounced. All are "bed-sitter" communities where high proportions of young people, single adults, and childless couples live in congested conditions. Westminster, Camden, and Islington are regarded as "trendy" boroughs noted for a liberal ambience generally attractive to squatters. Conversely, Greenwich, as an outlier borough, is atypical, removed physically and socially from the pulse of city center. Lightly squatted Lewisham and Southwark lack major squatter advisory groups important in organizing and supporting collective squatting.

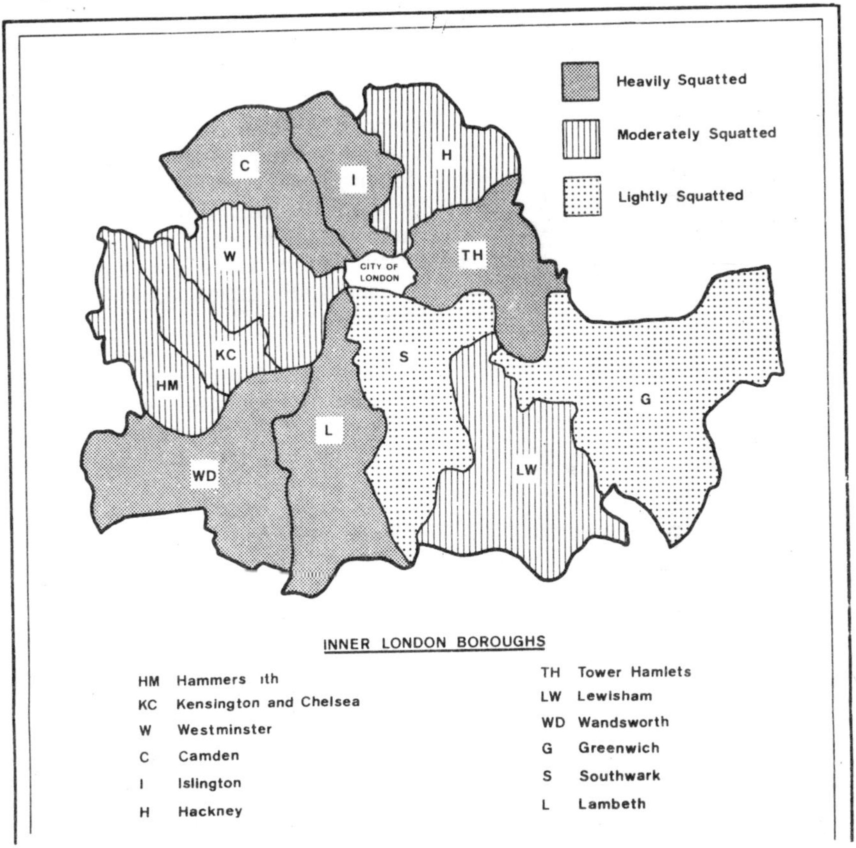


Fig. 10.5 : Relative rates of squatting in the twelve boroughs of Inner London.

The processes of urban change and renewal which have

created vacant structures in London are essentially duplicated in other squatted European cities. In Amsterdam squatting has been cencentrated in the inner city redevelopment area of Niewmarkt, and in Copenhagen it is found along the older central city waterfront district. Much the same applies in Turin, Paris, Madrid, and Stockholm. Though squatting is most closely associated with older, inner-city areas in varying degrees of transformation, it is by no means restricted to "blighted" Zones. It also pervades healthy, stable neighborhoods where property parcels scheduled for conversion have been left in vacancy. Squats are commonly found amid patches of gentrification or contiguous to thriving commercial districts (Fig. 10.6)

## CONCLUSION

Squatting offers a viable alternative form of housing tenure in the urban ecology of cities experiencing redevelopment and demographic change. In many inner urban zones of transition there exists a growing need for such "experiments in alternative forms of tenure".[28] One urban analyst of London, noting that the traditional unplanned city had a space for everyone, but that planned "redeveloped, improved" cities admit only a restricted range of citizens, postulated that:[29]

> The squatters movement . . . is a completely legitimate and natural expression of the principle of requisite variety, filling part of the gap, since there are whole categories of people who will never be housed by the (regular) modes of tenure.

Intraurban squatting has not been confined to the European realm. For example, there has recently been a significant emergence of squatting in the central urban district of Sydney, Australia, where conditions of urban renewal, population displacement, and housing allocation inequities seem to fit the European pattern.[30] There have been several manifestations of group squatting in large cities of the United Staes, most notably New York, Boston, Newark, and Philadelphia. In the early 1970s squatting in New York City was recognized as having "become a movement ... an open challenge to the planning process".[31] New York squatters were referred to as "people pushed to the limit" by the housing bureaucracy. Hence, the parallels between squatting in London and elsewhere are readily apparent.

Squatting is now favourably viewed by many housing authorities on the basis of its economic merits. That squatters are capable of "restoring and improving houses ... at an infinitely lower cost and much more rapidly than the councils" has

Fig. 10.6 : Unauthorized, 160-member Huntley Street Squatters community, in occupation of vacated inner city block for nearly three years, fully barricaded against anticipated eviction stage during summer of 1978.

become an economic verity.[32] Within this context, squatting is increasingly regarded as an eminently sensible and economical use of unoccupied urban structures. Squatters serve a valuable function by efficiently renovating short-life property for temporary occupation. More important, they fully rehabilitate large residential parcels for parmanent habitation. The transformation of squatter communities into legalized, permanent-tenure housing cooperatives brings about a better utilization of physical and human resources. Furthermore, this is consistent with the incipient philosophy, now widely embraced by urban planners, of preserving older buildings and "saving" neighborhoods. By their economic and social revitalization of moribund neighborhoods, squatters often halt local degenerative trends.

Ward concludes that squatting has now become one of the "normal modes of tenure in London and many other cities".[33] Whether or not squatting is "normal" is highly arguable; but it has irrefutably become widely "accepted" by authorities as an alternative tenure form. That all Inner London boroughs now license squats, and fully forty per cent of the city's squatted properties have been authorized, is testimony to the acceptance and approval being accorded to squatting. This is further buttressed by the fact that squatting is well entrenched in other European countries and at least three, Spain, Denkark, and the Netherlands, have adopted squatter licensing policies similar to Britain's.

## FOOTNOTES

1. There is an almost total absence of reliable information on intraurban squatters. London squatters are highly cautious and skeptical of inquiry because of the fragility of their legal and tenure situation. Most of the communities I located were detected in three ways. First, through forays into areas "generally reputed" to be squatted; second, with assistance from the London Squatters Union, Advisory Service for Squatters, and the Squatters Self-Help Housing Resource Library—a method particularly valuable since these organizations are staffed with squatters or ex-squatters; and third, by tapping the squatter's "bush telegraph." Of the fortynine communities located, eighteen were visited and inspected. A balanced sample was sought in terms of squat type, location, population size, longevity, and legal status. Communities chosen had been in existence from six months to over eight years, allowing for observation of the evolutionary process.
2. Mark Gimson, Caroline Lwin, and Nick Wates, "Squatting: The Fourth Arm of Housing?," **Architectural Design**, April, 1976, p. 211.
3. Gimson, op. cit., footnote 2.
4. "Housing Quagmire," **The Economist**, Jan. 1, 1977, p.27.
5. "Council Concerns," The Economist, Jan. 1, 1977, p.30.
6. **Shelter Report on Bed and Breakfast** (London: A Shelter Publication, 1974), p.40.

7. In Britain homeless families are officially regarded as "those without a home, however inadequate, that they can call their own." The problems of housing stress and homelessness are graphically described and fully documented in: Ron Bailey, **The Homeless and the Empty Houses** (Harmondsworth, England: Penguin Books, Ltd., 1977); **Shelter's Submission to the Department of the Environment: Review of Homelessness** (London: A Shelter Publication, 1975); and **Blunt Powers—Sharp Practices: A Survey of Local Authority Policies on Homelessness** (London: A Shelter Publication, 1976).
8. "The Ghosts of Landlords Past," **The Economist**, Jan. 1, 1977, p. 30.
9. Jane Morton, "Who'll House the Single?," **New Society**, March 25, 1976, p. 664.
10. For a lively and detailed historical account of the early squatting compaigns of the late sixties refer to Ron Bailey, **The Squatters** (Harmondsworth, England: Penguin Books, Ltd., 1973).
11. Unauthorized squatting first erupted in the Borough of Camden where university students, unable to secure housing through normal channels, squatted several council flats. This promptly tiggered squatting in adjacent boroughs. Though seizure and occupation of private property was on a very limited scale, it was highly publicized and often grossly exaggerated.
12. Bailey, op. cit., footnote 7, p. 51.
13. Interview with Stephen Platt, staff member, Squatters Self-Help Housing Resource Library, July 31, 1978.
14. The general squatter population also reflects a high proportion of artists, musicians, and craftsmen who do not conform to normal full-time employment categories and who often have an especially difficult time finding rental accommodations.
15. These organizations, staffed largely by squatters, provide both practical and moral support. They organize and conduct individual or group squats, provide legal and economic advice, and publish useful, informative newsletters and newspapers.
16. This information may be obtained easily from various planning or tax departments and from the Land Registry Office.
17. Many borough housing councils have devised "counter-squatting" tactics, such as camouflaging their more valuable, empty properties with curtains and window artifacts to create an authenic "lived-in" appearance; such counterfeit ploys seldom fool squatters. Some authorities have a policy of "gutting" structures as a deterrent to squatting by removing stairways and floorboards, dismantling plumbing fixtures, and tearing out electrical wiring. This "municipal vandalism" has been effectively exposed by squatters and has created public backlash against housing authorities.
18. Whether the term "occupiers" includes squatters is legally uncertain but most gas and electricity companies have a policy of supplying them with service. Many squatters prefer to use color gas tanks, electrical generators, paraffin stoves, and oil lamps since they are portable and may be conveniently moved from one squat to another.
19. Bailey, op. cit., footnote 7, p.15.
20. Several squatter communities have removed exterior walls and paved terraces to establish large flower and vegetable gardens, creating a rural ambience amid the sterility of surrounding urban structures.
21. Robert Fichter, John F. C. Turner, and Peter Grenell, "The Meaning of Autonomy," in John F. C. Turner and Robert Fitcher, eds., **Freedom to Build: Dweller Control of the Housing Process** (New York, Macmillan Co., 1972), pp. 241-54; reference on p. 242.
22. **Department of the Environment Consultation Document: Squatting** (London: London Boroughs Association), Sept. 10, 1975, p.1.

23. Squatting is also commonly referred to as "lawful" and "unlawful" or "legal" and "illegal." These designations are inappropriate since squatting is not technically an illegal act under British law; it is better viewed as extralegal.
24. This permission is usually given in writing, but sometimes it is simply granted verbally. Squatters may refuse to vacate the premises when requested to do so and demand to be rehoused or resquatted before relinquishment of their present squat. Also, when evicted, it is possible to resquat the same property, thereby initiating the entire legal process again.
25. Stephen Platt, **Self-Help, Squatting, and Public Policy: A Discussion Paper** (London: Squatters Self-Help Housing Resource Library Publication, 1977), p. 6.
26. **Department of the Environment Consultation Document: Squatting,** op. cit., footnote 22, p.1.
27. This process requires registration with the Housing Department, including a fee of $170, acquisition of legal service, written definition of objectives, and adoption of a formal constitution. Normally only the better organised squatter communities are able to fulfil such requirements and it demands a long-term group commitment.
28. Colin Ward, **Housing: An Anarchist Approach** (London: Freedom Press, 1976), p. 171.
29. Ward, op cit., footnote 28.
30. "Squatting in Australia," **Squatters News** (London: London Squatters Union Publication), Nov. 9, 1977, p. 5; and "Sydney Squatters," **Squatters News** (London: London Squatters Union Publication), Nov. 23, 1977, p. 5. Sydney squatters are well organized, highly unified, and already have a squatter newspaper in publication.
31. Lisa Jorgenson, "New York's Squatters: Vanguard of Community Control?," **City**, Vol.5, No.5, 1971, p.35.
32. Ward, op. cit., footnote 28, p. 96.
33. Ward, op. cit., footnote 28, p. 33.

ELEVEN

Detlev Ipsen

# HOUSING CONDITIONS AND INTERESTS OF FOREIGN WORKERS IN THE FEDERAL REPUBLIC OF GERMANY

## IS THE PROBLEM OF FOREIGNERS A MINORITY PROBLEM?

"On 27th October at 2 a.m. a fire broke out in a tenement house in Elmsbuettel, Hamburg. The fire spread very rapidly and reached the upper storeys. There were more than 50 occupants, all of whom were emigrants, and seven lost their lives. How did this happen? An electric cable between the ground floor and the cellar had begun to smoulder and had then set fire to the wooden staircase . . . . The landlord had overcrowded the house with tenants. According to official regulations each foreign worker should have eight square metres living space, which means that only 24 persons should have been living in the 4 apartments. There were, however, 52 officially registered persons and perhaps another dozen unregistered. The staircase was stuffed and therefore the fire could spread and the way out for the occupants was blocked up . . . . The wooden staircase was not plastered underneath and it burned like tinder. In addition, several windows at the staircase were broken: that meant an effect of a well drawing chimney. The wooden partitions in the apartments caught fire at once . . . . The rent per square metre amounted to approximately DM 40."[1]

The description of this disaster in a newspaper, edited by and intended for foreign workers, gives a striking impression of the pitiableness those foreign workers have to live in: poor equipment, inadequate sanitary arrangements and electrical installations, overcrowded rooms and exorbitant rents.

Not only the results of our own research in Mannheim[2] but also numerous results of research already published verify this description quantitatively.[3] Once can, therefore, assume that the relatively poor standard of housing and living conditions of foreign workers and their families is generally accepted as a fact.

Nevertheless, differences do arise in the interpretation and theoretical classification of these descriptive reports and subsequently in the proposed political and socio-political measures and in reactions to the so-called foreign labour problem. Most of the sociological publications known to myself treat foreigners as a Randgruppe or a minority.[4]

The paper in hand puts this problem to the test, whereby I shall chiefly refer to a publication of the Konrad Adenauer Foundation with the title "Minorities in industrial districts—a comparison between Germany and America"[5] in order to illustrate the minority paradigm.

This German-American comparison is of particular interest as the minority theory represents a development in American sociology. In a critical exposition of the American minority theory M. Seltzer outlines the conditions for its origin in Chicago:[4] "In 1892, still another massive strike among miners, railroad workers and iron workers was put down only after thousands of military troops, police and private detectives were mobilized and set to the attack. During this period, an English visitor found wealthy Americans 'pervaded by an uneasy feeling that they were living over a mine of social and industrial discontent . . . and that some day this mine would explode and blow society into the air . . . .' The University of Chicago, established in 1892 on J.D. Rockefeller's millions, was the site for this (first sociological) department . . . . It was here that much of the construction of the minority paradigma occurred....[6]"

Institutionalized sociology and, with it, the minority theory is regarded as the reaction of liberal Americans in the middle and upper classes to the problems connected with immigration, urbanization and industrialization. The preoccupation of German authors with minorities is also linked to concern about social conflicts. J. Stingl points out: "As history shows, for long duration the discrimination of individuals because of a certain group affiliation, or more precisely because of the common characteristics of this group which became the source of discrimination, leads to a social conflict." If no possible solutions can be found, "the accumulation of unsolved problems can give rise to social dynamite which could shake the foundations of our society."[7]

The advantage of regarding social problems as those of a minority (Randgruppenproblematik) is that an investigation of the societal causes can be neglected or even completely excluded. The problem is serious but slight because it only concerns a minority and first of all it can be treated as a pragmatic and particular problem, the solution of which is only a matter of time and goodwill. The advocates of the theory have a certain amount of difficulties when they attempt to give a theoretical definition of a "minority".

N. Glazer stresses the point that minorities and majorities are not a question of quantity but one of discrimination and objective indications of poor living conditions. "There are (to sociologists) 'minorities' that are actually 'majorities' (the blacks in South Africa, women in almost all countries)".[8] The attempt to avoid the category of the ruling classes is laborious, but succeeds. In this way the same author can conclude his discussion of socio-political measures that, if it is the case that the poor conditions of a minority are the result of discrimination, the task is ". . . to force the majority to give up its discriminatory practices".[9] This juggling with the concepts of majority and minority at least makes it possible to point an accusatory moral finger at the majority of the population who should finally renounce their prejudices. Discrimination becomes a problem between particular groups of the population and, if occasion arises, the state must take action to resolve it; the state and capitalism are far from being regarded as the source of the problem. The minority paradigma allows several political conclusions, its advantage lies in the very "limited flexibility".

Robert Park's Law of Race Relations whereat he maintains that the development moves irreversibly from "contact" and "conflict" via adaption on one side (which leads to the majority's advantage over the minority) to assimilation, justifies any status quo as a necessary stop. The oppression of the black Americans can be regarded by the conservatives as a necessary phase in the process of development, the liberal can console himself that it is only a temporary stage. The limited flexibility of the interpretation of the minority paradigma is generally of use in three ways. As the minority theory is not sheer invention but built up on existing cultural and ethnic differences in status, the emphasis of these differences causes division in industrial disputes and other social conflicts. J. Brecher reports a directive of the management given to private detectives employed during a strike: "We want you to stir up as much bad feeling as you possibly can between the Serbians and the Italians. Spread data among the Serbians that the Italians are going back to work . . . . Urge them to go back to work or the Italians will get their jobs."[10]

A spontaneous strike at the John Deere agricultural machinery factory in Mannheim in 1973 ended in a brawl between Germans and foreigners which had obviously been instigated by the management. During the strike rumours were circulated that Turks had made violent threats to Germans who did not participate in the strike according to their wishes.[11] Similar reports came from a strike at Ford's in Cologne.[12]

This pragmatic application of the minority is seldom found in sociological literature, although as a social reality it should be the central object of research. The classic programme of the minority theory, however, is not the clearly reactionary application of it as a strategy of division, but the liberal individualization of social problems. "This is for public policy to ignore any group definitions, and to simply help the poor, those who do poorly in school, those without skills or good skills, the individual who has met discrimination."[13]

M. R. Lepsius has a less moral point of view. "The main aim must be the prevention of institutionalization of ethnic groups and their continual relegation to underprivileged economic, social, political and cultural spheres of existence".[14] The main aim, therefore, is not the prevention of poor socio-economic conditions, the curtailing of political rights, and culturally impoverished forms of existence, but the prevention of the institutionalization of such conditions as ethnic ones. The consent of status ascription contrasts with the ideological core of capitalism: an open society founded on achievement and equal opportunities. Pragmatically expressed: "Indeed, the assignment of dirty work and the delineation of the position of outsiders still play an important role today but in the meantime, it is more important for the survival of soceity to integrate minorities by education and culture . . . .[15]

Mueller describes a dilemma: on the one hand there exists the desire to have available a reservoir of cheap laborers constantly at disposal, i.e. a desire for social segregation. On the other there is the desire to maintain the ideology of equal opportunities. It has been correctly recognized that individualization impedes social conflicts; at this point the positions of the right-wing and the liberal bourgeois diverge. The attractiveness of the liberal position is its aspect of pragmatic help, which appeals to many who wish to bring about change. The limitations of this position are shown clearly by N. Glazer when he refuses to grant collective rights to minorities, in other words, to advance to institutional solutions. "Because the United Staes is an open society that offers a field of action for the enterprising individual, because it has steadily moved away from creating an official majority . . . . I believe to proceed to a society organized on the basis of group affiliation and group rights will be divisive and harmful to the interests of most

Americans, including those who were part of deprived groups".[16]

To regard the foreign labour problem as a minority phenomenon makes it difficult to consider this problem as a macrosociological one; this, firstly, to analyze it in the context of expansion of the capitalist labour market while centralizing industry at the same time;[17] secondly, following from that, the integration of this phenomenon into the strata and class structure of society. By doing so the interests of social groups will be converted into individual problems on the one hand, and on the other the same social group interest will disappear in favour of the functional interest of survival of society as a whole.

The approach of the minority paradigma is the empirical manifestation of the problem, which can be fairly easily ascertained by inquiries.

At any rate I am of the opinion that opinion polls can contribute to a critical evaluation of the theory even if their perspective is easily limited to an individualizing view of social facts. In view of this I should like to concentrate on five relevant themes within the frame of the minority theory. In considering the problem a short description will be given first of all of the particular disadvantages of the foreign worker as regards housing conditions. Secondly I will examine to what extent the situation of deprivation is a question of time, which can be solved by the ability of the individual to adapt. Thirdly it will be considered whether or not the housing situation is accepted by those concerned and whether the situation can ultimately be traced back to particular cultural standards. Fourthly, some of the mechanisms of deprivation will be studied and the question will be raised whether these mechanisms are particular to the group of foreign workers or not. Finally, I shall, once more, take up the question of the particular disadvantages of foreign workers and I shall attempt to incorporate the foreigners housing situation into the stratified structure of the general housing provision.

The analyses given here are based on a study carried out in Mannheim in 1975. The 800 persons who were interviewed included minor employees and labourers as well as some self-employed craftsmen and businessmen; those interviewed people consisted of four nationalities: Greek, Italian, Turkish and German, two hundred of each country. Three residential areas were selected for research; these differed in terms of the standard of housing and density of foreign population, but as working-class areas only fell into the lower grades of residential areas. Mannheim itself is a medium-sized industrial town in the middle of an industrial conurbation with approximately half a million inhabitants. If one disregards rural and metropolitan conditions, the housing conditions in Mannheim may be considered typically for the Federal Republic of Germany. The description of the housing situation is drawn exclusively from the information gathered in this study which is, however, valid for the housing conditions of emigrants altogether. It is to be noted that the study did not include barracks, which are often rented by companies to unmarried workers.[18]

## THE HOUSING SITUATION OF FOREIGN WORKERS

As I have already mentioned the particular disadvantage of a certain group is the basis of the minority theorem. I wish to outline and examine briefly this premise by means of three questions:

1. Are there discrepancies between the housing conditions of the Germans and those of the foreigners?

2. What discrepancies exist between the different nationalities and is the housing situation of the Italians in particular better than that of the other foreigners?

3. Does the housing situation of foreign workers improve the longer they stay in the Federal Republic of Germany?

Four criteria were used in the description of the housing situation. The housing standard includes the equipping of the living quarters with a toilet, bath or central heating. Deficiencies in living conditions refer to inadequate electrical installations and sanitary arrangements, etc. The density of inhabitation is measured by the number of persons per room and the number of square metres per person. The fourth criterion is concerned with the cost of the accommodation; the cost is calculated by the rent and subsidiary cost for garbage disposal, street-sweeping, etc., referred to the number of square metres of each appartment (square metre rent).

Table 11.1 shows clearly that the housing conditions of the Germans in the areas investigated are better than those of the foreigners. One should bear in mind that the Germans referred to in this study like the foreigners live in relatively poor residential areas. The Germans to a larger extent had a toilet, bathroom and running warm water (heated by a boiler); even the German workers seldom have central heating. There are striking differences in the proportion of occupants to living areas, the accommodation of the foreigners being three times more densely inhabited as that of the Germans; as far as the

TABLE 11.1

**A Comparison of the Housing Situation of Germans and Foreigners in three working-class areas (the results given as percentages if not otherwise indicated):**

Following characteristics mark the living quarters of:

| | Foreigners | Germans | Italians only |
|---|---|---|---|
| Inside toilet | 69 | 93 | 72 |
| Bathroom | 43 | 84 | 51 |
| Central heating | 17 | 21 | 27 |
| Hot water | 28 | 63 | 40 |
| Inadequate electrical installation | 21 | 08 | 08 |
| Dampness | 24 | 10 | 18 |
| Damaged sanitary equipment | 21 | 08 | 20 |
| Number of beds per person* | 0.76 | 1.05 | 0.71 |
| Number of persons per room* | 3.26 | 1.13 | 3.83 |
| Rent per sq. metre* (in DM) | 4.63 | 3.97 | 5.28 |

*Arithmatical average

foreigners are concerned it is not even the rule that each person has a bed to himself. However, the foreigners have to pay far higher rents than Germans for accommodation of a minor quality.

There was no study made of the consequences of bad housing conditions, but it is not difficult to think of a considerable number. If inadequate electrical installations have been found in more than 20 per cent of the foreign households then the disaster outlined at the beginning of this article is no mere accident; the possibility of rest and relaxation in an overcrowded apartment is slight, and in the long run repercussions on the health of those foreigners engaged in heavy (manual) work are to be expected. The insufficient sanitary appliances and the dampness of the walls also contribute to this. Of course, the housing situation of all foreign workers is not uniform, as differentiation in living conditions is a basic principle of capitalist society. The housing situation of the Italians in particular could be better. To begin with the Italians were the first group of emigrants to settle in the Federal Republic of Germany (FRG), then their status is higher as far as the right to reside and work in Germany is concerned, because Italy is a member of the Common Market. As Table 11.1 shows, the Italians are better off than the average foreign workers (including Italians) in many respects. A high proportion has an inside toilet, bathroom and central heating. The overcrowding of living quarters, however, has remained a severe problem, particularly with Italians. It is worth noting that the particularly high rent the average Italian pays for his somewhat better living quarters necessarily leads to smaller apartments being rented.

Three reasons can be assumed for the better housing situation of Italian workers: First of all, it is possible that the housing situation is connected with the wave of immigration: the earlier a nation settles in a country the sooner the members of this nation find better living quarters, as a national sub-culture is built up whereby apartments and other advantages are mediated. Secondly, it is probable that the legal status plays a role, as Italians can plan for a longer stay due to the absence of limited permits for work and residence; therefore, it is more logical to strive for better living conditions and to devote a lot of time and money to the search for living quarters. Finally, it is conceivable that the length of residence of the individual Italian is longest; this leads to greater contact with the strange environment of the host country, an improved knowledge of the language and the establishment of social connections etc., which increases the chance of finding better living quarters. If this thesis is correct, one could assume that the housing problems of foreign workers will resolve themselves in time and that it is only a matter of the time required to overcome difficulties in adaption.

Table 11.2 confronts this thesis with the data collected by us. The study concerns not only Italians but all foreign workers, as the theory of individual difficulties in adapting does not relate to any particular nationality but to the length of individual residence.

The categories used to describe the housing situation refer to the standards of the living quarters. If the accommodation is described as good, this means it contains a toilet, bathroom and central heating. The designation of "poor" means that none of these facilities exist. Other criteria such as the density of inhabitation and deficiencies in living quarters produce similar results.

The table shows that the duration of individual residences has practically no bearing on the housing situation of foreign workers. It would, therefore, appear that the poor living conditions of foreign workers are not a short-term problem of in

TABLE 11.2

**Length of Residence and Housing Situation (in Percentages)**

| Quality of living quarters | Period of Residence More than 10 years | 6-10 years | up to 5 years | German control group |
|---|---|---|---|---|
| Poor | 15,4 | 19,4 | 18,0 | 1,5 |
| Simple | 31,6 | 36,0 | 31,1 | 16,0 |
| Average | 33,8 | 22,7 | 31,1 | 64,0 |
| Good | 10,5 | 11,8 | 13,7 | 18,3 |
| Number of persons interviewed | 228 | 209 | 160 | 198 |

Cramer's V = 0,08 p = 0,33

dividual difficulties in adapting; the relatively better situation of the Italians does not depend on the longer duration of individudal residence, but can be accounted for either by their legal status or by the establishment of an Italian sub-culture which counterbalances discrimination on the housing market.

To sum up: the poor provision of accommodation for foreign workers even within the same residential area is clearly in evidence. This seems to justify the premise of the minority theory. At the same time there is evidence of differences in the living conditions of the foreigners themselves, another point which the minority will fully substantiate. It is, however, problematic that the housing conditions do not improve with duration of residence. Even this is no contradiction of the minority theory. On the contrary, it is in fact a question of the nature of the problem of the theorem: discrimination seems to establish itself ethnically.

## THE HOUSING INTERESTS OF FOREIGN WORKERS

Whoever lives in poor conditions has to blame only himself. The argument can often be found, especially in non-scientific discussions and publications, that foreigners have no desire to have normal living conditions, first of all because "modes of accommodation" are different in the Mediterranean countries, and secondly because foreign workers are interested only in saving money as fast as possible and then returning to their home countries. There is something in this argument, even if it justifies and makes subjective the objective conditions of bad housing conditions in a cynical manner. The economic situation in their native countries compels the foreigners to emigrate, their economic function as a varying reserve of labour leads to a legal status without any guarantee of security. Viewed subjectively, that means that one is uncertain as to the duration of one's stay (53 per cent of the interrogated persons were of this opinion), and that the condition of existential uncertainty diminishes the motivation to exert onself as far as housing is concerned.

This speculation can be supported by data. Despite the fact that most living quarters are rather overcrowded, only 48 per cent of the workers questioned were dissatisfied with the size of their accomodation; despite the fact that living quarters are frequently badly fitted, only 49 per cent were dissatisfied with the facilities and despite the exorbitant rents only 30 per cent were of the opinion that they paid too much.

However, doubt arises if the simple question is asked whether they intend to move or not: over 60 per cent gave a positive reply, although partly with the qualified sense: "Yes, I like to move, but there are no lodgings".

The question whether or not they are satisfied with their living quarters does not give a clear indication of their interest in accommodation. It can often be proved that dissatisfaction with relatively poor housing conditions is no more than a resigned adaption to a situation which one as individual cannot alter. It would be more accurate to inquire about the concrete ideas of foreign workers about accommodation and then deduce therefrom their housing interests. Table 11.3 shows the actual distribution of certain features of accommodation and alongside this the distribution which the occupants would like to have.

**TABLE 11.3**

**Effective and required situation of housing standard for foreigners and Germans (in percentage)**

| | Foreigners | | | Germans | | |
|---|---|---|---|---|---|---|
| | Effect. | Requ. | Difference | Effect. | Requ. | Difference |
| Toilet | 68,5 | 86,2 | 17,7 | 93,0 | 99,0 | 6,0 |
| Kitchen* | 12,0 | 86,7 | 74,7 | 87,0 | 96,0 | 9,0 |
| Bathroom | 43,1 | 86,8 | 43,7 | 84,0 | 98,0 | 14,0 |
| Centr. heat. | 16,9 | 77,7 | 60,8 | 21,5 | 84,5 | 63,0 |
| Balcony | 10,1 | 35,8 | 25,7 | 45,5 | 84,0 | 38,5 |

Existence of a kitchen was recorded only when it was used exclusively by one household. Of course, almost all foreign households have the permission to make use of a kitchen.

Here the first striking fact is that the discrepancy between the effective and required situation is much greater for the foreigners than for the German workers, the average difference being 44,5 for foreigners and 26,1 for Germans (this discrepancy can be viewed as a guage for the typical inadequacy of accommodation in working class areas). Neither foreigners nor Germans have unreal expectations of living quarters, their wishes are modest: a standard apartment with a toilet, bathroom and central heating is desired, and many foreigners are prepared to do without balcony. A large number of the German occupants live in such a standard apartment, although there are quite a few without central heating.

The inadequacy of the foreigners accommodation is considerable; they are frequently without their own kitchen, bathroom and central heating although specified as lodging requirements. At the present time the average foreign household has almost 2 rooms at his disposal (1.9 rooms per household); desired are 2—5 rooms per household. If the effective and the required number of rooms per apartment are compared, it shows that especially 3- and 4- room apartments are required, but too many families are compelled to live in one- and two-room apartments. If one considers the average number of persons per room for the households of foreign workers (almost 5) the desire for a larger apartment is very modest, but this is determined more by the possibilities open to them than by necessity. In this study, as in many others, it could be seen that a large majority (63 to 66 per cent) aspired to a house of their own. Most architects and town planners seem to be unaware of this long-established fact. While it is accepted without question that the upper strata should live in their own, well-situated houses, this is denied to the lower strata with reasons that range from the ruination of the landscape by too many single houses to the definition of these needs as 'petit bourgeois'. The widespread desire for a house of one's own is a reaction to the unsatisfactory living conditions of the lower and middle strata in large cities. This desire is shown systematically in the need for housing units which are:

—well situated

—made up of autonomous units suitable for the family

—enabling the occupants to furnish the house according to

their own inclination

—built in peaceful green zones.

—ensuring a high degree of safety

These characteristics are not necessarily related to the present form of the single family house. Indeed, they must assume another form in order to have the advantage of high density of inhabitation and economic use of available space, the provision of a social and technical infrastructure and a good system of communications.

It is established that the housing interests of foreign workers are similar to those of Germans, although it is plausible that uncertainty as to the duration of the residence in the host country reduces subjective housing interests. It is evident that housing interests are the result of objective necessity rather than subjective requirements; industrial work and the poor climatic conditions must lead to a standard of housing which at least facilitates regeneration of one's ability to work.

Or in other words: the poor housing conditions of foreign workers cannot be interpreted by a low level of expectations conditioned by their culture; nor does their particular existential uncertainty lead to a demand for temporary accommodation; the conditions of employment and life in general are the most important factors which determine the housing interests.

One could, therefore, maintain that although foreigners have the desire for better living quarters, on the other side they are not willing to defray an adequate rent as every penny is saved for their life in their native country. In order to test this theory the housing requirements of the foreign workers have to be compared with the amount of rent which they would be prepared to pay for such accommodation and the effective rent. Judging from the wishes already expressed as regards housing standard it can be concluded that for a foreign worker the ideal apartment should be equipped with a kitchen, bathroom and central heating and consist of two or three rooms. This would correspond to an apartment of approximately 70 sq. metres. The costs for it would amount to about DM 300,[19] according to present rates in Mannheim. At the moment, foreign households pay an average rent of DM 198. per month, but would be willing to pay DM 237. Nevertheless, the difference between the actual market prices and the amount that could possibly be raised for rent is considerable: a discrepancy of 26 per cent. If a similar study is made of the German occupants, the market price for the desired quarters would amount to DM 419 due to the interest in a larger apartment and a remarkable non-acceptance of defects in the building. In fact, the German households in question pay DM 245 for rent and would be prepared to pay DM 319 in this case the difference between the possible and the required rent is even greater than that one of the foreigners, namely, 31 per cent.

These figures show that neither German nor foreign workers are in a position to spend a sufficient amount of their salary on an apartment which would meet their requirements; moreover, the housing interests are not based on unrealistic dreams which cannot be fulfilled, but on basic requirements. Without interpreting this result in detail, it is, however, an indication of the general nature of the housing problem, which is more than only a problem for foreigners.

## MECHANISMS OF PARTICULAR DISADVANTAGE TO FOREIGN WORKERS ON THE HOUSING MARKET

The causes of the poor provision of housing for the lower strata are economic and not specifically valid for individual groups of the population, such as the foreign workers but characterize a system of housing provision. It is obvious that a profiteering organization for housing provision will result in accommodation being built in those places for these people who, by their rents, can guarantee the greatest possible returns. The demand for accommodation is only relevant when there is the possibility of a corresponding high rent. At present in the FRG there are some 500,000 luxury flats vacant while there is simultaneously a considerable demand for accommodation in the lower strata. What makes the situation even worse is that the number of moderately priced and relatively simple apartments is steadily decreasing: the number of older buildings is being reduced by re-development, or they are allowed to fall into disrepair because the owner does not want to invest any more money into the building for reasons of speculation; at the same time public housing is becoming more and more expensive, as there is a system of subsidized mortgages, which cease after a few years. The high interest rate is carried over to the rents and thus frequently produces prices far beyond the rents on the private housing market. These general conditions of a relative lack of accommodation are extremely complex and are not to be discussed in this article.[20] Here, we merely wish to indicate which mechanisms maintain the particular discrimination against foreign workers in the housing market. Discrimination exists first of all insofar as foreigners have to pay more than Germans for living quarters of similar quality. As regards poor accommodation the price per sq. metre is on average 37 per cent higher for foreigners than for Germans. Then again discrimination exists in that foreigners do not even obtain the accommodation which they are looking for or require.

Thirty per cent of German workers, but 72 per cent of Italians, 70 per cent of Turks and 64 per cent of Greeks stated that they had taken the accommodation they were living in because they have had no alternative. It can be supposed that two mechanisms sustain (but do not cause) this discrimination: in the majority of cases a new apartment is procured by acquintances or relatives and not by newspaper advertisements or estate agents. This is true for Germans and for foreigners. However, while this informal arrangement has the effect that accommodations obtained by Germans are cheaper as if being procured by a newspaper or an estate agent, the opposite is true for foreigners. They remain confined to a partial market where a steady demand increases the prices for accommodation of poor quality. If a foreigner wishes to avoid this limited market, his inadequate knowledge of the German language makes him dependent on the assistance of an estate agent. In this case, not only does he have to pay a high fee to the agent but also the accommodation offered is very expensive. The duration of residence is the second mechanism. The longer a tenant lives in an apartment the cheaper the rent becomes. For the landlords of small properties, who mostly know the tenant personally, it is obviously difficult to raise the price for the lease of an apartment from year to year when the condition of the apartment at best stays the same, but often is more and more subject to wear and tear in the course of time. Therefore a tenant who lives in an apartment for less than two years will pay DM 6.48 per sq. metre for accommodation with poor standard, while if he lives there for 16 years or more, the average price per sq. metre is DM 1.99. As regards good quality accommodation, the difference is not so much but still considerable (DM 4.85 to DM 3.40 per sq. metre).

It is obviously that foreigners do not usually have a long period of residence; firstly, they often do not live abroad for a long time, secondly, because the poor quality accommodation they fall into compels them to move frequently. Therefore, no open forms of discrimination are necessary to regulate foreigners to a poor accommodation market and keep them there. These types of "impersonal" mechanisms occur more often than outspoken discrimination and can also be found in the industrial sector. Young, unmarried workers are dismissed sooner than a family man. The fact that especially many foreigners are young and single is then a "coincidental" effect of the "actual" reason for dismissal.

These points cannot prove that there is no specific discrimination whatever against foreigners. In my view, however, those examples are important because they show that disadvantage can be directly incorporated into a system of differential chances on the market. Simply because of its extent, disadvantages become something more than normal differentiation in a similar way as usury is different from profit and thereby is subject to a particular moral evaluation.

## THE HOUSING SITUATION OF FOREIGNERS WITHIN THE FRAMEWORK OF THE SOCIAL STRATA

Is the foreigners housing situation simply a problem for foreigners? If one goes by the minority theorem, the presuppositions give a positive answer. From a strictly immanent viewpoint, if the minority theorem is brought to bear on housing provision, one should be able to determine a clear discrepancy between the standard of provision for foreigners and the standard for the rest of the population. One should then examine whether such a surmise can be empirically supported in relation to the housing situation. So far, only the data which were collected in the study of the housing conditions of German and foreign workers have been discussed, whereby the differences in the situation of the native and foreign workers were emphasized. However, if one continually examines the differences and movements in one sector only, one does not achieve an impression of the whole. The inquiry which has already been cited, also conducted in Mannheim in 1975, which reflects the situation on the private housing market, allows us to analyze the foreigners situation in the context of the social stratification of the town.

The situation of the foreigners is only marginal if it stands out clearly against that of the German workers, or to express it in other words, if the difference between foreign and German workers is greater than that between the German working and middle classes (the upper class is so small that it cannot be included in this inquiry).

In Table 11.4, the professional status is taken as the criterion for a class hierarchy, with foreign workers at the lower end and German civil servants at the upper end.

The number of foreign workers and of German unskilled workers who live in good conditions is more or less equal; Ger

TABLE 11.4

**Social strata and housing situation**
**(Results in per cent)**

| | Accommodation facilities | | | | |
|---|---|---|---|---|---|
| | Good | Average | Simple | Poor | N |
| Foreign workers | 16,0 | 25,3 | 37,3 | 21,3 | 75 |
| German semi- and unskilled workers | 18,3 | 48,3 | 21,7 | 11,7 | 60 |
| Skilled German workers | 35,0 | 46,6 | 12,6 | 5,8 | 103 |
| German employees | 53,0 | 39,4 | 4,5 | 3,0 | 198 |
| German civil servants | 51,7 | 37,9 | 5,2 | 5,2 | 58 |
| Foreign and German workers together | 24,4 | 40,3 | 22,7 | 12,2 | - |
| German employees and civil servants together | 52,7 | 39,1 | 4,7 | 3,5 | - |
| N= | 194 | 196 | 66 | 38 | - |

Cramers V = 0,27 P = 0.000

man skilled workers are found almost exactly in the middle and then there is a clear demarcation with the German middle classes. It is a different matter with poor quality accommodation: the quota of foreign workers is considerably greater than any class of the native population. Yet, there is a marked difference here between unskilled and skilled workers. Foreign and German Semi-skilled workers are equally excluded from good housing conditions, which gives them something in common. There is a clear discrepancy between the foreign workers and the total German population, the former being far below the latter. If one takes the group of workers, both German and foreign on one side, and the employees and civil servants on the other side, it is quite evident, despite all internal differentiation, that housing conditions correspond to a clearly defined unequal class structure.

The housing situation of foreign workers, therefore, is firstly a general phenomenon as part of the unequal living conditions which are a basic principle of capitalist societies and, secondly, a specific phenomenon as discrimination against a particular category (not class) of society. This is not one of the familiar and openly advocated basic principles of capitalist society, but is a structural effect of competition on the market whereby the weaker parties are defeated; the remarkable and repellent aspect of it is that as far as foreign workers are concerned, it is quite clear that in competition on the market whole groups and not single individuals are the weaker parties; this means that the ideological thesis of the system "everyone receives according to his output" can no longer be maintained.

## SUMMARY

The foreign analysis shows four aspects of the housing situation of foreign workers. The class status and stratum membership go a long way in determining the housing situation so that the situation of foreign workers can be seen within the framework of the general housing situation of the working class. Secondly, the distribution of opportunities is differentiated within a fixed framework. In other words, within the housing situation of the workers there are considerable gradations, but in every respect the foreigners are subjected to a much worse situation. Thirdly, I have tried to demonstrate by some examples that the process of discrimination occurs automatically and impersonally, primarily market mechanisms and not persons cause or mediate the disadvantages. Finally, the study has shown that the accommodation requirements of the foreigners are very similar to those of the Germans, the cultural standards of their native countries, and the uncertainty about the duration of their stay in the Federal Republic of Germany are, therefore, of less consequence than the compulsion to a particular level of reproduction which stems from a homogeneous mode of work and life.

In relation to the empirical validity of the minority theorem, the study has demonstrated in our empirical case that numerous results tend to indicate another direction: the housing situation of foreign workers can be integrated into the general system of provision which varies according to class and stratum membership. It is therefore quite possible that the situation of single groups, i.e. the Italians, will improve in the course of time but their present position will be occupied by other immigrant workers or deposed strata. The political conclusions can be easily formulated from the premise (as it is very difficult and complex to outline this in detail, I cannot enter into it within the framework of this essay).[21]

The housing problems of foreigners must be solved within a political framework which is based on the interests of the working classes as a whole and which comes to grips with the system of housing provision. This is the opposite of minority strategy.

## FOOTNOTES

1. Die neue Stimme, Oktober/November 1976, S.14
2. D. Ipsen In Zusammenarbeit mit H. Beyerlein, H. Glasauer und R. Schreieck: Wohnsituation, Wohninteresse und Interessenorganisation auslandischer und deutscher Arbeiter, Forschungsbericht Mannheim 1975.
3. Es liegen zahlreiche Studien zur sozialen Lage der auslandischen Arbeiter in der Bundesrepublik vor. So hat fast jede Grobstadt eigene Berichte erstellen lassen, als Beispiel: Maria Borris: Auslandische Arbeiter in der Grobstadt, Frankfurt 1975. Die Bundesanstalt fur Arbeit hat eine Reprasentativerhebung durchgefuhrt (Reprasentativehebung 1975, Nurnberg)
4. siehe dazu als besonders treffendes Beispiel: K. Bingemer u.a.: Leben als Gastarbeiter, Koln/Opladen 1970
5. M.G. Eisenstadt/W. Kaltefleiter: Minoritaten in Ballungsraumen - ein deutsch-amerikanischer Vergleich, Eichholz Verlag 1975.
6. M. Seltzer: Some critical reflections on American minority theory, Institute of Organisation OG Arbejdssociologi, Kopenhagen 1975, S. 9 ff.
7. J. Stingl, Probleme der Beschaftigung auslandischer Arbeitnehmer in der Bundesrepublik in: MG Eisenstadt, op. cit. S. 56.
8. N. Glazer: The Integration of Minorities from the Point of View of Social Science in: M.G. Eisenstadt, op. cit. S. 25.
9. N. Glazer: op. cit. S. 30.
10. J. Brecher, Strike, San Francisco 1972, S. 162.
11. R. Eck, D. Ipsen, W. Kleber, G. Portele: Der gescheiterte Streik bei John Deere: Zur Frage der Streiktaktik, unveroffentl. Manu.
12. Gruppe internationaler Marxisten (Hrsg.): Der Streik bei Ford, Eigendruck 1975.
13. N. Glazer, op. cit. S. 29.
14. M. R. Lepsius: Strategien fur die Eingliederung der Gastarbeiter in der Bundesrepublik Deutschland in: M. G. Eisenstadt, op. cit. S. 16.
15. H. Muller: Bildungs - und Erziehungsprobleme von Minderheiten und Randgruppen in der Bundesrepublik in: M. G. Eisenstadt, op. cit. S. 33.
16. N. Glazer, op. cit. S. 31.
17. Konkret beschreibt K. Hottes die Wellen der Einwanderung ins Ruhrgebiet:

    1. Welle: Bevolkerung aus den deutschen Mittelgebirgsregionen Mitte des 19, Jahrhunderts.
    2. Welle: Bevolkerung aus Oberchlesien bis Anfang des 20. Jahrhunderts.
    3. Welle: Samtliche Hilfsarbeiterbevolkerung aus Galizien, Russisch-Polen und Slowenien bis 1914.
    4. Welle: Sustrom von Heimatvertriebenen
    5. Welle: Hilfsarbeiter aus Sudeuropa, Turkei und Nordafrika;

    Der Autor Vergisst die Zwangsarbeiterbevolkerung wahrend des Faschismus. Siehe K. Hottes, Die Integration ddr Gastarbeiter in die Stadt als soziales System in: M. G. Einsenstadt, op. cit. S. 78.
18. Die Wohnsituation in Betriebsunterkunften wurde von E. ZIERIS untersucht; siehe: Ernst Zieris: Betriebsunterkunfte fur auslandische Mitburger in Nordrhein-Westfalen, Dusseldorf 1972.
19. B. Bachmann. D. Ipsen, G. Kurtz-Solowjew: Ortsubliche Vergleichsmieten in Mannheim 1975, Veroffentlichung der Stadt Mannheim 1975.
20. Fur eine neuere und ausfuhrliche Analyse zu diesem Thema siehe H. BREDE, B. DIETRICH, B. KOHAUPT, Politische Okonomie des Bodens und der Wohnungsfrage, Frankfurt 1976.
21. Wir selbst sind im Rahmen des schon zitierten Forschungs- berichts der Frage der Moglichkeiten und Probleme der Selbst-organisation auslandischer Arbeiter machgegangen.

TWELVE

DeWitt Davis, Jr. and Rickie Sanders

# EMPLOYMENT PROBLEMS FOR BLACKS
## Labour Segmentation and Different Geographic Scale

### INTRODUCTION

For years many economists who were and are a part of the neoclassical school have strongly advocated human capital and margin productivity. In recent years much has been written regarding labor market segmentation in the United States and other more developed countries (MDCs) with a similar economic structure.

The late 1960's was the beginning of research in labor market segmentation; however, Kerr (1954) was one of the first to discuss labor market segmentation in his stimulating article on balkanization. There tended to be a correlation beteeen segmentation and social dissatisfaction. The economists did not take the spatial aspect into account.

During the 1960's the civil rights groups and others brought their dissatisfaction with the pace and direction of social change, especially in relation to equal employment opportunities for women, minorities, and teenagers. Along with this dissatisfaction in the social arena was also a heightened concern for the theory and methodology of economics, the types of questions asked, and the explanations offered by the orthodox schools.

As a result of this concern, a new body of literature emerged which not only attacked the neoclassical tradition by suggesting that it was incapable of providing adequate explanations for what was occurring, but it also led to major policy disputes (Averitt, 1968; Baron and Hymer 1968; Doeringer, 1969; and Blueston, 1970). It was recognized that the dualist interpretation offered a successful and innovative line of inquiry when evaluated as an empirical description of the working of the lowest wage sector in a traditional segmented model (Cain,

1976).

The formal and informal labor market theory applied to the less developed countries (LDCs) of Africa, Asia, and Latin America is a similar form of labor market segmentation. However, the dissimilarities are of significance to the theme of this work. A review of the dual market theory which emerged from the social reform movements of the late 1960's and early 1970's in the United States and the formal and informal labor market theory created from the experiences in the LDCs will be presented in the following two sections.

This paper puts forth the idea that there is a need to analyze the cause of illegal employment and migration among blacks at different geographic scales by utilizing the structure of the formal and informal labor activites carried out in the most LDC's paired with the MDC structure. The paper is constructed around the black population because that group has the largest unemployment problem. Between the fourth quarter of 1977 to the fourth quarter of 1979, the average national unemployment rate was 6.1 per cent, 5.2 per cent for the white population, and 12.6 per cent for the black population (U.S. Department of Labor, 1980).

## SEGMENTATION IN MDCs AND LDCs

### The Dual Labor Market Theory

The theory of the dual labor market was developed in the late 1960's when it was found that 60 per cent of all workers in the inner cities failed to earn enough to support a family at minimum levels of decency. At this time, all of the conventional explanations of poverty became obsolete (Vietorisz and Harrison, 1972), and it was clear that the standard policy prescription of creating more jobs would in no way address the basic issues of ameliorating poverty. However, some economists argued that the supply side of the labor market was the focus of policy, and manpower programs were the implement.

This reality prompted social scientists, particularly economists, to seek other explanations for the poverty, unemployment and under employment that was occurring in the black ghetto. Orthodox economic theory *a la* the human capital school already existed, buts its explanation for what was occurring in the ghetto was merely an extension of conventional thinking, and it appeared ill-equipped to handle the puzzling features of these newly perceived problems (Gordon, 1972). Becker (1957) and others suggested that poverty was a function of low levels of education and occupational training caused by the quality of education in neighborhood schools of the impoverished worker.

The radical economic theorists, who surfaced during this time, devoted much of their energy to the concept of economic class (Gordon 1972; Edwards et al., 1975; Beck et al., 1978). While class may play a critical role in explaining poverty, unemployment and underemployment, one must be able to establish some relevant measures of class boundaries, i.e. how does one divide society into distinct classes? Without these measures, comparisons of behavior between classes are impossible, and although radical economic theory might have been capable of answering some of the basic questions, its solution (the classless society) was distasteful to the general American economic and political system. Therefore, the different schools of economic thought were incapable of providing an acceptable solution to what was occurring in the black ghetto.

During this time, a series of studies emerged which provided evidence that the labor market in the United States is divided into discrete segments across which mobility is severely restricted or even totally hindered (Gordon, 1972). On the one hand, there is a primary labor market (Bluestone, 1970) labelled primary and secondary as "the core" and "'the periphery", respectively, which functions more or less in keeping with public perceptions of work. It is characterized by high wages, high productivity, stability, opportunity for advancement, good working conditions, job security, equity, and due process in the administration of work rules (Wachter, 1974; Piore, 1975; and Edwards et al., 1975). There is also an opportunity for upward mobility. On the other hand, there is a secondary labor market, characterized by a vicious cycle, which will be discussed in detail below. This sector keeps wages, productivity, and stability at very low levels and many persons in this sector are underemployed. Upward mobility is practically impossible.

A more concise explanation of the existence of the segmented labor market is given by Piore (1969). He suggests that: (1) certain workers who could operate efficiently in the primary jobs are trapped in secondary markets because their physical characteristics resemble those of secondary workers, who are primarily blacks, other minorities, women, and teenagers; (2) the distinction between the primary and secondary sectors is not so much technologically determined as it is the product of a vicious cycle that has been perpetuated by historical forces; (3) behavioral traits, e.g. tardiness, absenteeism, apathy, etc., associated with the secondary sector are reinforced by living among others whose life-styles are accommodated by that type of employment; and (4) a wide variety of historical forces have interacted to increase the likelihood of sharp separations between the two labor markets (Gordon, 1972). Briefly, according to the dualist, "there are good jobs and there are bad jobs." For the most part, the attractive employment is offered to young adult and older white males; unattractive jobs are offered to women, blacks, minorities, and teenagers.

This explanation of a dual labor market as it exists in the United States is seen as totally unrelated to formal and informal labor markets or the explanations of the labor market segmentation that exists in LDCs for several reasons. First, the conditions which have given rise to segmentation in the two contexts are seen as different. In the LDCs, segmentation is recognized as the result of structural imbalance (closely related to if not caused by the rapid increase in rural-to-urban migration) which decreases opportunities for employment. In the United States, segmentation is seen as the product of the historically determined vicious cycle which structures jobs as if certain people do not matter.

When this occurs, employers typically do not encourage job stability, they give no additional compensation for investments made in human capital, they hire employees without screening, and, in general, they make no distinctions between individuals. A second reason why the LDCs and MDCs are recognized as different may be the degree to which the excluded groups are incorporated into the system of industrialization. In LDCs, persons in the informal sector are totally excluded from all of the accruements in institutionalization. They do not come under the protection of social welfare legislation, are not guaranteed sick leave, and are not paid minimum wages. They are excluded from job advancement.

This is contrasted with the situation in the United States, where persons in the secondary sector share in many facets of institutionalization, such as social security, hospitalization, and minimum wage, even though these persons may be excluded from union memberships. These ideas lead to the following discussion on the formal and informal labor market theory.

**Formal and Informal Labor Market**

Much of the research showing parallels between LDCs and MDCs has treated this subject matter by using colonialism and racial/ethnic discrimination as strong causes for labor market differences (Blauner, 1972 and Geschwender, 1978). For several decades, another group of researchers has taken a more labor specific approach to the existence of a formal and informal labor market in the urban theory of LDCs (Lewis, 1954; Ranis and Fei, 1961; Hart, 1971; Merrick, 1972; and Berry, 1976).

Even prior to Hart's seminal work in which he introduced the notions of "formal and informal income opportunities," most cities of the Third World were seen as being divided between two juxtaposed systems of production—one in the Western section, employing Western forms of production and the other in the indigenous section, employing peasant systems of production, i.e. a firm centered economy versus a bazaar type economy or a legal economy versus an illegal economy.

The formal section in the LDCs includes activities such as government, the liberal professions, manufacturing, etc. These activities are protected and institutionalized, pay high wages, operate on a large scale, and utilize Western oriented and/or derived technologies. The informal sector includes activities such as casual day laborers, the self-employed and small-scale craftsmen. They are highly competitive and easy entry occupations with flexible working hours. More specifically, informal activities are those which occur outside the system of benefits and regulations instituted by government legislation. Many of these activities are illegal or carried out illegally in urban areas.

In LDCs, this segmentation can be explained, in part, by the path that economic and technological development has followed and in part by the pace and scale of urbanization. With regard to the path that development has taken, it can be postulated that urban based production units were established to satisfy a small and highly diversified demand for consumer goods (Souza and Tokman, 1976). Moreover, since most of the industries were, in fact, subsidiaries of giant multinational corporation, the type of goods produced and the technology employed were determined by MDCs. As a result, while many techniques appeared to be capital saving, they were labor saving (Souza and Tokman, 1976), and the demand was for small numbers of quality, skilled workers rather than quantities of unskilled laborers who were most in supply (Mazumdar, 1975). The effect of this was to concentrate wealth and jobs in the hands of a few, and rather than modernization "trickling down," it has given rise to the dual economy—segmented in terms of people, activities, and spatial manifestations.

The rapid pace and enormous scale of urbanization have exacerbated this problem. Since the supply of labor from the rural hinterland to the urban area has exceeded the wage-earning employment opportunities available in industry, a large proportion of the labor force is compelled to seek its livelihood by buying and selling almost anything that will generate an income (Hart, 1971).

In the following section, the labor market segmentation theories have been constructed in a model to illustrate the functions of secondary labor, unemployment, illegal employment, informal labor, and migration to locations of different geographic scales.

## ANALYZING THE MODEL

The model in Fig. 12.1 shows the processes of the secondary labor market and unemployment of the MDCs and informal labor market and illegal employment of the LDCs. The deprived worker gets caught in the vicious cycle of secondary labor or unemployment.

The first stage in the vicious cycle occurs when employers offer jobs that do not provide job mobility and do not pay adequate wages. In the second stage, employees respond by quitting to earn more money elsewhere. As a safeguard, employers begin to structure jobs and production in such a way that instability is not a great catastrophe. In stage three, eventually, the behaviors on the part of both employer and employee become fixed and the vicious cycle is then institutionalized. Once this occurs, job discrimination is perpetuated.

The vicious cycle operating here is practically identical to the notion of circular causation which characterizes agricultural productivity in LDCs. When circular causation results in a downward spiral, a poor farm family, faced with a minor crop failure, subsequently eats less, works less, and produces less. An upward spiral is also possible, but it rarely occurs. This is a vicious cycle. In the model, the worker may manage for economic enhancement and/or internal or peer recognition to move into the illegal labor sector.

If the worker survives the illegal employment socially, psychologically, and physically, the worker may remain there, but if the worker has a value conflict, the worker may be satisfied by returning to the secondary vicious cycle. The push factor may eventually cause the worker in the secondary labor box or the illegal labor box to migrate or return to another place or the place of origin for better opportunities and a

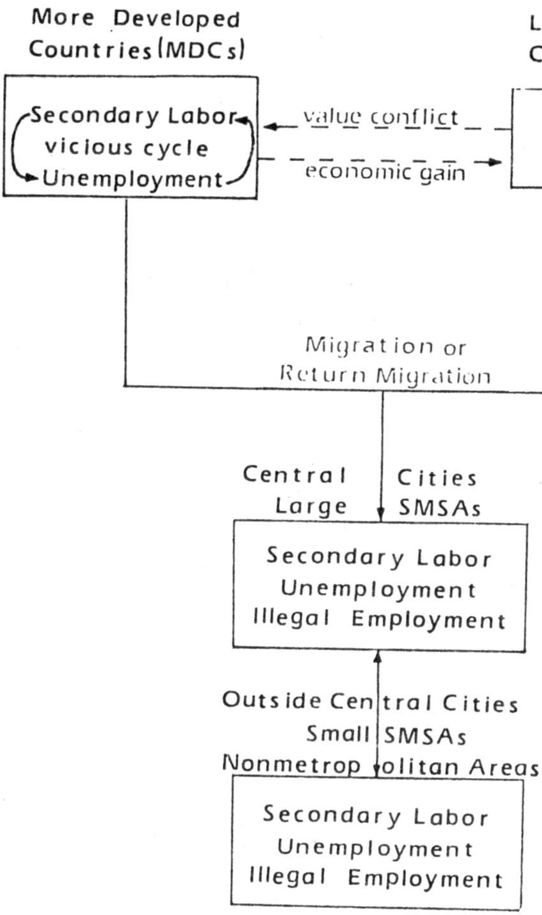
More Developed
Countries (MDCs)
Less Developed
Countries (LDCs)
Secondary Labor
vicious cycle
Unemployment
value conflict
economic gain
Informal Labor
Legal/Illegal
Employment
Migration or
Return Migration
Central
Large
Cities
SMSAs
Secondary Labor
Unemployment
Illegal Employment
Outside Central Cities
Small SMSAs
Nonmetropolitan Areas
Secondary Labor
Unemployment
Illegal Employment

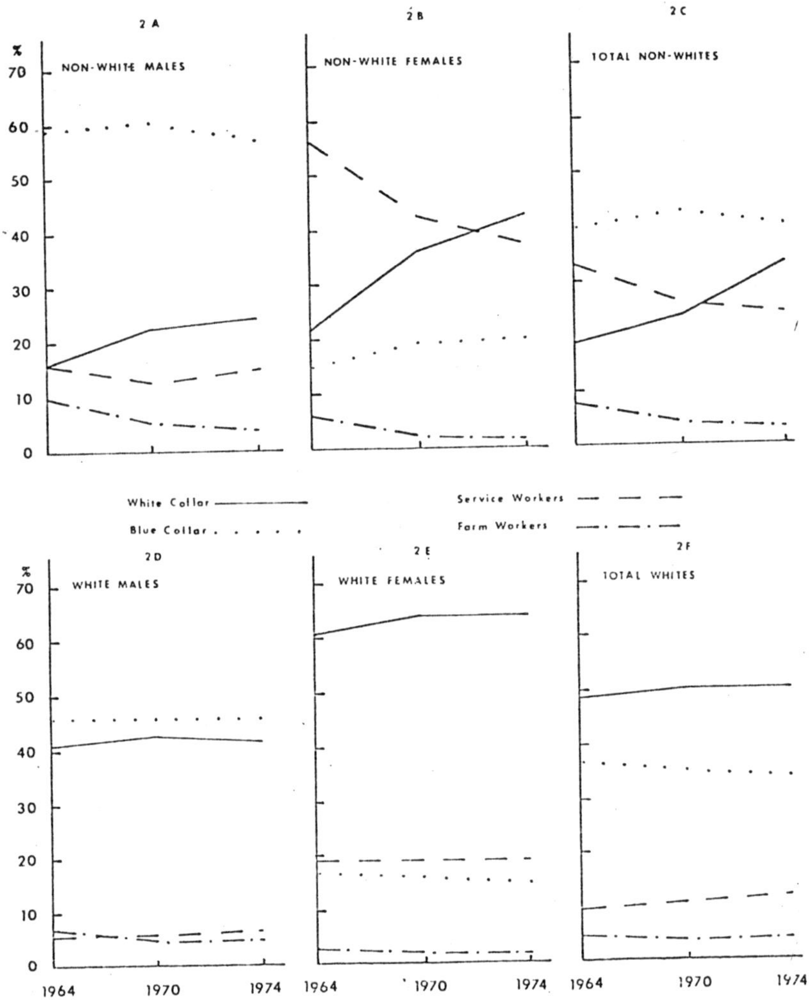


Figure 2. The occupations of the employed population of the United States: 1964, 1970, and 1974 (annual averages).

more secure life. The model focuses on large and small Standard Metropolitan Statistical Areas (SMSA) in central cities and outside central cities, and nonmetropolitan areas (i.e. different geographic scales as well as geographic regions). Migrating to a smaller geographic scale may reduce competition and increase recognition by the internal group.

The informal sector box in the model is part of the dual labor market theory in the LDCs and functions much the same way as the illegal employment of the MDCs. However, in the LDCs this sector may also be composed of legal activities, but the informal activities functioning in the MDCs are always illegal because they are not sanctioned by the Federal government. However, the migration patterns are somewhat different because the movement is basically from rural to urban areas in LDCs. Also, stepwise migration is clearly distinguishable.

## TREADMILL OF EMPLOYMENT

Although the United States is characterized by a dualistic structure, it differs from LDCs in that a barrier has been erected which separates the poor people from the mainstream and for all practical purposes makes them invisible. "The average traveler on speedy freeways does not see the rundown company town where the permanently unemployed loiter on street corners and in bars. Suburbanites at shopping centers no longer glimpse the poverty of the central cities" (Harrington, 1962). A hidden subculture is created in the American society which cannot be precisely described because it is hidden from the major group's view. Its inhabitants are considered reprobate persons who are, according to Harrington (1962), beyond the reach of the welfare state.

Contrary to popular belief, most of the poor in the United States are employed. "Most of the poor who are able to work do in fact work, but usually in low-paying and sporadic jobs" (U.S. Department of Labor, 1980).[1] They are restaurant workers, hospital employees, clerks in small shops, janitors and menial jobholders. The most observed ones are black Americans, long time inhabitants of the poverty subculture, working, if at all, in the most unattractive and poorest paying jobs. Table 12.1 describes, from 1964 to 1974, that the blue-collar occupations were 10 per cent of the employed non-white labor forces. Within the blue-collar category, the largest proportion of workers were non-farm laborers and operatives. This is a strong indication that the secondary laborers caught in the vicious cycle are not progressing.

TABLE 12.1

**Occupation of Employed Population: 1964, 1970, and 1974 (Annual Averages)**

| Occupation | 1964 Black & other races | 1964 White | 1970 Black & other races | 1970 White | 1974 Black & other races | 1974 White |
|---|---|---|---|---|---|---|
| Total employed (thousands) | 7,383 | 61,922 | 8,445 | 70,182 | 9,315 | 76,620 |
| Per cent | 100 | 100 | 100 | 100 | 100 | 100 |
| White-collar workers | 18.9 | 47.7 | 28.0 | 50.8 | 31.9 | 50.4 |
| Blue-collar workers | 40.4 | 36.3 | 42.3 | 34.9 | 40.6 | 34.2 |
| Service workers | 32.4 | 10.4 | 25.9 | 10.8 | 24.8 | 11.6 |
| Farm workers | 8.4 | 5.7 | 4.3 | 3.9 | 2.7 | 3.9 |

Source: U.S. Bureau of the Census, Current Population Reports, Special Studies, Series P-23 No. 54. The Social and Economic Status of the Black Population in the United States 1974, Table 48, p. 73, and Table 49, p. 74.

The data in Table 12.1 are expressed graphically in Fig. 12.2A through 2F. This illustrates that, with the exception of non-white females, minimal or no employment shifts took place over the decade among other groups. For non-white females, however, the most noticeable changes took place within the service category where participation decreased from 56 per cent in 1964 to 37 per cent in 1974. Since the white-collar category for non-white females increased from 22 per cent in 1964 to 36 per cent in 1974, on the surface, it would appear as though non-white females over the ten-year period benefited from the higher wages and better jobs to be found in the white-collar category.

More detailed examination, however, reveals that the majority of jobs obtained by non-white females in the white collar category was in the clerical workers subgroup (U.S. Bureau of the Census, 1974). This subgroup possibly affords 'high status' but probably offers less in terms of wages and, even more important, offers little opportunity for occupational advancement. With the lack of opportunity for upward job mobility and constant low wages, it can be concluded that the jobs in the clerical subgroup are not very attractive in relation to economic advancement.

The argument frequently cited today is that the number of persons being employed have increased in recent years, and the poor people today are impoverished due to defects in their character, lack of will, effort, or skill. Strong support for this argument is that the Irish, Italians, or Jews overcame their bewilderment, seize the opportunities, and eventually climbe the ladder to success without federal assistance or wars on poverty.

What is not acknowledged in this argument is that poverty today has a new form which is substantially different from that which existed fifty or sixty years ago. The earlier poverty accompanied the unfolding of the Industrial Revolution in the United States. Though not much more pleasant than the situation facing today's impoverished, it was at least surrounded by a layer of hope. Not only were these industries to absorb the newcomers (i.e. steel, railroad, and textiles), but the economy's need for sheer labor obviated any prospective demand for great skill or education. Job opportunities were plentiful; further, there was an internal ladder of opportunity allowing a young man to climb, for example, all the way from floor sweeper to skilled machinist (Willie and Riddick, 1970). Even if such instances were not rampant, they were enough to lend a measure of reality to the American dream.

In recent years, despite the improved employment numbers, jobs with built-in ladders of opportunity are declining. Further, some dramatic changes are taking place in the manpower profile of the nation and although total employment has been increasing, clearly the exogenous factor that provided the impetus for the increase was the post-war population explosion. Together with the larger consumer market and vast growth of national output, the expansion of population indeed created jobs.

It must be recognized that most of these created jobs have been in the government and services sectors. The long-term net effect of this is that a displaced factory worker is more likely to secure employment not in a factory but in a gas station or a repair shop. If the worker persists in looking for something to which he is accustomed, he may very well remain unemployed indefinitely. In fact, most of the new entrants to the workforce find no jobs or go to work part-time at low pay, generally in services, trades, or some other occupation in the secondary sector.

As a result, a sizable industrial worker or employee surplus is created that has no palpable relation to the affluent, functioning segments of society. Willhelm and Powell (1964) have emphatically stated a depressing truth about specific members of this labor group:

> With the cost of automation, the black American is moving out of his historical state of oppression into uselessness. Increasingly, he is not so much economically exploited as he is irrelevant. And his anxiety is an anxiety that will spread to others in society as automation proceeds . . . .
>
> The tremendous historical change for black American is taking place in these terms—he is not needed. He is not so much oppressed as unwanted; not so much unwanted as unnecessary; not so much abused as ignored. The dominant society no longer needs to exploit him. If he disappeared tomorrow he would hardly be missed. As automation proceeds, it is easier and easier to disregard him.

This compelling quote applies not only to black Americans, but also to others who are affected by increasing automation. Consequently, much of the unusable labor supply is forced into activities that take place outside the knowledge of government, or they are illegal activities similar to the informal activities in LDCs.

## ILLEGAL EMPLOYMENT IN THE UNITED STATES[2]

The widening gap between the primary and secondary labor markets has resulted in dissatisfaction and unemployment, and there is the notion that illegal employment comes about because of this. Although there are many different types of employment not sanctioned by the Federal government yet not considered illegal, there are many that provide jobs for a substantial group but are legally unacceptable. The former would be such jobs where the employer refuses to withdraw taxes from the employee (e.g. babysitting, maid service, house cleaning), and there are jobs such as aluminium can collecting, etc. The illegal categories discussed below are major ones which generate much money in the American economic system.

Numbers gambling is one of the major illegal activities in the black community. The numbers gambling institution acts as a loan agency for ghetto residents and employs a sizable group. In fact, the numbers gambling enterprise is second only to the Federal government in the provision of jobs for unemployed ghetto residents (McKay, 1940; Drake and Cayton, 1962; Lasswell and McKenna, 1972; and Light, 1977).

Light (1977) suggests that "numbers gambling is a remedy to the chronic malfunction of the larger society's financial institutions." If this is indeed the case, the similarity between numbers gambling in the United States and activities like medicinal herbalists in some LDCs becomes more apparent. In both cases the activities: (1) are indigenous remedial measures designed to compensate for imbalances in the system; (2) offer no protection such as social security and hospitalization to their employees; (3) are not sanctioned by the government; and (4) offer an income to persons who would otherwise be supported by the state.

"Prostitution, another major illegal activity, was the largest illegal industry of the late nineteenth and early twentieth centuries" (Bell, 1960, 164; Light, 1944, 467). Black females were employed in this illegal enterprise. The males served as "go-betweens" in sexual encounters. The business had a tendency to increase during the First and Second World Wars. During that period prostitution acted as a means to an end and prevailed until the person was legitimately employed. For years black brothels were owned by white businessmen and racketeers. Indications show that white control of the industry has diminished during the latter half of the twentieth century. Recently, more blacks have infiltrated this illegal activity.

## MIGRATION

Migration and size of location put the segmented labor market theory in better perspective. If it is accepted that job opportunities cause people to move more readily than for other reasons, then it is imperative to discuss migration as an essential part of the illegal employment and secondary labor argument (see Fig. 12.1).

Migration patterns and processes go a step further in contributing to our understanding employment and labor market segementation in both LDCs and MDCs. As indicated earlier, in LDCs it is primarily the high levels of rural-to-urban migration which have constructed job creating capability of governments and private organizations. It has been argued that while rural-to-urban migration is no longer the dominant direction of internal migration in the United States, it existed for many decades, especially among blacks.

The initial waves of black migrants from the South did not strain job creating ability. In fact, it actually provided the North with a cadre of workers who were quite willing to work in the most menial jobs. Bonacich (1976) contends that blacks were offered lower paying, "bad" jobs for several reasons: (1) lack of white labor (whites were unwilling to accept some types of employment); (2) decrease in immigrants from Europe; (3) blacks could be temporarily promoted from janitor to machinist to act as a buffer between the employers and the white "troublemaker" employees and unions; and (4) with no other employment opportunities available, blacks were forced to work for low wages. This suggests that, in the short run, both the black employees and the white employers benefited from the migration.

Second generation blacks in the North, however, are less willing to work in secondary jobs and prefer to leave the active labor force entirely rather than endure the frustration of being at the bottom. This reluctance to accept the menial jobs that were worked by their fathers has manifested itself in two ways: first, as the central theme of this paper suggests, in a migration or reverse migration trend away from the industrial North to large and small SMSAs in different regions of the United States (Campbell, 1974; Long, 1975; and Davis, 1976). Table 12.2 illustrates that between 1970 and 1974, both blacks and whites began migrating out of the Northeast and North Central industrial regions, whereas the South and West experienced net migration for both groups.

Between 1950 and 1960, the twelve largest cities in the United States lost over two million whites and gained nearly two million black residents. The percentage of the white population has continued to decrease since 1940 within the central cities, whereas the percentage of the black population has increased. This is indicated in Columns 2 and 4 of Table 12.3. Interestingly, Table 12.3 also shows that relative to whites between 1960-1970, there was proportionally an equal percentage of the black population outside the central city. The change of black population was greater outside the central city between 1970 and 1974 (see Columns 3 and 5). These data are somewhat misleading since some of this increase is not attributable to in-migration but to natural increase. Further, three out of four of the black males who migrated to the central cities worked in unskilled or semiskilled occupations in the secondary sector.

After the 1960's, in the 48 cities with black populations of 40,000 or more, there has been a growing visible trend toward out-migration and a return to the South. In a work on reverse black migration, Davis (1976) showed that approximately 33 per cent of the black migrants who moved South settled in nonmetropolitan areas.

TABLE 12.2

**Interregional Migration of the Population 4 years Old and Over: March 1970 to March 1974 (number in thousands)**

| Migration Status & Race | South | Northeast | North Central | West | North & West* |
|---|---|---|---|---|---|
| Black | | | | | |
| In-migrants | 276 (43.7)** | 88 (13.9) | 96 (15.2) | 172 (27.2) | 356 (56.3) |
| Out-migrants | 241 (38.1) | 143 (22.6) | 199 (31.5) | 49 (7.8) | 391 (61.9) |
| Net migration | 35 (5.6) | -55 (-8.7) | -103 (16.3) | 123 (19.4) | -35 (-5.6) |
| White | | | | | |
| In-migrants | 3055 (40.3) | 930 (12.3) | 1692 (22.3) | 1913 (25.2) | 4535 (59.7) |
| Out-migrants | 2041 (26.9) | 1799 (23.7) | 2284 (30.1) | 1466 (19.3) | 5549 (73.1) |
| Net migration | 1014 (13.4) | -869 (-11.4) | -592 (-7.8) | 447 (5.9) | -1014 (-13.4) |

* Columns 2, 3 and 4 are added together to form column 5. A comparison is made between South and North & West.

** The per cents are in parentheses.

Source: U.S. Department of Commerce, Social and Economic Statistics Administration, Bureau of the Census, 1974.

TABLE 12.3

**Population Inside and Outside Central City or Cities of Standard Metropolitan Statistical Areas by Race: 1920 to 1974**

| Population | White | | Black | |
|---|---|---|---|---|
| 1 | 2 | 3 | 4 | 5 |
| Per cent of Change | Central City | Outside Central City | Central City | Outside Central City |
| 1920 - 1930 | 22.2 | 33.3 | 52.5 | 16.5 |
| 1930 - 1940 | 4.3 | 15.1 | 19.9 | 9.2 |
| 1940 - 1950 | 10.9 | 36.4 | 48.1 | 28.5 |
| 1950 - 1960 | 4.7 | 49.3 | 50.3 | 30.9 |
| 1960 - 1970 | 0.1 | 26.1 | 33.2 | 26.4 |
| 1970 - 1974 | -4.4 | 7.3 | 6.7 | 19.5 |

Source: U.S. Department of Commerce, Social and Economic Statistics Administration, Bureau of the Census,1974.

Ironically, the South to which the reverse migrants are returning is now the new South. Where the black American was unprepared for the cosmopolitan North, together with sophisticated job discrimination, the black is also unnecessary in the mechanized and automated and highly technical industries of the new South. The original intention to migrate outside the central city or to the South did not prove to be as promising as first imagined. If the blacks become a participant in the manpower training programs and consider them a "temporary source of income" (Harrison, 1972, 122), they become a part of the vicious cycle and may eventually move into the illegal activities.

Increasingly, the new South resembles the urban North complete with numbers gambling, prostitution, and other illegal activities which no doubt generate millions of tax-free dollars. On the one hand, when competition becomes too competitive in the large SMSA, the illegal workers take their talents to small or non-metropolitan areas. On the other, they may find business too slow or their jobs become too compelling or obvious so they migrate to a large SMSA.

## CONCLUSION

While the preceding discussion has explored the nature of the relationship between employment, migration and poverty in the United States, several issues stand out as important. First, with increasing mechanization in the society and greater specialization in labor skills, it becomes more difficult for one to be substituted for another. Further, because specialized on-the-job training is increasingly becoming more important, the likelihood of transferring skills from one employment to another is also decreasing.

In the absence of skills, there is a continually widening barrier between primary and secondary labor employment. The consequence is that the pool of the unskilled workers becomes a stagnant one, untapped by society because it has no function or a collection of economically useless persons.

It is here that the similarity between theories developed for use in LDCs became relevant. Faced with low wages, no hope for advancement, few skills, and little education, the impoverished Americans are forced to supplement their incomes. Persons engaged in secondary employment supplement their incomes by engaging in informal activities. Informal activity, then, functions as a maintenance device by supplementing the incomes of the poor and thus allowing them to remain in urban areas. Increasingly, overt illegal activities are emerging as the dominant type of informal activity to be found in the urban ghetto (i.e. numbers gambling, prostitution, loan sharking, aluminium can collecting, etc.).

These informal activities are illegal only in the sense that they occur "outside the watchful eye of government." In other words, they are untaxed and offer none of the accruements dictated by modern society (e.g. sick leave and social security benefits). Involvement in these activities is in many ways a natural outcome of a system that excludes the vast majority of its minority population or relegates them to secondary employment. In fact, it can be argued that these illegal informal activities offer not only opportunities for high wages, but another important factor, they offer opportunities for recognition.

More substantial empirical research dealing directly with samples involved with illegal activities is needed before any definite conclusion can be reached. The immediate goal is to show the relationship between labor segmentation in MDCs and LDCs and migration in order to better explain unemployment and illegal employment at all geographic scales in the United States. Perhaps from this, government policies will be initiated to enforce pending laws and create other laws for preventing the vicious cycle or lessening the number of people who are forced into illegal activities after treading too long in the secondary vicious cycle.

12.7

## FOOTNOTES

1. This is a message from the Secretary of Labor, Ray Marshall to President Carter in 1980.
2. Ferman (1968) called illegal employment "the irregular economy" and argued that it has as much structure as the so-called legal employment.

## REFERENCES

Averitt, R.T., **The Dual Economy: The Dynamics of American In dustry** Structure. New York: Norton, 1968.

Baron, H. and B. Hymer, "The Negro in the Chicago Labor Mar. ›t," in **The Negro and the Labor Market Movement.** Edited by J. Jac bson. New York: Doubleday, 1968.

Beck, E.M., P.M. Horan, and C.M. Tolbert, "Stratification in a Dual Economy: A Sectoral Model of Earnings Determination," **American Sociological Review,** 43, October, 1978, pp. 704-720.

Becker, G.S., **The Economics of Discrimination.** Chicago: University of Chicago Press, 1957.

Bell, D., **The End of Ideology.** New York: Free Press, 1960.

Berry, R.A, "Wage Employment, Dualism and Labor Utilization in Columbia - Trends Over Time," **International Labor Review,** Vol., 114, No. 3, 1976.

Blauner, R., **Racial Oppression in America.** New York: Harper and Row, 1972.

Blueston, B., "The Tripartite Economy: Labor Markets and the Working Poor," Poverty and Human Resources, 5, July-August, 1970, pp. 15-23.

Bonacich, E., "Advanced Capitalism and Black/White Race Relations in the United States: A Split Labor Market Interpretation," **American Sociological Review,** Vol. 41, February 1976, pp. 34-51.

Brimmer, A.F., "The Economic Position of Black American:1976," **A Special Report of the National Commission for Man Power Policy,** Special Report No.9, Washington, D.C., 1976.

Cain, G., "The Challenge of Segmented Labor Market Theory to Orthodox Theory: A Survey," **Journal of Economic Literature,** Vol. 14, No. 4, 1976.

Campbell, R.R., D.M. Johnson, and G. Stangler, "Return Migration of Black People to the South," **Rural Sociology,** Vol. 39, No. 4, 1974, pp. 514-527.

Clark, C., **The Conditions of Economic Progress.** London: Macmillan, 1940.

Davis, D., "Reverse Black Migration," **Discussion Paper,** No. 53, Ohio State University, 1976.

Drake, St. C. and H.R. Cayton, **Black Metropolis.** New York: Harper and Row, 1962.

Doeringer, P.B., **Programs to Employ the Disadvantaged.** Englewood Cliffs, N.J.: Prentice-Hall, 1969.

Edwards, R.C., M. Reich, and D.M. Gordon, **Labor Market Segmentation.** Lexington, Massachusetts: D.C. Heath, 1975.

Emmerij, L. "A New Look at Some Strategies for Increasing Productive Employment in Africa," **International Review,** Vol. 111, No.2, 1975.

Fisher, A.G.B., "Capital and the Growth of Knowledge," **Economics Journal,** 43, 1933, pp. 379-389.

Geschwender, J.A., **Racial Stratification in America.** Dubuque, Iowa.: W.C. Brown, 1978.

Gordon, D.M., Theories of Poverty and the Underemployment.Lexington, Ma.: Heath, 1972.

Harrington, M., **The Other America.** New York: Macmillan, 1962.

Hart, K., "Informal Income Opportunities and Urban Employment in Ghana," **Journal of Modern African Studies,** Vol. 11, 1973.

Harrison, B., **Education, Training, and Urban Ghetto.** Baltimore: Johns Hopkins University Press, 1972.

Kerr, C., "The Balkanization of the Labor Market," in **Labor Mobility and Economic Opportunity.** Edited by E.W. Bakke, et. al. Cambridge: MIT and Wiley, 1954.

Lasswell, H.D. and J.B. McKenna. **The Impact of Organized Crime in an Inner City.** New York: Policy Sciences, Inc. Distributed by U.S. Department of Commerce, National Technical Information Service, 5285 Port Royal Rd., Springfield, Va. 22151, 1972.

Lewis, W.A., "Economic Development with Unlimited Supplies of Labour," **Manchester School Economic Social Studies,** 22, May 1954, pp. 139-91.

Long, L.H. and H.A. Hansen, "Trends in Return Migration to the South," **Demography,** 12 (4), 1975, pp. 601-614.

Light, I. "The Ethnic Vice Industry, 1880-1944," **American Sociological Review,** Vol. 42, June 1977, pp. 464-479.

Light, I., "Numbers Gambling Among Blacks: A Financial Insti tution," **American Sociological Review,** Vol. 42, December 1977, pp. 892-904.

Mazumdar, D., "The Rural Urban Wage Gap, Migration and the Shadow Wage," **International Bank for Reconstruction and Development,** No. 197, Februrary 1975.

McKay, C., **Harlem: Negro Metropolis.** New York: Dutton, 1940.

Merrick, T., "Employment and Earnings in the Informal Sector in Brazil: The Case of Belo Howizonte, "**The Journal of Developing Areas,** Vol. 10, April 1978.

Munnel, A.H., "The Economic Experience of Blacks: 1964-1974." **New England Economic Review,** January/February 1978, pp. 5-18.

Piore, M.J., "On-the-Job-Training in the Dual Labor Market," in **Public Private Manpower Policies.** Edited by Arnold R. Weber, Frank Cassell, and Woodrow L. Ginsberg. Madison: Industrial Relations Research Association, University of Wisconsin, 1969.

Piore, M.J., "Notes for a Theory of Labor Market Stratification," in **Labor Market Segmontation.** Edited by R.C. Edwards, M. Reich, and M. Gordon. Lexington, Mass." D.C. Heath, 1975.

Ranis, G. and Fei, J., "A Theory of Economic Development," **American Economic Review,** September 1961.

Seligmann, B.B., "Poverty and the Economy", in **Modernization, Urbanization, and the Urban Crisis.** Edited by G. Germani, Boston: Little, Brown, and Co., 1973.

Sethuraman, S.V., "The Urban Informal Sector : Concept, Mea surement, and Policy," **International Labor Review,** Vol. 114 No. 1, 1976.

Souza, P. and V. Tokman, "The Informal Sector in Latin Ame rica," **International Labor Review,** Vol. 114, No.3, 1976.

U.S. Bureau of the Census, Current Population Reports, Special Studies, Series P - 23, No. 54, **The Social and Economic Status of the Black Population in the United States,** 1974.

U.S. Department of Labor, **Employment and Training Report of the President.** U.S. Government Printing Office, Washington, D.C. 1980.

Vietorisz, T. and B. Harrison, "Labor Market Segmentation: Positive Feedback and Divergent Development," **American Economic Review,** Vol. 63, No. 2, 1973, pp. 366-376.

Wachter, M. "Primary and Secondary Labor Markets: A Critique of the Dual Approach," **Brookings Papers on Economic Activity,** 3, 1974.

Willhelm, S.M. and E.H. Powell, "Marginality: Black and White," in **Modernization, Urbanization, and the Urban Crisis.** Edited by G. Germani. Boston: Little, Brown, and Co., 1973.

Willie, C.V. and W.E. Riddick, "The Employed Poor: A Case Study," in **Poverty as a Public Issue.** Edited by B.B. Seligmann. New York: The Free Press, 1968.

THIRTEEN

Jean-Paul Levy

# THE REHABILITATION OF TOWN CENTERS AND OLD QUARTERS/NEIGHBORHOODS IN FRANCE

## Rationality and interpretations Using the Example of Toulouse

Even without going back to the famous experiments in the restoration of historical monuments carried out in the 19th century by the architect Viollet-le-Duc, the rehabilitation of town centers and old quarters/neighbourhoods in France already has a history.[1] A decisive period was begun in 1962 by the Malraux Act on protected areas. But it was in the seventies that important procedures for the resorption of insanitary housing and the legislation leading to the creation of the National Agency for Housing Improvement (Agence Nationale pour l'Amélioration de l'Habitat, ANAH, 1971) and the Urban Development Fund (Fond d'Aménagement Urbain, FAU, 1976) were instigated,—a period when heavy, socalled "bulldozer", renovation was changing in no uncertain way the hearts of cities and towns, from the regional metropolis to the medium-sized town. This much is common knowledge. However, in a conglomeration the size of Toulouse (5th largest city in France), the programmed rehabilitation has still not been started in 1983.[2]

One wonders about the reasons for this discrepancy, for the slowness and delays in the progress of projects. The needs are however just as important here. After all, did not the public census of 1975 reveal that 43.5 per cent of the housing in Toulouse dated from before 1948, that 36.1 per cent was considered uncomfortable, and that nearly 10 per cent was unoccupied (most of which being situated in the town center)? With regard to these needs, subsidized rehabilitation may well appear modest: only 507 dwellings benefited from the National Agency for Housing Improvement grants between 1976 and 1978.

How can this slowness in the case of Toulouse be explained? A study of this case confronted with the problem of the rehabilitation of the town center and the old quarters proves to be most instructive: this local case becomes more accessible in the light of the recently passed laws concerning political and administrative decentralization. The question arises as to whether this local case is not in fact particular to Toulouse with regard to France and its social institutions in general. If we are talking about an exception, this would stem from the peripheral position of Toulouse vis-a-vis the movement of capital and the economic machinery affecting France if not Europe. This position allows local protagonists and certain strata of Toulouse society to deploy themselves and to occupy the economic ground of rehabilitation by their property strategies, taking advantage of the local repercussions resulting from the transition of the French economy from the phase of competitive capitalism to that of monopoly capitalism, a transition accompanied by an important development of the tertiary sector.

## TOULOUSE—BACKGROUND

Like a number of French cities, Toulouse has undergone serious modifications, both quantitative and qualitative. These modifications concern urbanization in general, but more specifically the tertiary sector, the spatial distribution of the population and the political line adopted by the local community.

### Urbanization—a slowing down process

With less than 350,000 inhabitants according to the census of 1982, the inner city of Toulouse is situated at the center of an industrial or urban population zone (ZPIU) of more than 630,000 inhabitants totalling more than a quarter of the population for the whole of the Midi-Pyrénées region. The last decade has seen an ever-increasing expansion towards the towns and villages of the second and third peripheral circles.[3] This growth has today slowed down as may be shown by the production of housing: in the three years 1978 to 1980 inclusive, barely more housing was built than during the single record year of 1972 (10,283 compared to 9,047). It is however interesting to note that since 1976 more housing has been built on the outskirts of Toulouse (2/3) than in Toulouse itself, with an overwhelming proportion of individual houses (73 per cent in 1978 compared to barely 30 per cent in 1974).

These general signs make it clear enough that this escape to the suburbs as found in the whole of Western Europe and even North America, has of necessity had catastrophic repercussions on the historical center of Toulouse. The population of the old center diminished by a global 20,554 inhabitants between 1946 and 1975. This depopulation has become ever-increasing with the passing years: 1.1 per cent from 1946 to 1962; 2.1 per cent from 1962 to 1968; 2.7 per cent from 1968 to 1975, in a steady annual decline. It is more than likely that this tendency has been accentuated since 1975 with a total loss of around 30,000 inhabitants, a deficit which largely corresponds to the continued depopulation of the old quarters/neighborhoods.

## The development of the tertiary sector

At the same time and apparently contradictory to this trend, the working center of town has reinforced its role in a certain evolution borne out by:

- retail specialization in clothes, shoes and leisure goods.
- the development of offices in relation with the regional and departmental prominence of Toulouse within the Midi-Pyrénées region, in both public and private sectors.
- the appearance of what may be termed an alternative counter-centrality,[4] established during the economic crisis. It is composed of cultural and leisure commerce and activities (restaurants, cafe-theatres, etc.) which have in their way contributed in reinforcing the centrality of Toulouse.
- on a wider level, we have witnessed a spectacular development of so-called "cultural activities".

However the essence of this new importance assumed by the town center does not come from the juxtaposition of functions or the sum of its activities. We can take a short-cut in saying that the center has entered a phase whose major characteristic resides in the constitution of what may be termed post-centrality, a no doubt incomplete expression but with the advantage that it reveals its late establishment, coming after the development of a traditional centrality. This post-centrality does not seem to need a functional dimension in order to establish itself. It expresses itself with a whole ensemble of signs and symbols borrowing heavily from regional architecture, certain shapes, colors (pink), and materials (brick).

On a socio-spatial level, a great segmentation of the old center has resulted, more apparent today than twenty years ago. Next to the commercial center which remains the living, active part of Toulouse (in spite of its modest dimension in relation to a conglomeration of this size), other quarters take their place, such as St. Etienne and la Dalbade, once inhabited by Languedoc Members of Parliament, the nobility and upper bourgeoisie.

## The constitution of proletarianized neighborhoods

It is understandable consequently that other parts of the central area should progressively become slums and poor neighborhoods. Toulouse participated in the general movement prevalent in French cities, whereby workers mainly of foreign origin (first Spanish, then Moroccan, Algerian and Tunisian) group together in areas of dilapidated housing. Examples of this in Toulouse are the Arnaud Bernard quarter in the north of the old city and Saint Cyprien on the left bank of the Garonne.

This rapid review of recent evolution is not peculiar to Toulouse. After all is not the situation in which the city finds itself similar to that of almost all large French cities?

## Local urban politics

Local urban politics reveals the difficulties facing the town in completing the major town-planning projects fixed upon in the late fifties, bearing in mind the narrow economic basis of Toulouse. Firstly, there is a small project of heavy renovation (in the Saint Georges quarter), completed after a quarter of a century of work and concerning approximately 1,300 dwellings, and secondly, the urban priority zone (ZUP) of Mirail (2,000 acres or 800 hectares) a local example of the new towns conceived in France during the sixties.

However, in the old town center, for a long time there has been no activity apart from the obvious failure of the combined property restoration operation undertaken near the abovementioned renovated area, in spite of its very advantageous location. This failure no doubt finds its roots in the property owners' lack of motivation towards the possibilities offered by this first example of rehabilitation in Toulouse, which says a lot for the adaptability of the interests at stake connected with rehabilitation. And besides, the building trade did not feel mobilized by this potential new front of working in the old fabric of town, already fully taken up by the capitalization of the individual housing market on the outskirts of town. As for local capital, no investment is made in this area, at least for the moment.

And so nothing happens until 1981 and 1982, which see successively:

- the launching on 55 acres (23 hectares) of the Compans/Cafarelli project on land previously belonging to the army (former barracks), aiming at establishing a directional center to the north of the inner town but in a pericentral position, nearly half of which is occupied by a park. This is the first creation of a park within the city since the latter half of the 18th century, with the exception of the four parks on the outskirts of town.

- the completion of research prior to the launching of a project for Arnaud Bernard, the first of its type undertaken by the city, when the same kind of project has already been started in quite a number of medium-sized towns in the region over the last five or six years.
- the inauguration of research with a view to a proposed project for Saint Cyprien on the left bank.
- in addition, the freeing of land in or near the perimeter of the old center, in providing new opportunities in a town where building space is becoming increasingly rare, has created a completely new situation and pushed the municipality to re-examine its policy and to look at the future of the center in a more global fashion.

It would appear simple enough to come to the conclusion that the same classic territorial expansion of the town center is taking place as in a number of other large cities such as Montpellier, Marseilles and Lyons. But what is striking and worthy of note is the manner in which this renewal policy of Toulouse centrality is moulded on a movement national in its extent, and more precisely its form and content, whereas the principle of rehabilitation continues its slow course. Its slow gestation thus throws light on a system of local protagonists whose mobilization is but gradual. It would not be going too far to assert that the rehabilitation of the old quarters of Toulouse provides an opportunity of seeing more clearly the reactivation of protagonists on a local economic level, protagonists who had been brushed aside from the economic game as well as from the production of housing, more or less eliminated by the arrival in the region over a decade or so of large individual housing, companies such as Phenix, G.M.F., Bouygues, etc.

## SPONTANEOUS PRIVATE REHABILITATION

One can only be surprised at the slowness in launching rehabilitation in Toulouse, when already at the end of the fifties a dozen or so quarters were drawn to the attention of municipal officers as generally having uncomfortable, decaying and unhygienic housing; when the municipal team taking office in 1971 maintained in many ways their preference for the town center and its population, a preference which the Land Use Plan (Plan d'Occupation des Sols, POS) confirmed as its priority for the coming years.[5] The actual principle of rehabilitation is developed progressively in stages. The first corresponds to the appearance of a few isolated protagonists. It was in the early sixties that the first attempts at property restoration were launched, comparatively few and dealing each time with a small number of dwellings. They affected old aristocratic residences of great value and private town houses protected by the Historical Monument Department, with the result that repercussions and a strong impact were felt in a town where, as will be seen later, a certain cultural model, that of Toulouse high society, has with remarkable regularity and great continuity left its

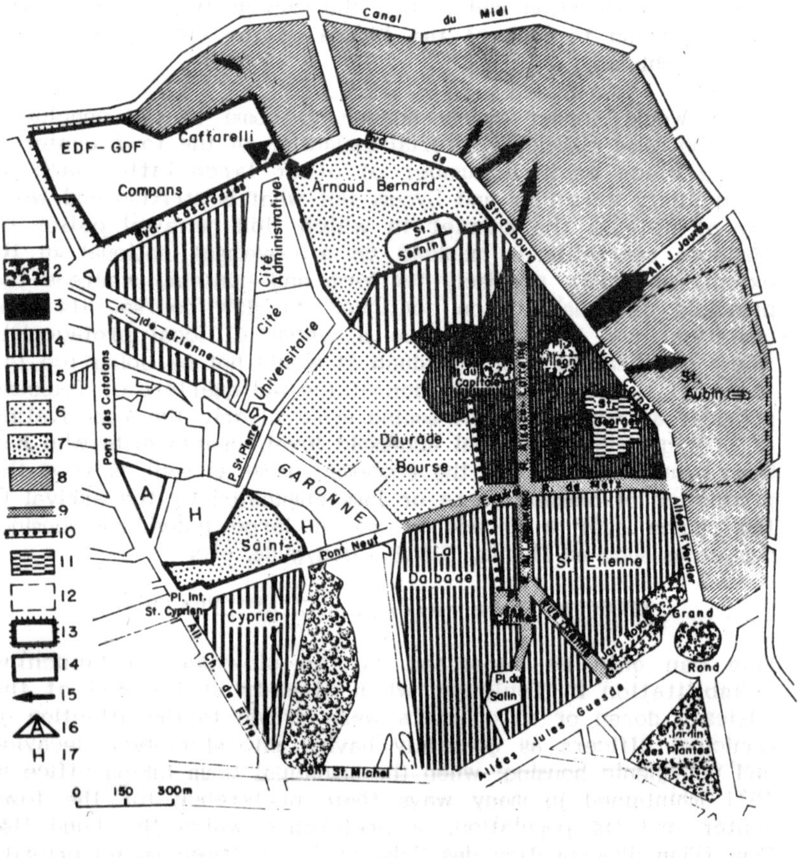

mark for more than two centuries.

However, at this time of reactivation of the culturalist model[6] only had a small effect in France, while town centers were witnessing the age of bulldozer renovation and urban growth was above all noticeable on the outskirts of town.

A second stage was inaugurated from 1977-1978 with the bringing in of what came to be known as the "rehabilitation connection" coming from private capital and intervention.

**The "rehabilitation connection"**

This phenomenon arose out of the simultaneous action of several categories of protagonists:

(i) First of all come the private individuals. If at the beginning these included families belonging to the middle class strata of Toulouse society, the general increase in property value, the rising cost of rehabilitation, the difficulties in finding buildings with the required advantages without great repair expenses have all contributed to their elimination from the "connection". More recently, the high price of credit has made this type of operation impossible for this category. The most-represented socio-professional groups are the trade and industry chiefs, the liberal professions, and managerial levels. The lion's share would seem to go to the medical profession. For all these categories, rehabilitation takes on a distinct patrimonial dimension. This explains why it is openly resembled to, even identified with the patrimonial strategy of the aristocracy and Toulouse bourgeoisie which, at least since the 18th century, had occupied the same neighborhoods as those sought after today. The similarity is too striking not to be pointed out. Do not both examples refer back to the same cultural model which, originating from the dominant classes, has strongly impregnated Toulouse society as a whole?

(ii) There are also the real estate agencies specially formed for this type of rehabilitation. An initial survey carried out with the aid of the files of the Office of the Court of Commerce and Toulouse shows that their number has been increasing since 1977-1978 and that between certain persons involved in several agencies at a time, there undobtedly exist connections which basically remain local or regional.

(iii) Then there are the property dealers, a vague and fluctuating category, difficult to pin down with accuracy in Toulouse. Their presence in the process of rehabilitation would seem to indicate an active participation on their part and that they assure its subsequent commercialization. They are indeed represented among the shareholders of the abovementioned agencies.

(iv) Finally, there is the building profession in its widest sense. Everything takes place as if, by a kind of process of vertical integration, rehabilitation short-circuited the division of labour, gathering together within one unit artisans, contractors, architects and salesmen.

What is more, a certain number of major features become apparent from an analysis of the role of these different protagonists. In the first place, one is struck by the almost total absence of large-scale operators. When they do exist at Toulouse, it is above all the outskirts that their presence is felt. A kind of market hierarchy has been formed : our pratagonists, chased away from housing production at the moment when the latter, becoming a mass production operation, demanded the implementation of greater capital, occupied the rehabilitation market with some hesitation, which accounts for the comparative lateness of Toulouse as mentioned above. Secondly, it has been observed that the housing areas aimed at by these protagonists are those which may be recuperated at the least cost. Private rehabilitation in Toulouse, as elsewhere in France, is only interested in a well-defined sector of the ensemble, whereas the most dilapidated sector is abandoned to its own devices, an abandon which only serves to accentuate the devaluation of the urban space in which it is situated. Certain protagonists have also sometimes been seen to intervene both in the old center and in the outskirts. Study of their present state of affairs reveals that rehabilitation would appear to be an attempt at diversifying the products they offer, thus reaching different sets of clientele, in what is a difficult period for construction and the building industry.

Is it not in fact an attempt at adapting the supply of housing to the difficulties and obstacles of acquisition represented by the rise in prices and the high price of credit which put a good number of families out of the financial running? The supply of rehabilitated housing is not however uniform. Saleable products vary in size from the large luxury flat to the tiny "studio", with in between the dwellings with mezzanine allowing an increased sales price for the same floor area. In an inquiry into old housing in Toulouse, the local Press came to the conclusion that the nearer the center, the smaller the surface area in dwellings became.[7]

The "rehabilitation connection" arrived to obviate the current risks of a housing market in difficulty in the region, a difficulty which pushed some local operators, brushed aside by large estate promoters and large-scale constructors, to take an interest in rehabilitation, "to survive", as one of them put it. An attempt is currently being made no less to structurize this market. It has been observed in fact that rehabilitation is often carried out after property has changed hands. After a period of intensive transactions from 1978 to 1980, things have since settled down corresponding, since 1981, to changing national politics and the passing of two Acts in Parliament (the Quillot Act and an Act instigating the taxation of large fortunes).

From the acquisition of a property its commercialization as flats after transformation, rehabilitation is of short duration (less than one year); it is comparable to that necessary to produce a housing estate of similar size on the outskirts of town. In the first case, the rotation of capital is much quicker, and the initial investment is often minimal bearing in mind the work investment necessary to propose a product supposedly aimed at the luxury market in Toulouse. Risk is reduced to a minimum, all of which would seem to suit the dimensions of the protagonists in the "rehabilitation connection".

## The local community in the face of rehabilitation

The local community, through the various actions which it has undertaken during this period, from pedestrian precincts to the restoration of fountains, the changing of street lighting, or resurfacing (paving, etc.) without a doubt stopped the process of devalorization of the old center. But is not the context as different throughout France, making creditable nowadays actions which were not so only a short time ago? These actions have one aim: to give the town a face-lift. Their seeming diversity must not give a wrong impression, bearing in mind that they successfully prepare the ground for rehabilitation. They evidently incite the property owners and protagonists of the "connection" to act. This is why, faced with the involvement of these protagonists, the community does not interfere in as far as the consequences thus incurred tend toward the same goal which the community itself is ultimately after. What's more, the local community makes an effort not to come in the way of these private strategies, limiting its land-buying to a minimum, trying not to falsify the market by use of its right of pre-emption, and leaving aside difficult and unpopular decisions such as the municipalizing of urban land or the right to control its sale in the center of town.

## REHABILITATION IN TOULOUSE—INTERPRETATIONS

The establishment of this "connection" has not been rapid. Some see in this obvious proof of the relative adaptability of local interest, as opposed to certain examples of cities (such as Paris) where the interests fired by rehabilitation are expressed with vigour. In the case of Toulouse, the root of the question is elsewhere, in the various interpretations and rationality of rehabilitation.[8]

It is in this combination of two social groups that resides the tacit agreement mentioned above, a compromise mode made possible by the absence of the dominant fraction of the French bourgeoisie in Toulouse. With the result that it is possible from this interpretation to examine how the central area of the town is organized hierarchically depending on the degree and form of penetration by the neo-bourgeoisie. We have already seen that the two neighborhoods it is most interested in . . . do not correspond to the active center of Toulouse, the commercial heart where the interests more closely linked with the exercising of commercial functions have constantly played a role for at least a century, in any case since the establishment of the Haussmann offensive (rue d'Alsace-Lorraine) at the end of the 19th century.[9]

Next to these two types of areas, there is a third type, seemingly left to one side, neither devalorized nor valorized. Some rehabilitation of property has been undertaken here, but insufficient to make it an area of interests as strong as in the case of the two preceding examples:

> either because the capital corresponding to the occupying owners and landlords is not enough to take care of irreversible rehabilitation.
>
> or because the neo-bourgeoisie is not yet interested in these areas, devoid as they are of the same cultural references and same symbolic points of anchorage susceptible of making them, like the previous ones, areas of power.

The differences between this type and a fourth type (exemplified in Toulouse by the neighborhoods of Arnaud Bernard and St. Cyprien) is great, this fourth type having become areas which receive the least well-off populations which seem to be, as it were, imprisoned by these dilapidated housing areas.[10]

It would appear that the municipality is at the moment most concerned with this fourth type of area, and it is here that future interventions should take place, though there is still a nuance of significance between Arnaud Bernard and St. Cyprien.[11] The former, by virtue of its intermediate position between the old center and the future directional center of Compans and Caffarelli, is taking on an importance hitherto unknown. The success of the proposed rehabilitation project will condition the integration of the directional center with the old center, and by extension, the entire rehabilitation policy of the municipality; it therefore raises a good many questions on its future and that of its populations.

## CONCLUSION

It is no doubt amusing to compare, as some writers have done, the rehabilitation of the old neighborhoods in France to a Spanish inn.[12] Each potential protagonist, each social group, arrives with its own motives and intentions which are therefore numerous and sometimes contradictory, whatever procedures and channels are opted for, and are the same throughout the rest of the country. However, if the State decides on the rules of the game and partially finances certain operations, the local cases and the results obtained are not necessarily identical. Therein undoubtedly lies one of the basic nuances between this urban policy and that of the sixties. It has been too fully dealt with elsewhere to dwell any longer on it here.

The policy of rehabilitation of old quarters/neighborhoods offers today, as in the case of Toulouse, a line of observation of great interest in understanding the remoulding of local private protagonists in a national context no longer resembling that of fifteen or twenty years ago. Not only does rehabilitation allow them to be revealed, but it is not going too far to maintain that it offers these private protagonists the opportunity of reactivating their involvement and bringing them to the force, through the patrimony interest at stake as revealed by the revalorizing of the old quarters.

Rehabilitation throws, if not new, at least clearer, light on the organization of social evolution. But the present reconstitution of power in the local case of Toulouse, the alliances thus authorized with the emergence of the neo-bourgeoisie, do they all actually comprise a new phenomenon? Three Toulouse writers,—C. Beringuier, A. Boudou and B. Jalabert—rightly answered this ten years ago: "In Toulouse, the same things are always done while giving the impression that new things are done.[13]

To sum up then, using the case of Toulouse, a good example in many ways, is not in fact the whole of urban society revealed in its recent transformations, in its relationships with the space it occupies in particular the center of town? With the exception of Paris, are not the same configurations to be found elsewhere in French towns? The question is worth asking.

## FOOTNOTES

1. This article makes use in part of results of research at present being carried out at the request of the Ministry of Housing (Ministére de l'Urbanisme et du Logement) in 1982 (Construction Plan). It has enjoyed the participation of Isabelle Bardaud and Eric Salord, scholars at the Interdisciplinary Centre of Urban Studies (Centre Interdisciplinaire d'Etudes Urbaines, CIEU).
2. In this article the distinction is make between proposed rehabilitation projects and spontaneous rehabilitation. This distinction is fundamental, even if both types tend towards the same objective, i.e. the revalorization of town centers and old quarters/neighborhoods. The former, undertaken by the local community, benefits partly from aid and the finance machinery of the State, and also of special organizations such as the Office for Low Rent Housing (Offices d'Habitation á Loyer Moderé, HLM) and the Organization for the Protection, Improvement and Conservation in the Transformation of old housing (PACT). The latter is undertaken by private individuals, without the aid and financing of the first type of rehabilitation.
3. For more information, see the "Travaux et Documents du CIEU, TOÙLOUSE, No. 9" ("Works and Documents of the CIEU"), published in 1982 on "la production de l'espace périurbain" ("production in the periurban domain"), under the direction of B. Kayser.
4. See J. P. Levy "Quartiers anciens et centre ville: nouveaux enjeux de la politique de réhabilitation" ("Old quarters/neighborhoods and town centers : new stakes in the policy rehabilitation"), Revue de Géographie des Pyrénées et du Sud-Ouest, Toulouse, 1983, 1, p. 101-126.
5. The Land Use Plan (Plan d'Occupation des Sols, POS), approved in 1981 after many vicissitudes, upheld the objectives for town centers of maintaining population numbers to check the process of civilization, the pursuit of the valorization of central activities, greater accessibility, and the usual reference to the preservation and restoration of the historical heritage, since the celebration in France of a National Heritage Year in 1980.
6. The working is that of Francoise Choay in "L'Urbanisme, utopies et réalités" ("Urbanism, utopia and reality"), Seuil, Paris, 1965, it is also to be found in the works of Camillo Sitte, especially in "Der Stadtebau" ("Town-building") published in Vienna in 1889, not translated in its entirety into French until 1980 ("L'art de batir les villes, l'urbanisme selon ses fondements artistiques", ("The art of town-building, urbanism according to its artistic foundations"), l'Equerre, Paris 1980, 190 p.).
7. The daily newspaper "La Dépeche du Midi", 18.1.83.
8. Cf. R. Ledrut "L'Espace en question" ("Space under Question"), Anthropos, Paris, 1976, especially p. 68 and after, and by the same author "Précis de Sociologie Urbaine", 1st edition, 1968.
9. See C. Beringuier, A. Boudou and G. Jalabert, "Toulouse Midi-Pyrénées, la transition ("Toulouse Midi-Pyrénées, the Transition"), Stock, coll. Villes en Liberté, Paris, 1972.
10. A. Bourdin, "Restauration-Réhabilitation : l'ordre symbolique de l'espace néo-bourgeois" ("Restoration-Rehabilitation : the symbolic order within neo-bourgeois space"), review Espaces et Sociétes, No. 30-31, Dec. 1979, p. 15 to 36.

11. It is, it is true, hard to imagine that a local community could start in various parts of its center several projects simultaneously, even with the opportunities provided by the freeing of a number of pieces of land, when one considers the economic foundations and financial capacities of a town like Toulouse, bearing in mind the projects already under way and the project for an underground railway within the next five years.
12. A. Bourdin, "Restoration-Rehabilitation", article mentioned above, p. 15.
13. C. Beringuier, A. Boudou and G. Jalabert, work quoted above, p. 319.

## KEY

1. River Garonne and canals (du Midi and de Brienne).
2. Green areas.
3. Commercial center.
4. Areas considered integrated thanks to the "rehabilitation connection".
5. Areas left waiting or in the process of being integrated.
6. Areas left waiting (La Daurade and La Bourse quarters).
7. Strongly devalorized areas (St. Cyprien and Arnaud Bernard quarters subject to an OPAH as from 1983).
8. Pericenter, residential, with infiltration of offices; present and future town center extension zone.
9. Haussmann offensive made after 1870.
10. Pedestrian axis completed after 1977, between two car-parks (in Capitole Square to the north and Carmes Market to the south).
11. St. Georges' renovation perimeter, 14.5 acres (5.80 hectares) from 1960 to 1980.
12. St. Aubin property restoration perimeter.
13. Project for a Directional Center on the 55 acres (23 hectares) vacated by the barracks. Already completed: Occitan park (25 acres) and Spots Hall.
14. OPAH projects at Arnaud Bernard and St. Cyprien.
15. Expansion of private tertiary sector into the outer center, at present towards the Allées Jean Jaurès, in the future into the approaches of Compans.
16. Abattoir triangle, soon to be vacated.
17. Hospitals of St. Cyprien on the left bank, remnant of the hospital tradition of medieval times, preserved today.

FOURTEEN

Hermann Borghorst

# CITIZEN PARTICIPATION IN URBAN RENEWAL IN BERLIN (WEST)

## INTRODUCTION

Representation democracy in the traditional sense has proved to be clearly insufficient. Political parties, interest groups, public administration and the parliament were not able to take up and articulate the different needs and interests of the citizens. Stronger than in the past there is an increasing claim among the citizens to directly participate in the shaping of their housing and living environment and to take part in the decisions on intended changes. The emergence of many citizen-protest groups and larger protest movements indicates that the political landscape has changed. The youth protest and the urban squatting that took place in Berlin during the last two years are the most radical expressions of a crisis-like development. Representative democracy must more than ever be completed by plebiscitary elements. New forms of citizen participation are especially suited to be applied in the context of local politics and at neighbourhood level.

In the following pages concrete experiences with and the practice of citizen participation in urban renewal in Berlin are described and analysed. In the focus of the analysis is the specific procedure of citizen participation in the neighbourhood of Kreuzberg SO 36 in Berlin. Four years ago an attempt was started to develop new goals and initiatives for the revitalisation of this old urban residential quarter in cooperation with the residents and to implement the results through continuous work.

## EXPERIENCES WITH CITIZEN PARTICIPATION IN URBAN RENEWAL

Urban renewal started in many West German cities as well as in

Berlin in the sixties after the removal of the large-scale war destructions. Extensive renewal projects however were carried out in the seventies on the basis of the Urban Promotion Law of 1971. The residents' participation in the planning process was a central component of this federal law. The purpose was to hereby increase the democratization of urban planning on the one hand and to secure a more efficient procedure on the other.

In the following years the interpretation and practical application of these legal provisions has brought up vehement and controversial debates on which one should be the proper form of citizen participation. During the implementation of the program different forms of formal and informal residents' participation developed in various urban renewal areas:

- public meetings and information offices in the urban renewal areas.
- formal public hearings before the committees of the district council.
- residents' associations, citizen-protest groups and self-aid groups.
- residents' council in the urban renewal area.
- urban renewal commission as a coordinating body between residents and urban renewal administration on the district level.

In the beginning different forms of citizen participation fulfilled the function of supporting the "official" urban renewal policy and of legitimizing it by creating symbolic consensus. Public hearings and public meetings are important instruments to disseminate information, but can easily be staged in a way to impress the audience and be misused against citizens' demands through a smokescreen of professional jargon, technical resources and rhetorical appeals to "city-wide" interests.

The residents' council in an urban renewal area of Berlin is an example of formally established citizen participation. This council consists of representatives of the tenants, the landlords, local trades and the employees. All are directly elected by the corresponding groups. This procedure is to assure a representative articulation of interests as well as the legitimacy of the residents' council. Since 1977 residents' councils have been constituted in several urban renewal areas of the different districts of Berlin. On the basis of the existing experiences with this Berlin model of participation strong and weak points can be summarized as follows:

(1) A concrete form of participation in urban renewal planning is offered to the residents of an urban renewal area. But the institutionalized form of representation develops to a formal and cumbersome procedure of little flexibility.

(2) Mostly voting of the tenants is extremely low (sometimes only 2%). Therefore the passive and resigned attitude of the overwhelming majority of the residents remains the basic problem of citizen participation.

(3) One reason for this development can be seen in the insufficient support of the residents' council by community organizers or advocacy planners. The participation could be much more intensified by personally addressing the residents.

(4) The residents' council and the urban renewal commission are in danger of being co-opted by public administrators. Preferences, articulated by the affected residents, are easily blocked by planning and administrative experts.

(5) Despite its merely advisory function the residents' council and urban renewal commission could sporadically gain influence on political and administrative decisions and thus achieve partial success. At the same time the lack of competence in the decision-making process leads to a feeling of helplessness and fatalism with many affected citizens.

(6) The political power of the residents' council increases if it does not concentrate on institutionalized activities only, but is fully integrated in the social and political processes of the neighbourhood and can rely on the support of locally active groups.

This analysis of the residents' council's functioning is reconfirmed by the experiences of citizen participation in Kreuzberg SO 36.

## STRATEGIES FOR KREUZBERG : GRASSROOT INITIATIVES

When the Berlin Model of the residents' council was implemented in formal urban renewal areas, it was paralleled by a new process of citizen participation which developed in a living quarter of the district of Kreuzberg. This process went far beyond the traditional concepts and procedures. The highly experimental and process-like nature of the procedure allowed for a clear definition of new priorities from the perspective of the residents.

## The Development of the Neighbourhood Kreuzberg SO 36

Kreuzberg SO 36 is a traditional working class neighbourhood, built during the industrialization in the second half of the 19th century ("Mietskasernen"). In the past the neighbourhood had good access to the old city centre of Berlin as well as to recreational areas in the vicinity. It got into an extremely unfavourable location at the edge of the inner city after the political division of Berlin, and increasingly so after the building of the Berlin Wall in 1961. SO 36 exhibits the typical pattern of a deteriorating inner city neighbourhood:

- an extremely high density of housing and severe deficiencies of parks and open spaces;
- an extremely high proportion of sub-standard housing (about 50 per cent of the apartments are without WC and 80 per cent do not have a bathroom);
- the apartment houses deteriorate and are not properly repaired (non-investment and house owners' speculation for public funds);
- a pronounced lack of provision with social facilities like kindergarten and day-care centres.

While mobile German tenants with high incomes migrated, the concentration of socially deprived population groups increased. The population loss in SO 36, which lies above the Kreuzberg and Berlin average (from 33,000 in 1973 to 27,000 in 1979), thus had a highly selective impact on the population structure. SO 36 as a whole and the northern part in particular with its 12,000 inhabitants became more and more a major living area for migrant workers (40 per cent). About 90 per cent of them are of Turkish nationality.

No distinctive planning perspectives for the development of SO 36 existed within the public administration before the "Strategien fur Kreuzberg" (Strategies for Kreuzberg) were initiated. This proved to be advantageous for the implementation of the residents' requests. The "urban development planners" within the public administration assumed an extensive depopulation of the area. They thought of letting part of the area "run empty" in order to tear it down and to redevelop it as recreational areas, which are badly needed.

## Goals of the Strategies Project

The main incentive for the revitalization of the neighbourhood came from a minister of one of the Protestant churches in the area. The negative social side effects of traditional renewal processes were avoided, and new and alternative solutions sought based on the resources within the area. The initiative was supported by the local Member of Parliament, committed urban planners and the local party organization of the Social Democratic Party. An open contest for the "Strategien fur Kreuzberg" was announced by the Department of Housing in Berlin against the resistance of urban development planners and urban renewal administrators. The project found the political support of the Senator of Housing who was in charge of the project.

The objective of the contest was to develop model strategies and applicable concepts for the social, economic and physical reorganization of the area. In particular, models for residents' participation were to be worked out including the whole population and activating the identification with the neighbourhood. The announcement of the contest provided only broad guidelines. This was done purposefully in order to appeal to all residents, citizen-protest groups, other locally active groups and institutions in the affected area as well as to other persons interested in the problems of urban renewal in general. They should all be integrated in a broad process of searching for new ideas.

## Results and Experiences of the Strategies Project

One hundred and twentynine proposals were submitted to the contest. The scope ranged from a simple letter to scientifically elaborated concepts. Among other subjects these proposals dealt with procedures of residents' participation, communication centres in the area, self-aid projects to ameliorate the housing situation, local business and the shaping of open spaces. Due to time pressures and low publicity in the beginning, the project did not succeed in attaining usable proposals from a large number of residents in the quarter (only 12 per cent of the participants). In its initial phase the strategies project remained largely unknown in the quarter. A large part of the participants nevertheless consisted of non-planners and non-scientists. The residents themselves were obviously overtaxed in submitting elaborate proposals within a short period.

However, the residents' influence was substantially different in selecting the proposals. This process was clearly dominated by them. Having a majority of votes in the Project Commission which simultaneously functioned as the contest's jury, the residents were able to pursue their perspectives for the area. The Project Commission consisted of 34 members: 22 residents of the neighbourhood and 12 members of the Department of Housing and the district administration of Kreuzberg. Eight of the 22 residents were named by locally active groups and 14 residents were drawn from lists, which included tenant employees, elderly people, local business, migrant workers, youth and teachers. The project was coordinated by a neighbourhood office of the Department of Housing and accompanied by an external group of experts.

From the perspective of the municipal bureaucracy of Berlin two major aspects have been most remarkable: firstly, the external presence of the central Department of Housing in the neighbourhood, which was the beginning of a decentrally organized quarter-oriented practice of urban renewal; secondly, the immediate dialogue with citizens in a local commission, where the citizens held the majority in decision-making processes. The neighbourhood office had to fulfil double role, on the one hand to pursue the goals of the Department in the residential area and on the other to assume a certain advocate position in favour of the neighbourhood inside the administration. At the beginning, the resistance has been especially big among middle-rank civil servants.

The public administrators in the Project Commission were confronted with an active and increasingly professionalized citizen group, able to coordinate their goals and perspectives. Local politicians and the involved planners were astonished about the high degree of social vitality in the neighbourhood. They realised how important it would be for the revitalisation of the quarter to accept the often time-consuming and conflict-stricken process of a growing consensus with the population of the area.

At the end of the contest 11 proposals have been awarded a prize. In discussions with residents, politicians and administrators these proposals have been made more precise and tested with respect to the feasibility ("testing phase"). Finally the Project Commission formulated its recommendations to the Senate of Berlin (city government) which, some months later, decided to finance most of the selected projects for a period of four years. The proposals of the Commission emphasize the fact that they are concentrating not mainly on the physical aspects of urban revitalization, but rather on the non-physical social aspects by promoting projects like a citizens' association, a self-managed organization of professional training for the youth, a counselling office for migrant workers and a neighbourhood meeting centre.

**Transformation in a Continuous Citizen Participation**

Already before the end of the contest the Senate of Berlin set up a program of housing modernization in order to start a specific, visible initiative for the renovation of this living quarter. The program was financed by conjunctural budget means of the 'Zukunftsin vestitionsprogram' (ZIP) (Future-Investment-Program). The strategies project soon gained such a high political importance and public attention that the funding of the area with 70 million DM in the context of this ZIP-modernization succeeded surprisingly fast. A "ZIP-Committee" was formed for the coordination of the program. Soon it emerged as an informal housing and planning committee at the neighbourhood level with general competence and open to the public. Again, the majority of this committee consists of residents. It still meets weekly and is consulted by planning experts paid by the public administration.

All rehabilitation and infrastructural projects as well as other public renewal activities are thoroughly discussed between citizens and administration in this voluntary committee. Although the committee was never formally sanctioned in a legal sense, it is fully accepted by all involved parties and therefore has a high degree of liability and legitimacy. Most of the resolutions are unanimous and the public administration hardly ever makes different decisions. The flow of information from the administration to the residents, however, often is insufficient. The bureaucratic routines of the administrative apparatus are incomprehensible for the citizen.

The perspective of problems viewed by the residents forces the different administrative departments to collaborate in the urban renewal process more closely than before. The structurally caused administrative fragmentation impeded adequate problem solutions. The citizens are not interested in political-administrative competences, but in quickly meeting their demands. Housing corporations, single landlords and architects in charge of them present their plans to the committee and face the dialogue with the residents. The enforcement of citizens' demands versus private investors can be accomplished best when the coordination with the ZIP-Committee is set up as a precondition for public funding.

House and block meetings of the residents have significantly contributed to including large parts of the population in the process of citizen participation. Concerning the rehabilitation of their house, for instance, tenants had the choice to agree or to refuse modernization by majority vote. Interviews with the tenants about this procedure revealed heavy deficits of information and a lack of time for discussion. The tenants were also asked when, according to their opinion, an apartment house should be modernized. The answers show a strong claim for a broad and active participation in the decision-making concerning the intended modernization:

- 53,8% "if all tenants agree",
- 41,4% "if more than half of the tenants agree",
- 4,8% "if a minority of the tenants agrees".

The coordination with the tenants facilitates the process of taking into consideration their different financial capacity as well as their various living preferences (type, extent and costs of the modernization). This goal could not sufficiently be achieved during the ZIP-modernization.

For the process of citizen participation the foundation of the "Verein SO 36" was a further important result of the contest. The citizens' representatives in the ZIP-Committee are members of the Verein, which has nowadays about 330 members, among them 15 locally active groups and initiatives. Its task is to realize the results of the strategies project and to pursue the interests of the neighbourhood versus the administration and the parliament. A staff of four full-time employees of the Verein are payed by the administration. For a year four other employees have been engaged in informing, counselling and supporting tenants in the process of urban renewal, in order to assure an independent procedure in favour of the residents. Good contacts and a satisfying working relationship between the Verein and the administration on the one hand fulfil the purpose to get necessary information early enough and to present citizens' demand more directly. On the other there occurs the danger that the Verein may become a professional citizens' elite and that a part of the citizens will there view them as "collaborators".

A certain division of roles developed between the "Verein SO 36" and the "Burgerinitiative SO 36" (citizen-protest group), which was formed by a group of oppositional citizens in the Project Commission. The citizen protest group edits a neighbourhood newspaper and tries to mobilize the residents especially by direct action. It remains in firm distance towards any cooperation with the administration, supports various forms of self-aid and uses manifestations, leaflet-actions and other activities with great publicity to call attention to neighbourhood problems. It hereby often creates the necessary political pressure that the "Verein SO 36" may use in bargaining with the public administration. The "Burgerinitiative SO 36" organized the first occupation of vacated apartments and thus created the term "Instandbesetzung" (squatting), i.e. occupation in order to repair the apartments.

These first squattings in 1979 were the starting point for a wave of further urban squatting actions (up to now about 150 apartment buildings). The protest opposed the fact that in spite of the housing shortage inexpensive apartments in older buildings were empty and deteriorating. The vacancy of apartments develops on the one hand through hasty and uncoordinated displacement of tenants, e.g. in the case of high standard modernization or of tearing down and constructing a new building. On the other, some investors consciously aim at destroying part of the building and subsequently tearing it down in order to erect more profitable new houses with public funds. The squatters oppose such ventures because they entail drastic increases in rent.

The criticism of insufficient maintenance of the apartment buildings of too expensive projects and of socially insensitive renewal procedures has been shared by broad parts of the population in the neighbourhood. The development to violent actions originated from a minority of the involved squatters. The eviction of squatters from some of the occupied buildings by the police has further boosted this process. Distrust between squatters and state officials has been increased by these actions and negotiations for a peaceful solution rendered more difficult. Due to the increasing political pressure the Senate of Berlin decided at the beginning of 1981 on a number of emergency actions, which changed previous urban renewal policies.

A comprehensive public repair program for apartment buildings was created especially to make vacated houses again habitable. The funding of housing rehabilitation by tenants was started. The government offered organizational and financial assistance to self-aid projects for juveniles. At the same time negotiations began on signing contracts of utilization with the squatters and on the take-over of occupied houses by trust companies and foundations. These proposals should secure that the squatters may stay in most of the houses and that they may shape their housing and living conditions autonomously. The further development of the issue is at present not foreseeable. Above all it is necessary to re-establish the broken-off negotiations.

## SUMMARIZING CONCLUSIONS

The present experiences can briefly be summarized with the following conclusions:

(1) In a deteriorating neighbourhood a stable and active citizens' group with growing expertise arises which, in the process of a dialogue with the administration and experts, is able to articulate and to successfully enforce its perspectives to the renovation of its living quarter. The most important precondition for success is a process-like development out of and an enduring support from the social and political activities in the area.

(2) During the process of participation an increasing circle of citizens can be reached, who usually are totally excluded from the procedure of urban renewal. The active participation of migrant workers remains a specially unsolved problem. The involvement of community organizers and social planners contributes to substantial expansion in participation.

(3) The administrative experts, planners and local politicians learn from the dialogue with citizens to take arguments of the citizens seriously, not to force upon them prefabricated planning concepts and to achieve as much as possible a consensus. The transfer of politically accepted decision-making competences to the mixed committee of citizens and administrators animates the citizens' interest to participate and stimulate their identification with the neighbourhood.

(4) The take-over of implementation tasks (tenants' counselling) by the citizens' association, the offer to promote self-aid projects and the decision-making power of tenants in case of their own apartment house strengthen the feeling of social responsibility for the development of their living quarter. The self-aid potential of the squatters could be included in this process, if they are to be successfully integrated in a process of communication with the quarter's population.

(5) More than ever the administration has to be willing to renounce or to flexibly implement big comprehensive city plans. Decentral strategies, which are developed in a dialogue with the citizens in the neighbourhood, assure a step-by-step and sensitive renaissance without effects of displacement. This kind of renovation allows a differentiated offer of detailed instruments and programs of public funding, which has to be coordinated in order to fit the single case.

(6) The experiences, which are presented in this paper, and especially the example of the "Strategien fur Kreuzberg", are the results of a long and conflict stricken process. A model of citizen participation, which has been developed in one neighbourhood, is not necessarily transferrable to another area.

The basic experience which has been gained, can surely be put into practice in multifold manners. Active citizen participation at the neighbourhood level can, in any case, meaningfully complement representative democracy.

## REFERENCES


Bottcher, Lutz u.a., "Strategien fur Kreuzberg". Bericht der Vorprufergruppe uber den Wettbewerb, in : Arch+, H. 37, 1978, S. 63f

Borghorst, Hermann u.a., Berliner Stadterneuerung: Erfolge und MiBerfolge der ZIP-Modernisierung, Projektbericht, Berlin 1981.

Bundesminister fur Raumordnung, Bauwesen und Stadtebau (Hrsg.), Burgerbeteiligung bei der Stadterneuerung. Beispiel: Strategien fur Kreuzberg. Bearbeitung: Volker von Tiedemann u.a., Bonn 1980.

Kodolitsch, Paul von, Schulz zur Wiesch, Jochen, Zur Erfolgskontrolle kommunaler Beteiligungsverfahren, Wettbewerb "Strategien fur Kreuzberg", in: Archiv fur Kommunalwis- senschaft, 1979, S. 26f

Senator fur Bau- und Wohnungswesen (Hrsg.), Stadtteilentwicklung. in Berlin Kreuzberg SO 36 (Strategiengebiet) 1977-1981, Berlin 1981

Senator fur Bau- und Wohnungswesen (Hrsg.), Strategien fur Kreuzberg - Verfahren und Projektergebnisse, Berlin 1979.

FIFTEEN

K. S. O. Beavon and C. M. Rogerson

# ASPECTS OF HAWKING IN THE JOHANNESBURG CENTRAL BUSINESS DISTRICT

## INTRODUCTION

In common with the situation in many Third World cities there occur a broad spectrum of street occupations in the latter-day South African city. The 'pavement people' of South Africa engage variously in a range of low-income earning activities which span retail distribution, production, transportation, begging and crime. Amongst an array of work activities which are conducted off the pavements are included the vending lof fruit, vegetables and flowers, street barbering, shoe-shining, hustling and prostitution. These precarious income generating niches have been recognized and recorded in many contemporary South African cities. Nevertheless, geographical studies largely have eschewed this significant facet of the national urban milieu (Rogerson and Beavon, 1980; Beavon and Rogerson, 1981). Street occupations are not, however, a new phenomenon in the fabric of South Africa's cities. Indeed, it has been shown elsewhere (Beavon and Rogerson, 1980; Beavon, 1981) that these activities have constituted ever-present features of the local urban environment.

It is the purport of this paper to focus attention upon one component of the many and varied street occupations that presently are manifest in the South African city. More specifically the objective here is to delineate the characteristics and conditions of existence of the street hawkers who ply their trade in the downtown or Central Business District (C.B.D.) of Johannesburg. This investigation constitutes, therefore, a contribution towards that expanding area of geographical study pioneered among others by Bromley (1978a, 1978b, 1978c, 1981; Bromley and Gerry, 1979), McGee (1971, 1974a, 1974b, 1976, 1978) and Santos (1976, 1979) which seeks to explicate the workings and conditions of the 'informal sector' or, more correctly, 'the casual poor'. Not surprisingly, in the context of the racial structuring of South Africa's 'forced-labour' economy (Legassick, 1977) almost all the participants in street occupations are members of the country's Black subordinate race groupings. It is an aspect of their daily struggles for survival amid the constraints of the apartheid economy that attention is centred here. In examining a street occupation such as hawking it is important to appreciate that the 'entrepreneurship' of these people is contingent upon their social conditions of existence under apartheid (Beavon and Rogerson, 1982). The survival strategy of working on the streets of South Africa is one which is essentially a replacement for an unavailable or perhaps inadequate wage income.

## A PROFILE OF JOHANNESBURG'S HAWKERS

The socio-economic characteristics of the people who hawk for their livelihood on the streets of Johannesburg were determined through a questionnaire survey administered during 1979-80. The survey provides the basis for detailing the characteristics of the hawker community operating in the city's Central Business District. The data collected in the study details not only the variety of goods sold but also yields insights into the varied backgrounds, incomes, educational levels and earning capacities of hawkers.

At the time of the survey there were between 200 and 250 hawkers operating on a regular basis in the central areas of Johannesburg. Excluded from this total are the community of licensed newspaper vendors who were not included the framework of the survey. Of the hawker community, a total of one hundred sellers were approached for interview. This yielded a set of 72 questionnaires that reflected successful interviews. It is on the basis of this sample of hawkers that the following profile of the city's hawker population is presented (Table 15.1).

TABLE 15.1

**Level of Education**

| | % | | % |
|---|---|---|---|
| None | 20.8 | Std. 7 - Std. 9 | 7.0 |
| Sub. A - Std. 3 | 32.0 | Matric | 1.4 |
| Std. 4 - Std. 6 | 38.9 | Post-Matric | 0 |

In the light of the discriminatory nature of the apartheid

system, it is perhaps not surprising that the survey revealed almost half of the hawkers of the Johannesburg Central Business District as effectively illiterate (Table 15.1). Schooling in South Africa is based on two years of pre-primary education (Substandards A and B), followed by five years of primary education (Standards 1 to 5) and five years of secondary schooling (Standards 6 to 10) the last year being the matriculation year. Given the fact that the quality of education among the Black population is poor, and that in the White sector attendance at school is compulsory until age 16 (usually the age of Standard 8 pupils) then it is reasonable to assume that persons with less than a Standard 4 qualification are essentially illiterate. More than fifty per cent of the hawkers fall into this category. Clearly such persons would find it difficult to proceed to relatively high paid job positions in the industrial sector. Indeed it became apparent during the interviews that many hawkers had opted for hawking because it offered them a better opportunity of earning money than was the case in other

TABLE 15.2

**Previous Occupations**

| | % | | % |
|---|---|---|---|
| Unemployed or Housewife | 37.5 | Scullery hand | 2.8 |
| Factory worker | 19.4 | Ticket collector | 2.8 |
| Domestic servant | 15.3 | Market labourer | 1.4 |
| Shop assistant | 8.3 | Plumber's assistant | 1.4 |
| Waiter | 5.6 | Cleaner | 1.4 |
| Driver | 2.8 | Hotel assistant | 1.4 |

TABLE 15.3

**Numbor of Years In Hawking**

| | % | | % |
|---|---|---|---|
| Up to 1 year | 8.3 | 11 - 15 years | 9.8 |
| 2 - 5 years | 33.3 | 16 - 20 years | 12.6 |
| 6 - 10 years | 25.0 | 21 years or longer | 11.2 |

unskilled occupations. This is borne out by the data in Table 15.2 detailing their previous occupations.

It was also apparent that hawking is not a transient occupation as almost sixty per cent of those engaged in hawking had been so engaged for more than five years (Table 15.3). The age structure (Table 15.4) tends to corroborate the previous finding with a remarkably consistent percentage of hawkers in the various ten-year age groups from 21 to 60. This

TABLE 15.4

**Age of Hawkers**

| | % | | % |
|---|---|---|---|
| 16 and under | 2.8 | 41 - 50 | 16.7 |
| 17 - 20 | 2.8 | 51 - 60 | 19.4 |
| 21 - 30 | 26.4 | 61 - 70 | 2.8 |
| 31 - 40 | 27.8 | 71 - 80 | 1.4 |

appears to support the notion that once a person has decided to become, or has been forced through circumstances to become, a hawker then such a person is likely to remain a hawker. Indeed only 16.4 per cent of the hawkers indicated that they would prefer a wage paid job. But the extent to which the choice is a free one is a moot point. From the data on previous employment (Table 15.2) it is clear that whereas hawkers have come from a wide range of previous job experiences the largest single group had not previously been gainfully employed. It appeared that hawking provided the means to ready cash at the same time providing security of such access and removing the previous threats of dismissal if due to recurrent illness or family problems a person was unable to report for work.

Details of the earnings by hawkers are set out in Table 15.5. It is important to note that many hawkers were reluctant to talk too frankly about this aspect of daily life on the streets. As such the question put to them was itself somewhat ambiguous. It asked simply, "What do you make per day?" The data so collected was computed to represent the average earnings per day for any day worked and from that to calculate average earnings per week. Bearing in mind that the data so collected has yielded what amounts to turnover figures, some indication of the costs incurred by the respondents must also be considered if any feel for the true financial gains of hawking is

TABLE 15.5

**Earnings From Hawking**

(a) Per Day :

Minimum R2.20; Maximum R82.28; Average R17.45

| | % | | % |
|---|---|---|---|
| Less than R 5.00 | 11.1 | R15.01 - R20.00 | 16.7 |
| R 5.01 - R10.00 | 25.0 | R20.01 - R30.00 | 19.4 |
| R10.01 - R15.00 | 16.7 | R30.01 or more | 11.1 |

(b) Per Week

Minimum R12.85; Average R109.67

to be obtained. A major drain on financial resources is the cost of getting to a 'pitch' with the merchandise. Computed figures are shown in Table 15.6. In addition the hawker faces the costs of purchasing his goods and from a limited set of data it has been possible to estimate the average cost at R66 per week. The implication is that incomes, or net earnings, from

TABLE 15.6

**Transport Costs For Hawker (Including Goods) Home To Work Only Per Day**

| | % | | % |
|---|---|---|---|
| Nil | 8.3 | R2.01 - R3.00 | 8.3 |
| Less than R1.00 | 43.0 | R3.01 - R4.00 | 9.7 |
| R1.01 - R2.00 | 15.3 | R4.00 or more | 15.3 |

Average cost per week of those that incur costs : R24.45

TABLE 15.7

**Size of Hawker's Household**

| | % | | % |
|---|---|---|---|
| Single | 8.3 | 7 - 9 persons | 20.0 |
| 2 - 3 persons | 18.1 | 10 - 12 persons | 7.0 |
| 4 - 6 persons | 45.9 | | |

hawking are meagre. This becomes even more clear when the size of household is considered as set out in Table 15.7.

Given the fact that hawking in central Johannesburg is mainly confined to parts of the CBD periphery adjacent to mass transport termini and the inner industrial zone, it is not surprising that most hawking is related to the sale of food items. It appears that many of the workers entering the city early in the morning buy items of food, frequently items of fruit, in lieu of a prepared breakfast or lunch. The other major categories of goods sold by hawkers are generally small fancy goods, items of clothing such as hats and scarves, as well as cosmetic items such as toilet soap, deodorants and toothpaste (Table 15.8).

TABLE 15.8

**Types of Hawker Business (Excluding That Conducted At 'Fixed Stands')**

| | % | | % |
|---|---|---|---|
| Fruit | 28.8 | Clothing | 11.4 |
| Vegetables | 15.9 | Leather goods | 5.3 |
| Cooked meat | 0.8 | Jewellery | 6.1 |
| Corn on the cob uncooked | 3.8 | Cosmetics | 14.4 |
| Corn on the cob toasted | 6.1 | Household items | 1.5 |
| Porridge | 0.8 | Other goods | 4.5 |
| Other cooked food | 0.8 | | |

It is the people presented in the above profile who were wont to ply their trade on the pavements of the city of Johannesburg.

## STREET HAWKING IN JOHANNESBURG

The underdevelopment of the street occupations in the apartheid city relative to the proliferation of similar occupations that have been observed in cities such as Hong Kong (McGee 1974a, McGee and Yeung, 1977), Cali (Bromley, 1978b, 1978c), and Nairobi (Westley, 1977) is inseparable from the several constraints that face the aspirant Black pavement trader. These constraints determine not only the geography of street trading in the central areas of Johannesburg but also assist in an understanding of the persistent poverty of the vast majority of the hawkers.

In the discussion that follows attention will be drawn to those constraints that create what is known as the 'defended space' of downtown Johannesburg, the policing of which in turn gives rise to certain spatial characteristics of the hawking scene.

A number of constraints in the form of national laws, provincial ordinances, and municipal by-laws together with the licensing procedures all serve to severely restrict legal hawking to a relatively small group of the casual poor. Indeed it can be argued that the very nature of the constraints on this income earning niche are in fact one of the causes for the prominence, from time to time, of large numbers of hawkers who find themselves through circumstances operating in defiance of the constraints and hence 'illegally'. As already evidenced in the earlier sections the majority of persons forced into the ranks of casual poor are Black. Consideration should therefore be given first to the role of national laws that affect not only hawking in Johannesburg but hawking activities in all the major cities and towns of South Africa.

## National Controls

In South Africa access to land and markets, or more exactly in the present context lack of access, is primarily exercised through the Group Areas Act (No. 36 of 1966). This legislation prevents Blacks from either buying land, owning businesses, or trading within a White Group Area. As the business districts of South African towns and cities are almost without fail part of a White Group Area the legislation not only prevents Blacks from being trader-owners within such areas, but naturally will also prevent the possible evolution of an enterprising hawker business into a retail business within fixed premises that can be owned by the hawker.

Whereas the Group Areas Act has an indirect effect on Black hawkers it is the Black (Urban Areas) Consolidation Act (No. 25 of 1945) that affects hawkers as such more directly. In the case of Black hawkers in Johannesburg the Act requires that they obtain the permission of the West Rand Administration Board (WRAB) in order to trade in the downtown area of the city. The Board in turn is required to be empowered by the Minister of Co-operation and Development to grant the permission. Only when such permission has been granted that application can be made to the local authority, in this case the Johannesburg municipality, for a trading licence.

## Municipal Controls

Application to the Johannesburg City Council for a trading licence must be accompanied by a fee of between R1 and R10 depending on the nature of the goods to be sold and how they will be sold. Before the licence can be granted the application is scrutinized by various municipal departments including Health, Traffic, and Planning. An objection from any one of these departments could result in the rejection of the application. Furthermore at the discretion of the Licensing Board the prospective hawker may be required to advertise his intentions to trade thr.ugh the medium of at least two newspapers in both official languages—English and Afrikaans. The advertisement will solicit objections to the intentions of the hawker. The total cost of the procedure sketched above including the cost of the licence if it is granted varies between R100 and R130. Even armed with a licence to trade as a hawker the individual seller may yet be thwarted by the regulations that govern street trading in the central area of Johannesburg.

## The Defended Space of Johannesburg

As is the case in many Third World cities Johannesburg has a variety of additional legal instruments and enforcement agencies that are designed and empowered to keep hawkers out of the prestigious areas of the city. In this respect the central business area of Johannesburg becomes the defended space of the city, a term that has been used by Bromley (1978b, 1978c). The defended space of Johannesburg is defined in the licencing and business control laws that are promulgated under the provincial authority of the Transvaal and is officially termed "the restricted area' of the city (Fig. 15.1). Within this defended space both national and local authority enforcement agencies are empowered to operate the controls on hawking activities. Furthermore the activities of hawkers, even those in possession on a license, are severely restricted. For example, the hawker who has successfully negotiated the maze of procedures already detailed and has obtained a licence finds that hawking is permitted only before 7 a.m. and after 6 p.m. in the restricted area. Furthermore, within this defended space there are defined 'restricted streets' where trading is prohibited between 7 a.m. and 9 p.m. on any Saturday. In addition on Christmas Eve and New Year's Eve, and on the Saturday preceding such days if they should fall on a Sunday, the prohibited hours of trading throughout the restricted area run from 7 a.m. to midnight! Consequently it is not surprising to find that even licensed hawkers frequently operate 'illegally' in the restricted area notwithstanding that they expose themselves to arrest, confiscation of their goods and fines of R100.

Control of the hawking activities in the defended space of the city is further complicated by the designation of 'fixed stands' and by invoking the municipal 'move-on' regulations in all

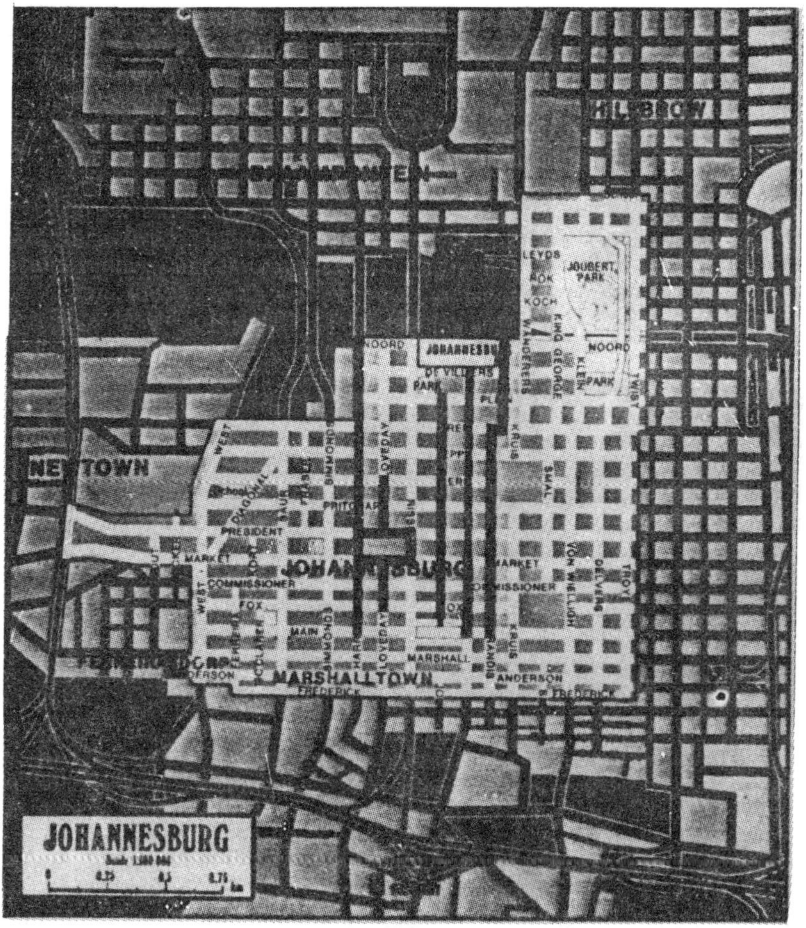


other areas. These latter regulations require the hawker to move, with his goods and his stall, a distance of at least 25 metres every twenty minutes. They also preclude the hawker from operating at any site so vacated within the next 24 hours. These legislative controls are the prime factors in shaping the geography of hawking in downtown Johannesburg.

## The Geography of Hawking in the CBD

Although hawking sites are widespread in the city the main body of hawkers in Johannesburg tend to cling to the fringes of the restricted area (see Fig. 15.2). It is here that the major termini of the railway system that links the CBD with the teeming Black townships such as Soweto, Alexandra, and Tembisa are located. In addition the bus stations and mini-bus-taxis that provide additional transport to and from the city are also found on the edge of the downtown area; more particularly along the northeastern, northwestern, southeastern and southwestern corners. With the exception of the Diagonal Street area (on the northwest side of the restricted area) the hawking activities are largely dominated by Blacks from the townships who sell their goods from pavement displays, off the tailgates of trucks and stationwagons or from small stalls made out of packing cases. The peak business periods are associated with those times

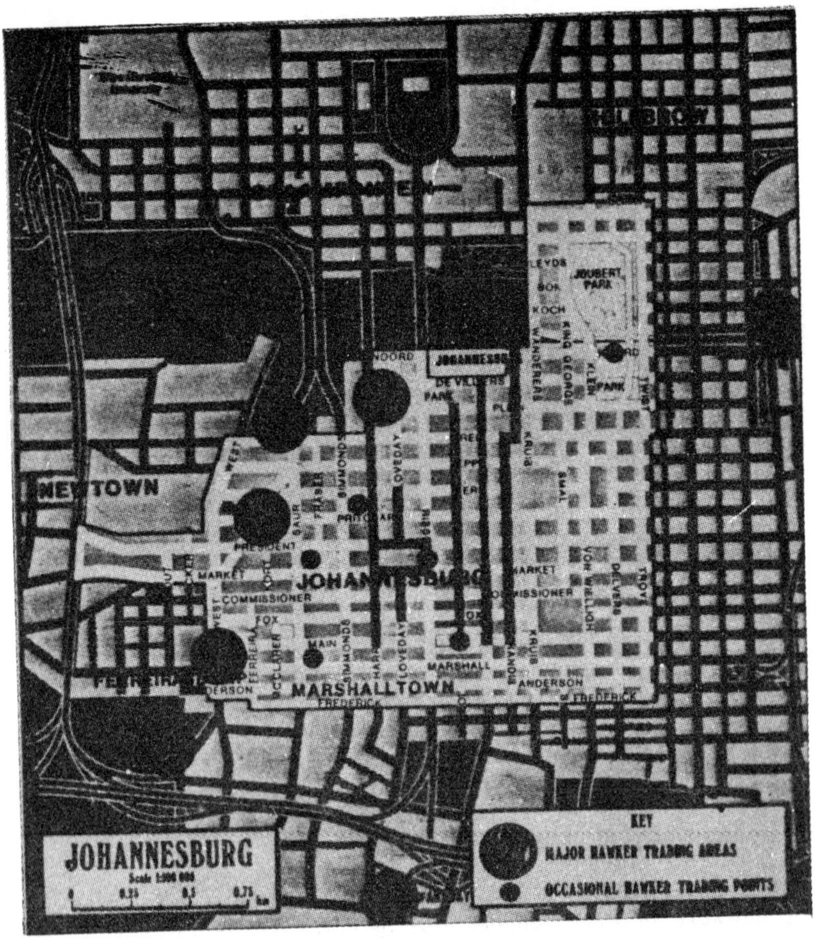

of the day when the thousands upon thousands of Black workers pour into the 'white' city from their segregated and distant residential areas. The early rising time and the rush for a place in the trains, buses and taxis contribute to the demand for the small snack items of fruit and other foodstuffs on display at the termini.

In the vicinity of Diagonal Street (cf. Fig. 15.1) there has for years been a resident Indian community, that traded from small shops, with goods spilling out onto the pavements. This style of trading gave to the area a distinctive air of a bazaar. Mingling with the permanent traders but operating from barrows parked in the gutter have been the Indian hawkers. Here too the sale of fruit and foodstuffs was characteristic but there was also a great variety of other items offered for sale by the hawkers of which small items of clothing were the most noticeable. Regrettably this is no longer the case. The relocation of the Johannesburg Stock Exchange from Hollard Street in the heart of the C.B.D. to Diagonal Street has seen the demise not only of the Indian hawkers of the area but of much of the bazaar economy of the street. The ruthless enforcement of the regulations, particularly the 'move-on' regulation has been the instrument by which the hawkers have been excised from the vicinity of the Stock Exchange.

It is the 'itinerant' hawker or more particularly the hawker who has not observed the 'move-on' regulations that has been the main target of officialdom. Those pavement traders that operate from the 'fixed stands' are far less harassed. An examination of Figures 15.3 and 15.4 shows that sites for a variety of pavement occupations are provided by the city authorities. In practice, however, it is only the sellers of flowers, vegetables and fruits that occur in any numbers (Tomaselli, 1981). Examination of the demand for sites has shown that the supply of 'fixed stands' for the sale of flowers in particular is far too low.

The 'fixed stands' in general may be hired from the Council for the specific designation they have given to the site. In the case of only a few of the flower-selling points does the Council rent a structure as well as the site. More usually the 'stand' is erected by the tenant. Notwithstanding the immunity a 'fixed stand' affords from the 'move-on' regulations the tenants face a different set of problems. In the first instance the number of sites is limited, and has been limited for some 27 years. Figure 15.3 shows the 'freezing' in the number and distribution of 'fixed stands' in central Johannesburg for the period 1953-1966, a period of tremendous growth in the city's population. During

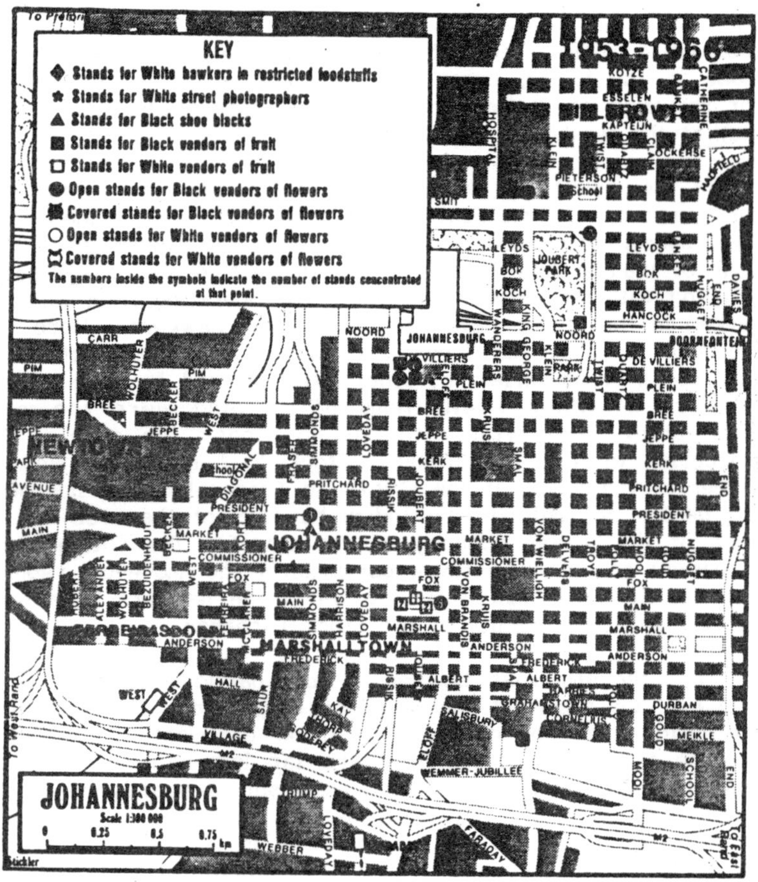


the period 1966–1980 (Fig. 15.4) a further 29 new stands were established. All of these additional stands, however, were for the use of White rather than Black hawkers. Indeed, the absurdities of allotting an increased number of stands for Whites is illustrated by the fact that there are a total of 16 stands available for White street photographers and 6 stands for White shoe-blacks, two categories of street operators that have long since disappeared from the streets of Johannesburg (Beavon and Rogerson, 1980). For the Black street vendors, the period 1966–1980 has been one of traumatic adjustment, occasioned by a net reduction in the number of fixed stands allocated to them by the Council. This reduction in the allocated stands occurred

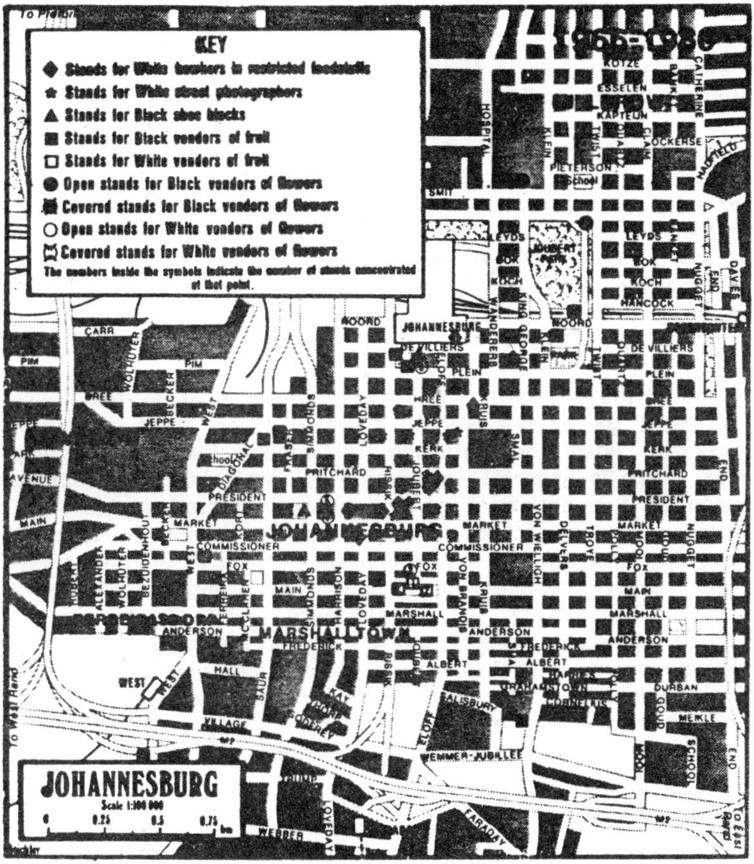


notwithstanding a great demand from Black hawkers for licensed fixed stands (Beavon and Rogerson, 1982). The decline in allotted stands available to Black or Indian tenants has been most strongly felt in the sector of flower selling in which the number of available stalls has been halved. Inevitably, this dramatic reduction of Black and Indian tenant flower stalls has heightened the competition for the remaining stalls. The burning issue is whether the stalls that are currently allocated on an annual basis should be allocated on the basis of priority of occupation, by lot, or by tender. All three schemes have been attempted by the Council and caused dissatisfaction of one type or another. Certainly the tender system whereby an amount of several thousand rands appeared necessary to acquire the central site near the City Hall has given rise to most cause for concern. The tender money allowing the tenant merely a right to acquire the use of the site for a year but in no way contributing to the cost of the licence or the monthly rental.

## CONCLUSION

There is a need for the greater acceptance of a 'grassroots' (McGee, 1974b) perspective on urban geography in order to encourage further investigations into the several activities captured by the 'informal sector' rubric. In particular, the adoption of such a perspective is imperative for examination of urbanization processes in the Third World.

The cities of South Africa manifest several of the characteristics of the archetypal Third World city. More specifically, in common with the situation throughout the underdeveloped world, there is presently occurring in South Africa a rapid expansion in the activities of the urban 'informal sector'. The present paper sought to offer a micro-level case study of life in the informal sector under apartheid through an investigation of the hawker community operating in the Central Business District of Johannesburg. The preliminary findings were presented of a survey which reveals aspects of the characteristics, modes of existence, life-conditions and spatial behaviour of the city's street hawkers. The current story of the hawkers of central Johannesburg is one of a struggle for continuing existence in the face of petty municipal regulations and the burdens of apartheid legislation.

## ACKNOWLEDGEMENTS

The authors are grateful to Mr. P. Stickler of the Geography Department at the University of the Witwatersrand for the preparation of the diagrams. The co-operation of the Town Planning Department of Johannesburg in providing some of the raw data is acknowledged. Financial assistance has been provided by the Human Sciences Research Council, Pretoria.

## REFERENCES

Beavon, K. S. O., From hypermarkets to hawkers : changing foci of concern for human geography. **Environmental Studies**, Occasional Paper No.23, Department of Geography and Environmental Studies, University of the Witwatersrand, Johannesburg, 1981.

Beavon, K. S. O. and Rogerson, C. M., The persistence of the casual poor in Johannesburg, **Contree** 7, 1980, 15-21.

Beavon, K. S. O. and Rogerson, C. M., Trekking on : recent trends in the Human Geography of Southern Africa, **Progress in Human Geography** 5, 1981, 159-189.

Beavon, K. S. O. and Rogerson, C. M., The 'informal sector' of the apartheid city: the pavement people of Johannesburg, in Smith, D M.(ed.), **Living Under Apartheid,** Allen and Unwin, London, 1982.

Bromley, R., Introduction - the urban informal sector; why is it worth discussing? **World Development** 6, 1978a, 1033-1039.

Bromley, R., Organization, regulation and exploitation in the socalled 'urban informal sector': the street traders of Cali, Colombia, **World Development,** 6, 1978b, 1161-1171.

Bromley, R., The locational behaviour of Colombian urban street traders: observations and hypotheses, in Denevan, W.M. (ed.) **The Role of Geographical Research in Latin America,** Conference of Latin American Geographers, Muncie, Indiana, Publication No. 7, 1978c, 41-51.

Bromley, R., Working in the streets: survival strategy, necessity or unavoidable evil?, in Gilbert A., Hardoy, J. and Ramirez, R. (eds.), **Urbanization in Contemporary Latin America,** John Wiley, Chichester and New York, 1981.

Bromley, R. and Gerry, C. (eds.), **Casual Work and Poverty inThird World Cities,** John Wiley, Chichester and New York, 1979.

Legassick, M., Gold, agriculture and secondary industry in South Africa: from periphery to sub-metropole as a forced labour system, in Palmer, R. and Parsons, N. (eds.), **The Roots of Rural Poverty in Central and Southern Africa,** University of California Press, Berkeley, 1977, 175-200.

McGee, T. G., **The Urbanization Process in the Third World,** Bell, London, 1971.

McGee, T. G., **Hawkers in Hong Kong: A Study of Policy and Planning in the Third World City,** University of Hong Kong, Centre for Asian Studies, Hong Kong, 1974a.

McGee, T. G., In praise of tradition : towards a geography of anti-development, **Antipode** 6(3), 1974b, 30-47.

McGee, T. G., The persistence of the proto-proletariat: occupational structures and planning the future of Third World cities, **Progress in Geography,** 9, 1976, 1-38.

McGee, T. G., An invitation to the 'ball': dress formal or informal? in Rimmer, P. J., Drakakis-Smith, D. W., and McGee, T. G. (eds.), **Food, Shelter and Transport in Southeast Asia and the Pacific,** The Australian National University, Canberra, 1978, 3-27.

Rogerson, C. M. and Beavon, K. S. O., The awakening of 'informal sector' studies in Southern Africa, **South African Geographical Journal** 62, 1980, 175-190.

Santos, M., Economic development and urbanization in underdeveloped countries: the two sub-systems of the urban economy, **Journal of the Geographical Association of Tanzania,** 14, 1976, 6-36.

Santos, M., **The Shared Space : The Two Circuits of the Urban Economy in Underdeveloped Countries,** Methuen, London, 1979.

Tomaselli, R.E., Johannesburg Indian flower sellers: a history of people on the street. Unpublished paper read at the **History Workshop 1981,** University of the Witwatersrand, Johannesburg, 1981.

Westley, S. B. (ed.), **The Informal Sector in Kenya,** University of Nairobi, Institute for Development Studies, Occasional Paper No. 25, 1977.

SIXTEEN

Farhat Gulzar

# SLUMIFICATION IN LAHORE

In the growing cities of Pakistan, millions of people are settling on public and private land and have raised temporary haphazard structures thereon popularly known as 'Slums'. Lahore is one of the fastest growing cities in Pakistan and is the Provincial centre of the Punjab. It received influx of population during Independence in 1947 and its total population reached 7,17,400. It increased to 8,49,476 in 1951 and 12,96,477 in 1961. By the year 1972 it rose to 21,69,742 and to 29,22,000 by 1981. Thus between 1951-1961 the total growth percentage was 62.65, between 1961-1972 it was 67.44 and between 1972-1981 it was 34.65. According to the official forecast, by the year 1991 the total population will reach 4,967,300 and by 2001, to 6,939,500. This increase in the population and addition of inhabitants will require at least 15,000 to 20,000 households per year.

The increasing numbers of poeple who have taken up residence in Lahore and the large-scale urbanization that has gained momentum due to the multifunctional character of the city has created serious problems in respect of urban facilities but the housing is worst affected. The migration of rural population to the city is due to the pull exerted by higher average income and job opportunities, better housing and health conditions, better education for their children and the accelerated pace of urbanization is faced with an acute shortage of housing and other civic amenities in the city. A large portion of the population which falls in the low-income bracket has no alternative but to live in improvised shelters which are devoid of even minimal civic facilities. These areas are known as slums which are scattered all over the city, and more or less resemble villages (Fig. 16.1).

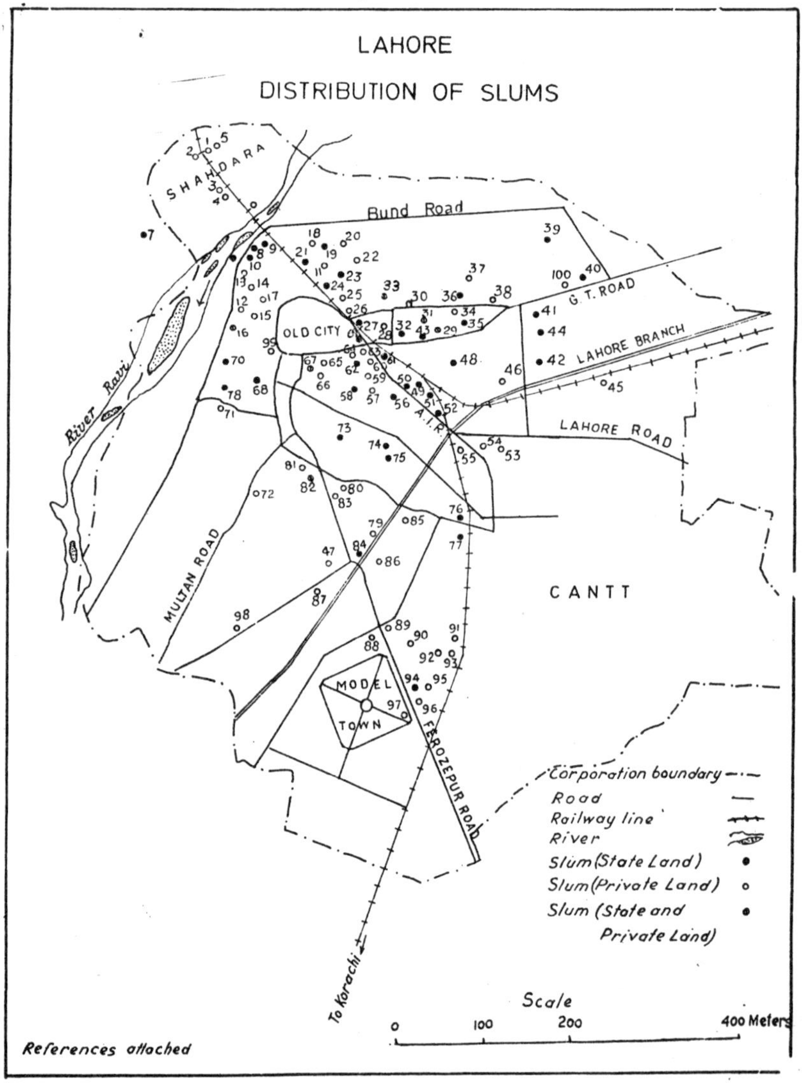
LAHORE
DISTRIBUTION OF SLUMS
SHAHDARA
Bund Road
River Ravi
OLD CITY
G.T. ROAD
LAHORE BRANCH
LAHORE ROAD
A.I.R.
MULTAN ROAD
CANTT
MODEL TOWN
FEROZEPUR ROAD
To Karachi
Corporation boundary
Road
Railway line
River
Slum (State Land)
Slum (Private Land)
Slum (State and Private Land)
Scale
0
100
200
400 Meters
References attached

**References to Figure 16.1**

1. Barkat People Colony
2. Islampura
3. Gharib Nagar Shahdra
4. Mill Area Shahdra
5. Piplan Wali Shahdra
6. Maqbra More
7. Bhutto Colony Tariq Abad
8. Albadar Colony
9. Siddiqi Colony
10. Alipur
11. Alipura
12. Mali Pura
13. Dhoban Pura
14. Feroze Pura
15. Amin Pura
16. Karim Pura
17. Samadi Ganga. Ram
18. Sher Singh Road
19. Data Nagar
20. Chah Matan Wala
21. Islampura Peco
22. Karim Nagar
23. Sheikhabad
24. Iqbal Park
25. Basti Hakim
26. Farooq Ganj
27. Iqbal Pura
28. Jhugian Faiz Bagh
29. Shuja Colony
30. Jamil Road
31. Katri Sheikh Mubarik
32. Jalar Sain Jewan
33. Marzi Pura
34. Mohammad Abad
35. Begum Pura
36. Gujjar Pura
37. Haji Pura
38. Yunus Pura
39. New Crole
40. Tanvir Abad
41. Mujahid Colony
42. Isa Abad
43. Sansi Quarter
44. Daras Barey Mian
45. Mohammad Pura
46. Phatak No. 7
47. Naqsha Bus Stop
48. Baja Line
49. Newan Toyya
50. Bringza Quarters
51. Jhugian Mir Allah Ditta
52. Gondi Pir
53. Dharampura
54. Basti Bhaley Masih
55. Mian Mir Colony
56. Bibi Pak Daman
57. Gari Shahu Scheme
58. Mela Ram Park
59. Charap Pura
60. Aqab Khaiyban Hotel
61. Jhugian Railway Station
62. Choor Shah Bhangi
63. Pathi Ground
64. Mayo Hospital Area
65. Mohalla Gwalan
66. Uchi Tibbi Gwalmandi
67. Habibia Colony
68. Liaqatabad
69. Katchu Pura
70. Ravi Town
71. People Colony
72. Janak Nagar
73. Kacha Mason Road
74. Patiala House
75. Shah Shamas Qari
76. Basti Saidan Shah
77. Siraj Colony (Qurab Lines)
78. Musafar Gali
79. Mental Hospital Area
80. Ahata Mool Chand
81. Chaudhri Colony
82. Chah Qurab Wala
83. Shah Jamal
84. Fazlia Colony
85. Canal Park
86. Jhugian F. C. College
87. Mian Wahdat Road
88. PRIB Garden Town
89. St.Mary Colony
90. Mustafabad
91. Guru Mangat
92. Theh Zaildaran

93. Ara Chanan Din
94. Nasir Abad
95. Gopal Nagar
96. Henry K.
97. China Hospital
98. Iqbal Town
99. Name not available
100. Name not available

Most of the slums date back to 1947 when influx of immigrants from India to Pakistan took place. Due to high demand for housing, squatting became prevalent on open lands of the city, the badly hit was the Government land. Rapid urbanization during the past 35 years further aggravated the problem. The quality of housing material and technology used for construction depends largely on the age of the settlement. These settlements are of varying size and material. The slums are sometimes located in areas invaded by floods and are often washed away during heavy rains. The major concentration of the slums is in the central part of the city. The older slum dwellings are made up of mud or brick walls and clay tiles or galvanized iron roofs. Plot sizes range from 200 sq. ft to 1,500 sq. ft. The densities are high and there are almost no street patterns or open spaces. In these 100 slum areas spread out within the limits of the Lahore city (Fig. 16.1) live 600,000 persons in 35,000 households. This makes up about 15 per cent of the total population of Lahore. Of the total numbers, 45 slums are situated on state land and 43 are on both state and private land. Fifteen areas, mostly on state land, have been ordered for shifting whereas the balance 85 are to be regularized as per decision of the Government.

As is evident from Fig. 16.1 most of the slum areas are located close to one another around the old city and are widely distributed over other parts of the city. In almost every instance the areas in which these communities are located had extremely poor drainage conditions and were subjected to severe flooding during the rainy season. This, of course, aggravates the already poor sanitation conditions since toilet facilities and proper methods of garbage disposal were absent or inadequate in all areas. One of the principal community needs in these areas is improved drainage and sanitation conditions. The major community need is more public faucets from which drinking and cooking water could be obtained. In general, conditions in a few of these areas can be described as deplorable and in all the areas at least as poor. This is not to say that constructive elements are poor in these areas but the fact is that the great majority of the people are better off now than before and that they do not want to leave their present communities signifies that one cannot simply evaluate the slum areas on the basis of such characteristics as housing conditions and physical site characteristics.

Preliminary analysis of reasons for migration of the low-income groups interviewed mostly indicates these to be pull-oriented, i.e. most of the slum inhabitants arrived with the idea that employment opportunities were easily available or they knew some-one in the city prior to their arrival. Push factors are of great importance, but the number of immigrants that entered the city in 1947 during independence is tremendous.

Another common characteristic of the majority of the slum community interviewed is that the place of employment and of residence are highly correlated. Thus, in formulation relocation plans for slums the Government should consider this factor carefully. The desire of most of the slum community residents is not to move their present community of residence to other parts of the city. A number of reasons account for this and one of the most important is that their jobs are presently accessible.

Slums are even found in the most sophisticated areas of the city like Gulberg, Civil Lines, Shadman, etc. The increase in the number of slums is usually imperceptible over a short period. But given proper chance they go on increasing with gradual appearance of activity by way of personal services and retail business to develop them into regular neighbourhoods.

The size of the slum varies with the area available for free development. It varies from a small cluster of 65 households in Najaf Colony, Phase II (Table 16.2) almost that of 1,500 households in Davis Road slum area (Table 16.3). The largest population of 7,000 is found in Daras Barey Mian, Phase II (Table 16.1) and Sukh Nehr which also has the largest land area of 500 kanals (Table 16.2). The sizes of slums close to the old city are small whereas they are large in the areas developed after independence. This is due to the non-availability of large vacant tracts of land in the pre-1947 period close to the old city.

List of Remaining Slums

| | | | |
|---|---|---|---|
| 1. | Barkat People Colony | 2. | Piplian Wali Shahdara |
| 3. | Albadar Colony | 4. | Albadar Colony |
| 5. | Siddique Colony | 6. | Mali Pura |
| 7. | Duban Pura | 8. | Ferozepura |
| 9. | Amin Colony | 10. | Karim Park |
| 11. | Sher Singh Road | 12. | Chah Motian Wala |
| 13. | Karam Nagar | 14. | Basti Hakeem Nayar Wasti |
| 15. | Farooq Gunj | 16. | Jhuggian Faiz Bagh |
| 17. | Katri Sheikh Mubari | 18. | Jalal Sian Jewan |

TABLE 16.1

**List of Slums Situated on State Land (Federal Land)**

| Sr. No. | Name of the Abadi | Area K M | Popu-lation | No. of houses | Ownership | Remarks |
|---|---|---|---|---|---|---|
| 1. | Jhuggian Rail-way Station | 24-00 | 1540 | 350 | Railways | In principle the transfer of the land has been agreed upon. |
| 2. | Iqbal Park | 175-00 | 5500 | 800 | " | - do - |
| 3. | Daras Barey Mian Phase I | 251-00 | NA | NA | " | - do - |
| 4. | Majahid Colony | 37-00 | 1200 | NA | " | - do - |
| 5. | Essa Abad | 48-00 | 2400 | 300 | " | - do - |
| 6. | Sansi Quarters Phase-I | 176-00 | NA | NA | " | - do - |
| 7. | Baja Lines | 28-00 | 8500 | 400 | " | - do - |
| 8. | Qurban Lines | 165-00 | 5000 | 550 | " | - do - |
| 9. | Tariq Abad | 42-00 | 1800 | 200 | " | - do - |
| 10. | Datta Nagar | 60-00 | 2500 | NA | " | - do - |
| 11. | Jamil Abad | 42-00 | NA | NA | " | Railway is not prepared to transfer the land. |
| 12. | Sansi Quarters Phase II | 111-00 | NA | NA | " | - do - |

| | | | | | | |
|---|---|---|---|---|---|---|
| 13. | Daras Barey Mian Phase II | 41-00 | 7000 | 900 | " | - do - |
| 14. | Maqbra More | 250-00 | NA | NA | " | Proposed to be shifted. Survey was not carried out. |
| 15. | Samadi Ganga Ram | 52-00 | 1500 | 129 | ETPB | ETPB has transferrred some proprietary rights to the occupants. |
| 16. | Gurudat Bhavan | 40-00 | NA | NA | " | - do - |
| 17. | Manzoor Abad | 94-00 | 3000 | 350 | ETPB/ Private | A portion of land for Park and School has not been handed over to LDA. The Case has been moved to Chairman ETPB for handing over the land. |
| 18. | Kachu Pura | 110-00 | NA | NA | ETPB/ Private | Some proprietary rights have been transferred by ETPB. LDA has no direct concern with it. |
| 19. | Gharib Nagar | 37-00 | 1000 | 150 | Nazul/ Railways | In principle the transfer of the land has been agreed upon. |
| 20. | Teb Zaildran | 300-00 | NA | NA | Civil Aviation Dept. | Land not handed over to LDA |
| | Total | 2083-00 | | | | |
| | | 260 Acres approx. | | | | |

TABLE 16.2

**List of Slums Situated on State Land (Provincial Land)**

| Sr. No. | Name of abadi | Area | Popu-lation | No.of | Ownership houses | Remarks |
|---|---|---|---|---|---|---|
| 1. | Basti Saidan Shah | 225-00 | 8000 | 930 | LDA | |
| 2. | Nasir Abad | 47-00 | 2500 | NA | LDA | |
| 3. | Sheikh Abad | 74-00 | 1200 | 170 | LDA | |
| 4. | Gujjar Pura | 65-00 | 950 | 150 | LMC | In principle the transfer of the land has been agreed upon |
| 5. | Shuja Colony | 195-00 | 1450 | 290 | Nazul/ Private | Proposed to be developed during the current financial year. |
| 6. | Begum Pura | 84-00 | 1900 | NA | Muslim/Auqaf | |
| 7. | Shah Shamas Qari | 33-00 | 2000 | 250 | Muslim/Auqaf | |
| 8. | Choor Shah Bandgi | 42-00 | 1500 | 150 | Muslim/Auqaf | |
| 9. | Mela Ram Park | 29-00 | 900 | 117 | Settlement Department | In principle the transfer of the land has been agreed upon. |
| 10. | New Crole | 48-19 | 2000 | 325 | Settlement/ Muslim Auqaf | |
| 11. | Liaqat Abad | 24-00 | 900 | 140 | Settlement Dept. | In principle the transfer of the land has been agreed upon. |
| 12. | Munafar Gali | 33-12 | 500 | 120 | " | - do - |

| | | | | | |
|---|---|---|---|---|---|
| 13. Patiala House | 74-00 | 1000 | 135 | " | - do - |
| 14. Davis Road | 86-00 | 5000 | 1500 | " | - do - |
| 15. Fazalia Colony | 127-00 | 6000 | 900 | " | - do - |
| 16. Mill Area Shahdara | 107-00 | 2000 | 350 | " | - do - |
| 17. Islampura Shahdara | 392-00 | 6000 | NA | " | - do - |
| 18. Katcha Mason Road | 41-00 | 900 | 150 | " | - do - |
| 19. Mian Mir Colony | 134-09 | NA | NA | Auqaf/ Private Settlement | Proposed to be developed during the current financial year. |
| 20. Najaf Colony Phase I | 73-00 | 1115 | 193 | LDA | |
| 21. Najaf Colony Phase II | 22-00 | 325 | 65 | LDA | - do - |
| 22. Chaudhry Colony | 72-00 | 2000 | 233 | Nazul | - do - |
| 23. Awami Colony | 180-00 | NA | NA | Health (Punjab) | - do - |
| 24. Dharampura | 75-00 | NA | NA | Settlement Dept | |
| 25. Sukh Nehr | 500-00 | 7000 | 1200 | " | |
| 26. Harbanspura | 75-00 | 900 | 160 | " | |

19. Marzi Pura
20. Muhammad Abad
21. Haji Pura
22. Younas Pura
23. Tanvir Abad
24. Muhammad Pura
25. Newan Toya
26. Barganza Quarters
27. Jhuggian Mehr Allah Ditta
28. Gondi Pir
29. Takia Sanaran Ghari Shahu
30. Bibi Pak Daman
31. Chappar Pura
32. Aqab Khabian Hotel
33. Mohallah Gowalian
34. Ucha Tibba
35. Habibia Colony
36. Ravi Town
37. Janak Nagar
38. Ahata Mool Chand
39. Chah Qubran Wala
40. Katri Atta Muhammad
41. Basti Chausia
42. China Hospital
43. Ahata Chiragh Din

**Slums Proposed to be Shifted**

1. Ara Chanan Din
2. Saint Mary Colony
3. Bhabra
4. Mustafa Abad
5. Ali Pura
6. Pathi Ground
7. Jhuggian F. C. College
8. Shah Jamal
9. Henry Key

Being a vast city, Lahore has long distances between its various areas and as such expensive in terms of time and money. Usually the slum dweller is a pedestrian or a cyclist and as such cannot travel long distances. He therefore chooses to live in a slum which is nearer to his place of work.

The general survey of these settlements shows the following special characteristics of slums:

(i) Water supply, drainage, sewerage, roads and electricity are almost missing.
(ii) There are no public facilities like schools, dispensaries, health centres, recreation, etc., thereby depriving children, women and men of essential social services.
(iii) The living conditions in slums are deplorable. They are mostly made up of mud without any ventilation and proper light.
(iv) A very small percentage of children go to school and there is a high rate of dropouts.
(v) There are no maternity and child care centres. Because of poverty and illiteracy only one per cent of the expectant mothers seldom go to hospitals and Mother Child Health (MCH) Centres. The local un-

trained 'daies' look after the delivery cases. On this account, it is estimated that in these areas, there is a higher rate of infant mortality compared to other parts of the city.

(vi) The poor living conditions can be directly attributed to low incomes of the families. There are hardly any employment opportunities available within these abadis. The male labour force comprises mainly workers and local artisans like labourers, vendors, Government servants, rickshaw drivers, sweepers, etc. Among women, few work in houses of adjoining developed abadis as house-maids, etc. It has been estimated that income per household ranges from Rs. 200.00 to Rs. 300.00 per month.

(vii) Children are mostly sent to small workshops and factories as apprentices where they earn Rs. 2.00 to Rs. 3.00 per day and thus supplement the family income. This is also one of the reasons for not sending children to schools. It is observed that there is frequent exploitation of child labour.

(viii) The participation of women in economic activity is poor considering the low earning capacity of each household. Those who work are house-maids who bring home some daily/monthly income to supplement the family income. Thus, there is hardly any skilled labour among women in these abadis.

A general characteristic of the growth of slums is the availability of land either free of cost or at very nominal rent. The lands in the central part of the city are always expensive. As a result, the earliest slum dwellers chose such lands which were available but were either not for sale or had no owners and were not supervised. These consisted of general evacuee vacant areas, vacant open lands and large compounds and quarters of evacuee trust properties, state lands and land held by local bodies. Most of the lands and properties occupied by slums are either evacuee, evacuee trust properties and state properties. Attempts by all concerned with such properties to get these lands and properties vacated have been successful. A large number of slums have developed over private lands where people have purchased small plots and constructed slums over them (Fig. 16.1). These usually occur at the periphery of the city and around such villages which have been or are about to merge with the main city. The land values over there are usually low and lands are purchased as agricultural lands which are generally much cheaper than urban lands. At many a place, clusters have developed over very unattractive lands or very marginal lands.

The present Government has laid great emphasis on the development of slum abadis, and the following decisions were taken:

(a) Priority should be accorded by the Provincial Government to the immediate conferment of provisional proprietary rights on the inhabitants of these abadis on state lands upon payment of a concessional cost by the inhabitants.

(b) January 1 should be fixed as the cut-off date regarding the regularization of these abadis on state land and conferment of proprietary rights thereon. Encroachments made after this date should not be recognized and the Provincial Governments should take appropriate steps to evict subsequent encroachers and prevent further encroachments.

(c) In the case of slums on state land under the ownership of Federal Government Agencies such as Railways and the Ministry of Defence, the Provincial Governments should ensure full consultation and coordination with the Federal Agencies concerned before conferring proprietary rights on the inhabitants of such abadis.

(d) Slums located on private land should be regularized through individual negotiations and compromise between the land owners and inhabitants of the slums with the assistance and close involvement of the local administration. In the alternative the interested parties may seek recourse to legal measures, if so desired.

In accordance with the aforesaid policy, the Government of Punjab has outlined strategies to solve the problems of slums on the following lines:

(i) Provision of basic infrastructure such as street pavements, construction of drains, approach roads and disposal of sullage.

(ii) Environmental improvements wherever possible in the existing slum areas and strict check on the unauthorized encroachments.

The Government of Punjab has taken a serious note of the unauthorised constructions/encroachments on public property and un-hindered growth of the slums in the province. With a view of discouraging this tendency, the following decisions have been taken by the Governor of Punjab:

(a) All slums which do not fall within the recognizable yard-stick laid down by the Government (viz. 100

household units and be in existence before 1st January 1978) should be removed in a phased manner.

(b) Housing and Physical Planning Department and Local Councils should immediately prepare new schemes for low-income groups. These colonies should be established in the peripheries of big towns, especially near the industrial areas.

(c) Big villages around major cities should be provided with electricity and other basic civic amenities.

(d) Small industrial units should be established in the rural areas to check the migration from rural to urban areas.

(e) All open spaces of plots belonging to Government Departments/Autonomous Bodies/Auqaf, etc., should be properly guarded and cleared of all types of encroachments. All such open plots which are not required by the Departments/Organizations for their use in the near future should be considered for transfer to the Development Authorities/Improvement Trusts/Local Councils concerned for maintaining as open plots.

(f) All encroachments on Government properties, roads streets and public places should be removed, if necessary by force.

The Lahore Development Authority carried out a comprehensive programme for the development of slums by carrying out physical surveys through private consultants and development plans in accordance with the principles of town planning specifying the width of the streets, etc. The Engineering Wing was assigned the execution of work in accordance with the development plans. The civic amenities being provided by the LDA are paved streets, open drains, water supply, street light and development of open spaces into parks wherever sites were available.

While undertaking the development activites, the first priority was assigned to those slums which had cropped up on state land. Second priority was assigned to the development of those which were established on the land under the Federal Agencies, and the third priority was given to those which were partially under the state land.

Lahore Development Authority (LDA) has made achievements in the development of slums by providing paved streets, open paved drains, water supply, disposal of sullage, street light, parks wherever sites were available. In a few slums the plots for the construction of mosques, schools, churches, community halls have been given by the LDA. Slums situated on Federal Government land are partially developed by the Lahore

Municipal Corporation and those situated on Provincial government land are partially developed by the Lahore Development Authority.

LDA has constructed 3,558 one-room quarters opposite the Packages Industries at Kot Lakhpat for the rehabilitation of those persons whose houses were demolished due to realignment of streets/roads or of those who were shifted from some slums, i.e. Shah Jamal, Mary Hospital, Punjab Road Transport Board Premises, Wahdat Road, etc. The gigantic and most difficult process of development was completed with the active assistance and cooperation of the residents in general and the Development Committees in particular. About 35 slums have been developed during the past four years at the cost of Rs. 13.12 crore.

In addition to that water supply will be provided to 10 slums. The LDA aims at commencing these works as early as possible so that these areas are handed over to the LMC for maintenance.

UNICEF indicated its desire to provide assistance in the field of social and economic development of the low-income people residing in slums. A workshop was organized by UNICEF in collaboration with P&D Department in November 1979 which was attended by the representatives of related agencies, i.e. Lahore Municipal Corporation (LMC), Social Welfare Department, Pakistan Family Welfare Council, Pakistan Medical Association and representatives of the slum abadis. A second workshop was held from 2nd October to 5th October 1981 for the preparation of a detailed Action Plan. This project will deal with only eleven such areas.

Slum clearance or improvement and amelioration involves physical as well as social and economic considerations.

The Government has been aware of the gravity of the problem and accordingly schemes have been prepared to rehabilitate the slum dwellers. The biggest housing project for these people is the Lahore Township Scheme, near Kot Lakhpat, which makes a provision of 35,580 quarters over an area of 4 marlas each for the low-income people. Out of the completed units a large percentage was allotted to the low-income groups of Government servants and a few hundred to the inhabitants of slums which had been cleared up.

## CONCLUSIONS

In conclusion, slums, a term used essentially to mean areas

with clusters of temporary tenements where a certain section of the population is forced to live in a squalid environment, devoid of the barest facilities and services. Slums located around the old city are old belonging to the pre-independence period and those in the fringes belong to the post-independence times and are fairly scattered. The inhabitants of the slums live in all sorts of make-shift arrangements using any kind of building material which they can lay their hands upon. Their dwellings are made of katcha bricks, mud, wood, straw, bambooo and pacca bricks. Some live in delapidated abandoned Hindu temples. The common amenities like drinking water, sewerage, electricity, latrines, bath rooms virtually do not exist. Most of them live in subhuman conditions. A large number of workers in the slums are unskilled or semi-skilled workers.

In order to provide them with the basic amenities of life the Government is taking all possible measures to provide them with pucca houses. The Town Planning Department has already developed a housing scheme called the Lahore Township near Kot Lakhpat. It is primarily meant to cater to the housing of the low-income group.

Note: The figures were obtained from the Lahore Development Authority and from the office of UNICEF, Lahore.

SEVENTEEN

H. M. Saxena

# THE PROBLEM OF SLUMS IN SMALL TOWNS
## A Case Study of Sriganganagar

In the developed world, when we talk of the problem of slums, we usually mean the slums in the big cities. But this is not true of the developing countries like India. Here we have an acute problem of slums not only in big cities but also in medium and small towns. Most of our small towns are much congested and unhygienic, although their effect on an individual's body is mitigated by the openness of the environment. For a planned growth of a small town it is essential to check the problem of slums at their primary stage.

The specific objectives of the present paper are (i) to explain the nature of slums, (ii) to examine the problem of slums in Sriganganagar, which is a small town, and (iii) to suggest remedies for the improvement of slums.

## NATURE AND CAUSES OF SLUMS

A slum is an area in an advanced stage of blight where (i) dwellings are unfit for human habitation, (ii) delinquency, crime and disease flourish, and (iii) social and economic liabilities so greatly outweigh assets that all hopes of rehabilitation have been lost. A slum is a menace to health, safety, morality, and a fertile ground for poverty, high rates of birth, infant mortality and crime. Actually these are the shelters of those poor people who are not integrated into the life of the city.

As suggested by Charles J. Stokes, slums can be classified horizontally as slums of "hope" and slums of "despair". The slum of "hope" is meant to be the one where the inhabitants are interested in improvements and welfare, while "despair" denotes lack of such intention.

There are several causes which aggravate our slum problem. One of the main cause of the development of slums is the rapid growth of industrialization in cities, that too without previous planning. With the establishment of factories dwellings are required for the workmen, who always prefer their habitation to be as near to the works as possible. Another cause of slum expansion is faulty planning and inadequate implementation machinery. Some of the other causes of the development of slums are : (i) lack of proper protection of residential neighbourhood from inharmonious uses and activities, (ii) lack of open spaces, (iii) lack of education among slum dwellers, (iv) growth of population and construction of houses, (v) dilapidation and decay of structures, due to age, neglect and faulty construction, (vi) poverty, and (vii) neglect of the city authorities, etc.

## TOWN GROWTH OF SRIGANGANAGAR

Sriganganagar ($29^{o}56'$ N : $73^{o}52'$ E) is situated in the northern-most part of Rajasthan and covers an area of 6.08 sq. km. It is a newly developed town of Rajasthan. Before 1927 there was nothing of modern Sriganganagar, but a small village known as Ram Nagar. Even Ram Nagar was 65 years old. This was a Dhani (hamlet) of Ramu Jat which thereafter was called Ramnagar. The development of the present town was started with the advent of the Gang Canal in 1927. After inauguration of the Gang Canal in 1927 Maharaja Ganga Singh named it as Ganganagar. The foundation of the new planned town was laid by the Maharaja in year 1931. In year 1931 its population was only 9,943. But afterwards there was a rapid growth of population resulting into rapid morphological growth. Due to partition of India in 1947, a large number of refugees settled down in the town. Therefore, the growth of the town intensified, followed by a rapid growth of industries. According to the 1981 census its total population was 1,23,692. Although Sriganganagar is a planned and a newly developed town, yet at some places slum locations have emerged during the past 15 years only.

## SPATIAL DISTRIBUTION AND SITE OF SLUMS

There are only eight slum areas in Sriganganagar because the town is newly developed. It is observed that all these slum areas have emerged during the past decade and a half only. The spatial pattern of these areas indicates that most of them are located in the peripheral regions of the town, while a few are along 'D' minor canal. The biggest slum area of the city is located in Ward Nos. 15 and 16 near the Sugar Mill. The other large slum areas are located in the western part of Ward No. 22 and the central part of Ward No. 23. The other slum areas are located along Karanpur Road near the Government Higher Secondary School, along 'D' minor canal and opposite the central ware-house. It becomes clear from the above description that out of all the slum locations only two are in the planned city, while the rest are in the Purani Abadi area.

The site of a slum denotes not only the actual space occupied by it, but also the functional characteristics of that area. The site does not only exercise its influence on the present pattern of the slum area, but it has been incessantly acting and reacting since its origin. The slum areas of Sriganganagar have various types of sites determined on the physical nature of the ground such as ponds, canal banks, undulating ground, open space near town, etc. The site of the biggest slum area, i.e. near, Sugar Mill is a low-lying area having three pits filled with dirty water. In Ward No. 22 also a similar type of site is occupied by slum dwellers, although in this case pits are small and shallow. The slum area of Ward No. 23 is having open space site. Undulating ground is a site for three small slum areas along the canal, while roadside slums can be seen along Karanpur Road near the H. S. School and opposite the Warehouse.

## HOUSING AND STREET PATTERN

The slum dwellers are economically backward people, and, therefore, occupy the area with physical obstacles and make their houses in odd surroundings. The houses in the slum areas are small, congested and of very sub-standard type. The dwellings are very close to each other, sometimes having only one metre space between the rows of houses. These houses are a slushy, smelly clutter of bamboo, straw and mud. It is estimated that the total number of houses in the slum areas of Sriganganagar are about 2,500, out of these 75 per cent are located in two slum areas, viz. near the Sugar Mill and in Ward No. 22. All these houses are single-storeyed and made of mud. The maximum and minimum height of a house in the slum area is 3.5 and 1.5 metres respectively. There is a lack of provision in these houses; generally two or three holes of 10 to 15 cms. diameter serve the purpose of ventilation. The streets are very narrow, their width varies from .75 to 1.5 metres. In all the slum areas drainage system is completely absent. Nearly 65 per cent of the slum structures in the town are owned by the slum dwellers. The land was allotted to them by municipal authorities mostly free of cost.

## OCCUPATIONAL AND SOCIAL STRUCTURE

The slum dwellers in Sriganganagar are engaged in various

occupations. There is a general tendency among slum dwellers of similar occupation to live together. Most of the slum dwellers in the town under study are engaged as labourers in industries as well as in agriculture, construction work, as domestic servants, cobblers, rickshaw-pullers, or as class IV employees either in government or semi-government establishments. In the slum area near the Sugar Mill, 90 per cent of the dwellers are industrial workers engaged either in the Mill or in cotton ginning factories or in saw mills. The remaining 10 per cent are engaged in construction or shoe-repairing job. The dwellers in the Sampat Basti area and opposite the warehouse are engaged in weaving and black-smithy work, but because of their low income they cannot afford the minimum living standard. In the slum area along Karanpur Road people are either class IV or domestic servants or agricultural labourers. The slum area of Ward No. 22 is having a mixed type of occupational structure, while in the Ward No. 23 area most of the slum dwellers are sweepers and rickshaw-pullers.

The educational and social structure in the slum areas is entirely different than in the entire urban area. Most of the slum dwellers in Sriganganagar are illiterate. Only five per cent of them are having primary education. It is wrong to think that the life in slums is nothing but evil. The slum dwellers exhibit a life pattern that bubbles with warmth and intimate contact. There are festivals, functions, dancing, and also fights and scandals. It is true that "the function of the slum at any movement in city development is to house those classes which do not participate directly in the economic and social life of the city". (Stokes 1970).

## SUGGESTIONS FOR IMPROVEMENT AND CONCLUSIONS

For a balanced growth of a town it is necessary to plan a strategy to eradicate slums this should be based on new policy of ecology and redevelopment. A definite programme of works should be noted. Some of the general suggestions for the improvement of slums are as follows:

(i) The population will have to be shifted from slum area to other areas.

(ii) Proper housing arrangements should be made. The work of acquisition of land and construction of houses should be taken up by the city authorities, because the cost may be heavy and the work may also take time. In the meanwhile, congestion may form again. This should be strictly checked and controlled.

(iii) The slum area should be decentralized.

(iv) Proper sanitary arrangements and other basic services should be provided such as water supply, electricity, medical aid, etc.

(v) In improvement schemes only such buildings as are really good should be retained and others demolished. The area thus cleared can be used for providing open space and sites for new buildings, etc.

In the case of Sriganganagar there is an urgent need to improve the slum area of Ward Nos. 15 and 16 near the Sugar Mill because the conditions in this particular area are of worse type from the point of view of health and habitation. The vast open space within the municipal boundary, in the vicinity of the slum area, can be used for rehabilitation of the slum dwellers. Further, half of the population of this area should be shifted to the southern part of the city, so that further congestion can be controlled. On the basis of the opinion of the slum dwellers we can call this slum area as the slum of "despair", but through proper planning conditions can be improved.

In other slum areas the conditions are not so bad. They require proper drainage, water supply, medical facilities, etc. These slums of Sriganganagar are the slums of "hope". Our strategy towards slums should be for slum improvement instead of slum clearance.

## REFERENCE

Stokes, C. J., A Theory of Slums, reprinted in **A Geography of Urban Places**, eds. Putnam, R. G & others, Methuen, 1970, p. 413.

EIGHTEEN

H. S. Mathur

# SOCIO-ECONOMIC PROFILE OF URBAN SLUMS
## A Case Study of Jaipur City

Slums punctuate almost every city of the world today. In India also every metropolitan city or industrialized town has slums where nearly one-fifth to one-half of the population lives in demeaning conditions. So without being pessimistic it must be recognized that slums have become an inseparable part of our urban life and more particularly of industrializing and fast growing urban centres. The urban planners have undoubtedly become conscious of their cancerous growth which is some gain, by itself, but it does not take us far, due to their ever increasing growth both in population and area. In the present work the socio-economic aspects of slums have been dealt with by taking Jaipur as an example.

Slum is a loosely applied term, very often taken to be synonymous to dilapidated houses and blighted areas of the city. Here it denotes only those residential areas which are characterized by overcrowding, insanitary conditions, having absence of civic amenities and facilities and which because of these substandard living conditions endanger the health, safety or moral of the inhabitants of the community.[1]

Studies is regard to Greater Bombay show that 1.2 lakhs or 15 per cent of all households reside in slums.[2] Nearly 23.8 per cent of the people live in slums in Madras.[3] The present estimates for Jaipur city show that out of a total population of 10.04 lakhs (1981) nearly 1.58 lakhs or 15.8 per cent live in slum areas. In the official jargon they are called as Katchi Basties having shanties and squalid settlements. The growth of slums in the city is a saga of rapid population growth mainly after 1951. The old walled city built in A.D. 1727 comprised an area of 6.25 sq. km. to contain a population of 1.5 lakhs as envisaged by the planners. The city remained away from evil consequences of deteriorated ecology for more than two centuries because the population never exceeded the limit.

It was only after 1947 that due to the influx of refugees, the city attained a population of 2.9 lakhs in 1951. Subsequent increases in the ensuing decades were tremendous in this capital city. Thus in 1961 and 1971 the city had 4.03 lakhs and 6.13 lakhs inhabitants respectively; the figure has now crossed the million mark in 1981. Simultaneously the areal sprawl of the city has increased to 155.4 sq. km.[4] but the attractive pull of the city is so great that the growth of slums continues.

The overcrowding of population is not entirely due to the natural increase, rather it is on account of immigration from rural areas and small towns where proper means of livelihood are not available. The influx of rural migrants is chiefly in the form of labourers employed in the construction of houses in scores of new colonies which are fast coming up, to work in factories and business houses or to gain self-employment in trade and transportation. To absorb them the city does not have low-cost houses and so a large section of immigrants are expelled out of the orbit of the city's life and by compulsion live in temporary huts.

## Growth

The first ever survey of the slum areas of Jaipur was done in 1971 when 109 Katchi Basties were identified, out of which 13 were earmarked for redevelopment.[5] It was found that 36 slums were in the walled city to be put under the jurisdiction of the Municipal Council and 73 in the extra-walled city under the Urban Improvement Trust. Enumerations showed that 15.8 per cent of the city's population resided in 28.4 per cent of the total households in slums.

The city has 50 municipal wards today, 29 in the old walled city and the rest in the new city. Estimates for 1981 show that the walled city has 44 slums with a population of 51,383 (5.1 per cent) in 8,664 households while the new city has 65 slums with a population of 107,390 (10.7 per cent) in 17,798 households. Thus the total number of slum dwellers has increased to 1,58,773 and the number of households to 26,462. The decadal growth of slum population has thus been 58.72 per cent. This shows that in spite of planned efforts for slum redevelopment the situation has worsened. It also shows that new colonies of Jaipur have now become the sites of the new rural immigrants and that slums are developing fast in such areas.

## Socio-Economic Survey

The schedule of present survey included investigations of the slum area with regard to their spatial distribution, family composition, housing, migratory status, education, employment and health. One slum from every municipal ward was selected. Out of 50 wards of the city 14 do not have any slum. So the survey was done only in 36 wards taking one slum of each ward. The entire survey was confined to 247 households taking only 1 per cent sample of the total slum population.[6]

## Spatial Distribution

In the old city the sites of slum dwellers are just along the city wall or in the north-eastern fringe. While in the extra-walled city they have made sporadic settlements on some vacant sites sometimes encircled by posh colonies also. Some of the slums in the new city are 15 to 20 years old. Later on when colonies developed in these areas they came to be surrounded by planned colonies.

The distribution shows that certain municipal wards have a very high number of slum colonies, for example Ward No. 8 has 9 slum areas. Fourteen wards have one slum each, 5 wards have one slum each, 5 wards have three slums each, 4 wards have three slums each, 4 wards have three slums each and so on (Table 18.1).

The highest population of slum dwellers is in wards 7, 15, 32 and 50 comprising 37.73 per cent of the total. Two of these wards are in the old city. The second highest percentage population is in 5 wards, viz. 1, 4, 5, 37, 45, the first three in the old city and the rest in the new city.

Enumerations show that certain municipal wards have a very high percentage of slum dwellers and so thay can be called as slum infested wards. Thus Ward No. 15 in Chowkri Topkhana Hazuri of the old city has a population of 14,678 slum dwellers (9.25 per cent) and Ward No. 45 in the Beni Park area of the new city has 12,220 people (7.70). In the remaining wards the percentage of slum dwellers varies from 0.28 to 5.81.

## Family Composition

The average number of persons per household in the slum areas is 6.8 while the corresponding figures for non-slum areas is 5.1. Thus the slum dwellers have a higher family ratio and suffer from greater congestion of space.

TABLE 18.1

**Distribution of Slums in Jaipur, 1981**

| No. of Slums | No. of wards | Ward Number | Population | Households | Percentage of Total slum population |
|---|---|---|---|---|---|
| Nil | 14 | 2,3,10,12,17,20, 21,24,25,36,40,41, 48,49 | NIL | NIL | NIL |
| 1 | 14 | 9,11,16,18,19,22, 26,27,28,29,34,35, 46 | 9,563<br>17,719 | 1,593<br>2,862 | 6.02<br>10.82 |
| 2 | 5 | 6,13,14,43,47 | 9,563 | 1,593 | 6.02 |
| 3 | 4 | 7,15,32,50 | 59,913 | 9,987 | 37.73 |
| 4 | 5 | 1,4,5,37,45 | 29,243 | 4,874 | 18.42 |
| 5 | 2 | 30,33 | 9,367 | 1,562 | 5.90 |
| 6 | 2 | 38,44 | 6,698 | 1,117 | 4.22 |
| 7 | 1 | 39 | 7,865 | 1,310 | 4.95 |
| 8 | 2 | 31,42 | 13,608 | 2,268 | 8.57 |
| 9 | 1 | 8 | 5,327 | 888 | 3.37 |
| | 50 | 109 | 158,773 | 26,462 | 100.00 |

Computed from the Census data, 1981.

The age-structure of surveyed households shows that nearly 35 per cent of their population is of the age-group below 10 and another 25 per cent is of 10 to 20 years age (Table 18.2).

TABLE 18.2

**Age-Structure of Slum Population, Jaipur**

| Age-group | Persons | Population |
|---|---|---|
| 0-10 | 581 | 34.6 |
| 10-20 | 420 | 25.0 |
| 20-30 | 272 | 16.2 |
| 30-40 | 215 | 12.8 |
| 40-50 | 113 | 6.7 |
| 50 and above | 79 | 6.7 |
| Total | 1680 | 100.00 |

Computations based on field survey.

It is obvious that the percentage goes on decreasing in the higher age-groups. It may, therefore, be discerned that on the one hand life expectancy among the slum dwellers is short while on the other their birth-rate is quite high. Nearly 60 per cent of the population is below 20 which shows a markedly high growth-rate in the last two decades. People of over 50 years age are less than 5 per cent forming an insignificant minority. Wiebe in a survey of Chennanagar slum area of Madras also found high birth and death rates in slum dwellers being 43 and 50 per cent higher than in the non-slum areas.[7]

## Migratory Status

Most of the slum dwellers are rural migrants having their own social polarities. Nearly all families coming from a particular village, tehsil or State prefer to live in the same slum thus forming social organization of their own.

The survey shows that 27 per cent of the slum dwellers had migrated from the rural areas of Jaipur Tehsil, 22 per cent from Jaipur District and 34 per cent from other districts of Rajasthan. Combined together 83 per cent of the slum population is from Rajasthan State while an insignificant minority of 17 per cent is formed by the residents of other States. (Table 18.3). In a similar survey by Singh and deSouza for Delhi 50 per cent of migrants were found to be from U.P., 30 per cent from Rajasthan, 14 per cent from Punjab and 6 per cent from other States.[8]

TABLE 18.3

**Migratory States of Slum Dwellers, Jaipur**

| Place of original residence | Percentage of Slum Dwellers | Year of stay in Jaipur | Percentage of Slum Dwellers |
|---|---|---|---|
| Jaipur Tehsil | 27 | 0–2 | 3 |
| Jaipur District | 22 | 2–5 | 8 |
| Other districts Rajasthan | 34 | 5–10 | 20 |
| Adjoining Statoo | 12 | 10–15 | 31 |
| Other States | 5 | Above 15 | 38 |
| Total | 100.00 | | 100.00 |

Based on field survey.

More important is the span of stay of slum dwellers in the city. It is discernible that a sizable proportion has been living in the city for more 10 years. The percentage of such dwellers is 69. Those living for less than 2 years are only 3 per cent. It denotes that the annual increase of immigrants is 1.5 per cent which is sufficiently high to pose problems of housing and sanitation. It is also notable that in spite of a great span of stay these large groups of immigrants have not yet been fully absorbed in the socio-economic milieu of the city. Disparities in their education, living standards and earnings with the more affluent urban dwellers has caused severe socio-economic dichotamies.

## Housing Conditions

The housing conditions of these areas present the appalling state of congestion, blight, insanitation and social impoverishment. In an industrial city like Ahmedabad over 54 per cent of slum dwellers live in single-room tenements with 4 to 9 people.[9] Still more horrifying conditions are in Bombay where 28 per cent of slum households are without any bath facilities and an incredibly high 22 per cent have no lavatory.[10]

The survey of Jaipur slums shows that the average number of rooms per household is 2.05. However, large variations exist. In the slum colony behind Sanischarji temple in the Station Road, the average availability of room per household is only one because of the high land values in the area while in the Brahmpuri harijan colony every household has three rooms. Most of the slum houses in the old city are pucca while in the new colonies they are kuchha made of mud walls and thatch roofings. Nearly 92 per cent of slum dwellers have their own tenements. Only those who have immigrated recently live in rented huts. The rental value of these huts varies from Rs. 15 to Rs. 45 p.m. depending upon the locality, its distance from arterial and trunk roads, place of work and the availability of civic amenities.

In Jaipur, only 42 per cent of slum households have lavaratory, 30 per cent have bath facilities and 50 per cent have separate kitchens. Thus a sizable proportion of residents are devoid of these basic facilities. It is imperative that most of the residents use open fields and uncovered drains for defecation and the public stand posts of water for bathing. Nearly all the Katchi basties have public water taps and the dwellers are entirely dependent upon them. The total number of public taps in these areas is 704 which shows that an average of 37.6 households and 225 people are dependent on one public tap. These spots are often the sites of unhealthy quarrels among the dwellers. In summers when water supplies deplete there is always a great rush on these sites. Quite often, these places are surrounded by mud and filth with no outlet for the flowing spilled water. The slushy water collecting into small pools thus becomes the potential foci of several diseases causing health hazards to the residents.

Invariably in all the slums insanitary conditions prevail with heaps of garbage piled near the houses, streaming filthy water on the roads and the pavements dotted with nightsoil. The lanes and blind alleys which become narrower and narrower are outworn and without any drains. Some of the slum hutments have even been built on either side of the ganda nullah, the main outlet for the city's sewers. The insufferable smell and squalor of these areas is obnoxious and unbearable and the herds of stray pigs and donkeys loitering about are an eye-sore.

**Literacv**

The poverty-stricken people are always unconcerned about their education. For them their immediate need—to search for means of livelihood—is more significant than education. Further, their style of life, social status and moral values do not encourage it. While literacy rates in the younger people are going high in the slums of south India.[11] it is not so in Jaipur.

In the Katchi Basties of Jaipur, children below 10 years have a literacy rate of 26.5 per cent while those in the age-group 10-20 years have a markedly low rate of 5.6. Adults above 20 have the most demeaning literacy rate of only 1.5 per cent. Compared to the overall literacy percentage of Jaipur which is 54.24, literacy among the slum dwellers is miserably low. This has far-reaching social implications and so murders, suicides, crime, prostitution and gangsterism are the attendant evils of these areas.

**Employment**

The problems of slums are intimately connected with occupations, work, employment pattern and the economy of the dwellers. Under-employment, unemployment and poverty coupled with lack of social awareness are admittedly the most potent compulsions which force these victims to congregate within and around the spatially stagnant urban core.[12]

In Jaipur, the average monthly income per household in the slum areas is Rs. 400.00 p.m. Considering the average size of the households to be 6, the per capita income works out to be Rs. 66.6 which is hardly sufficient to sustain oneself in a metropolitan city. The average workers per household is 1.6 which shows that a large percentage is unproductive. The occupations of working population are varied. Starting from beggars who constitute 0.4 per cent of the slum population, the dwellers have an income of up to Rs. 1800.00 p.m.

A sizable proportion (41.7 per cent) of the working population is self-employed working as fruit and vegetable hawkers, butchers, doll makers, foothpath sellers, craftsman etc., Another big section is of government employees working as peons, cleaners, chowkidars, drivers, hospital ward boys, etc., constituting 17.8 per cent of the total. Nearly 13.5 per cent have gained self-employment as rickshaw pullers and thela pullers and 10.5 per cent work as masons, labourers and factory workers. Those driving taxis, auto-rickshaws, trucks and tongas are 9.3 per cent while the rest are engaged in miscellaneous jobs like livestock raising, domestic servants, handicrafts, etc. It shows that a large bulk of the population is low paid and the dependency ratio is very high.

## Health Problems

The survey leaves us with the impression that slum dwellers are not quite "health conscious". Due to the problems of overcrowding, congestions, insanitation, scarcity of water, absence of civic amenities, poverty, etc., the heatlh problems assume astounding dimensions.

Almost all the people suffer from undernutrition particularly the children who suffer from Xerophthalmia, anaemia, scurvy and rickets and appear to be pale and sickly. A high percentage of these people report themselves to medical centres for diseases like amoebiasis, helmenthiasis, diarrhoea, dysentery, viral hepatitis and typhoid all of which are water-borne diseases. Scarcity of water in summer and frequent disruption of water pipes and sewage pipes in the rainy season in these low-lying areas cause acute contamination of drinking water supply. Moreover, the total apathy of the people towards hygeinic living makes them more prone to diseases.

Amongst the working population tuberculosis, asthma, peptic ulcers, hypertension and various types of carcinoma are common. Due to their constant living in sub-human conditions and physical exertion beyond physical limits especially in the polluted atmosphere of the city they are more susceptible to such diseases.

The study shows that ecological and socio-economic aspects of slum areas are inseparable. They both have a mutually causal relationship which perpetually tends to cause deterioration of the situation. The problem is not merely of unhealthy urban ecology; it is a much larger one concerning the socio-economic status of human beings who have been condemned to inhabit the city's plague spots.

It makes it imperative that in order to evolve an integrated plan of action for the social and economic betterment of slum areas, a total assessment of problems of slum dwellers has to be made. The redevelopment plans should be so framed and executed as to cause no harassment, no coercion and no adverse effect on the status of the slum dwellers. Simultaneously active cooperation of the residents has to be sought for devising means to raise their socio-economic status. The new immigrants should be absorbed in the urban milieu most effectively otherwise the city will be "ruralized" in many ways.

## REFERENCES


1. A slum as defined by the United Nations in **Urban Land Policies.** New York: U.N. Secretariat, Document ST/SCA/9 April 1952, p. 200.
2. Ramachandra, P. The Slum: A Note on Facts and Solutions, In: Desai, A. R. and Pillai, S. D. (eds.) **Slums and Urbanization.** Bombay: Popular Prakashan, 1970, pp. 161-70.
3. Nambiar, P. K. "Slums of Madras, City", **Census of India 1961**, Vol IX, Madras, Part XI-C.
4. **Master Plan - Jaipur**, 1971-91. The Chief Town Planner and Architectural Adviser, Government of Rajasthan, Jaipur: May 1976, p.19.
5. Sethi, N. K. "Slum Redevelopment in Jaipur: Policies and Performance", **Prashasnika.** H.C.M. Institute of Public Administration, Vol. VII. No.1-2, June 1978, p. 64.
6. Arora, R.K., Hooja, R. and Mathur, S. **Jaipur: Profile of a Changing City.** Jaipur, H.C.M. Institute of Public Administration, 1977, p. 27.
7. Wiebe, P. D. **Social Life in an Indian Slum.** Delhi: Vikas. 1975, p. 28.
8. Singh, A. M. and de Souza, A. **The Urban Poor: Slum and Pavement Dwellers in Major Cities of India.** Delhi: Manohar Prakashan, 1980, pp. 28-29.
9. Desai, A. R. and Pillai, S. D. (eds), **Slums and Urbanization**, Bombay: Popular Prakashan, 1970, p. 149.
10. Ramachandran, P. op. cit., p. 163.
11. Wiebe, P. D., op. cit., p. 144.
12. **Slums of Old Delhi**—Report of the Socio-Economic Survey of the Slum Dwellers of Old Delhi. Bharat Sewak Samaj, Delhi Pradesh: Atma Ram, 1958, p. iv.

NINETEEN

Puspha Agnihotri and D. S. Shrivastava

# GEOGRAPHICAL SURVEY OF SLUMS
## Case Studies in Cities of Madhya Pradesh

Urban slums are generally understood to be the places where conditions of housing fall much below the general levels of the urban places. This term is comparative and means various things in different countries. In the United States, for instance, a blighted area is defined (by an Act of 1947) as any area located within the territorial limits of a municipality where buildings by reason of dilapidation, absolescence, overcrowding, poor light and sanitary facilities, etc., are detrimental to public health, morals or welfare. If the above definition was to be employed to urban areas in India or in any other developing country with a longer history of urban development, most of them are likely to fall within the term of urban blights (slums).

The types of slums, as Charles Abrams describes them, vary from place to place, as does the definition. They include metropolitan and rural slums, new slums, hand-made and pre-fabricated slums, etc. Some are in shacktowns, others are found in the back alleys of mansions, while some are made of scrap; others are put together with mud, thatch, or wood findings (Abrams 1970 : 9). Lewis Mumford traces the origins of the slums to the expansion of factories. The main elements in the new urban complex were the factory, the railroad and the slum. By themselves they constituted the industrial town (Mumford 1970 : 15).

Why people live in the slums is answered by Desai and Pillai (1970 : 3). They point out that our cities are overcrowded mainly by the immigrants from rural areas and small towns which lack proper means of earning a livelihood. Unemployment among villagers creates serious social and economic problems. The population drain from rural areas to urban centres has created difficult problems of housing and other construction such as public buildings, streets, transportation, water supply and sewage disposal system. The increasing overcrowding in cities has given rise to slums. The problem of slum living has recently acquired new dimensions and the phenomenon has become extremely important today. The study of slums pays explicit attention to the urban-rural relationships. The influence of slums in urban society is becoming socially crucial as well as a scientific problem for which no permanent solution has yet been found. There are two fundamental ways of dealing with the slums. One is to rebuild them and the other is to simultaneously prevent them from ever coming into existence. In a short, the aim is to learn whether city planning can hopefully act as a birth-control upon slum conditions.

The house construction activity in the cities is largely controlled by the rent-minded property owners. They obviously do not build for the poor who cannot pay the market rent for even small residential accommodation. Thus a large section of the poor population in cities is forced to either sleep on the pavements or live in slums. The slum-dwellers generally consist of casual labourers, hawkers, beggars, lepers, rickshaw-pullers, unlicensed railway porters and people with no apparent trade, who find it difficult to obtain better accommodation elsewhere. Housing in slum areas is both "land-crowded" and "use-crowded". The people from both outside and from within the cities have contributed to the deteriorating conditions in those settlements. Slums are not only the breeding centres for but also the cradleland of crimes, diseases and immoral trafficking. Three "ds" seem to be related with the slum-dwellers, viz. "despair", "decay" and "death". But can we let this happen? This question deserves deeper analysis and understanding because it ultimately relates to the question of the fundamental rights of every person to have a proper home.

Slums are areas of social, economic and physical deterioration relative to other parts of the city and consist of temporary hutments called "Jhuggis". By Indian definition these are self-contained as far as the local needs are concerned. These are the places where people live in squalor, without even basic amenities, causing grave health hazards to themselves as well as to the rest of the city's population. These are the depressed areas full of dirt, noise, disease and ugliness.

The process of urbanization deeply affects the future of the city and the latter has become of great concern to the urban planners. The enormous gains in technology and material would not be possible without the economics of scale the city provides.

The rate and scale of urbanization have been increasing fast since the early sixties. The population increase in urban centres is notably faster than in rural areas. In Madhya Pradesh, as a whole, the urban population continues to grow in cities of the state. The two decades, 1961 to 1981, witnessed two general population trends, viz. large flow of rural population to urban areas thereby resulting in faster growth of large urban centres.

The total population of the State, according to the provisional Census figures of 1981 is 52,138,467. The urban proportion of the population of the state, i.e. 20.3 per cent, is considerably below the national average of 24 per cent. The number of class I cities in M.P. increased from 11 to 14 during the last census decade and the population which in 1971 amounted to 45 per cent of the total urban grew to about 47 in 1981. Whereas the total population of Madhya Pradesh increased only by 25 per cent in the decade 1971-81, the urban population grew by 56 per cent in the same period. Moreover, there is every indication that the pace of urban growth is continuing at an increasing rate.

The three cities under study contain 29.6 per cent of the class I cities. These three in order of size are Indore (1981 pop. 827,071), Bhopal (672,329) and Sagar (207,401). The decennial increase in the population of these cities varies considerably. Indore, the largest city of the state, has grown by over 47 per cent during the past two decades, while Bhopal and Sagar cities registered 75 and 34 per cent growth respectively. The construction of independent dwelling units on the other hand, has not kept pace with this population increase. According to the 1971 census there were over twentysix per cent families in Indore who lived in shared households. Similarly over 40 per cent families were without independent dwelling units of their own in Bhopal city.

The number of persons sharing residential accommodation does not include those people who live in temporary shelters or in slums. Their number is considerably high. At Indore city, for instance, it is estimated that a fourth of the total population (nearly 200,000) lives in slum areas. Similarly 11 per cent in Bhopal and 8.5 per cent in Sagar cities live in slum areas.

The survey of slum-dwellers of the three different types of cities shows that the average number of days of employment in rural areas declined from 210 in 1974-75 to 180 days in 1980-81. Linked with these figures is the sharp rise in rural indebtedness. Droughts and famines though are no longer the causes of out-flow of the people, it is rather the high unemployment ratio which pushes the villagers into the cities. The authors, through sample surveys, have studied the relationship between the uneven economic and social development and the direction in which the villagers are pushed.

## INDORE

None of the other industrial cities in the state have been surveyed as extensively as Indore during the past few years. It is one of the sixteen largest cities of India, according to the Slum Clearance Board, which have been selected for the urban environmental improvement scheme launched in 1974. Indore is the only city of the state to benefit from the different improvement schemes. The Madhya Pradesh Urban Community Project with UNICEF assistance was aimed at investigating the slum areas of the city.

The city is densely populated and is the richest urban centre of the state. According to the UNICEF report there were 2000,595 people living in slums. This makes roughly 25 per cent of the city's current population. The city has 75 slum localities which cover an area of 275 hectares (Maps 19.1 and 19.2). Slums are located either on Government land or on the land owned by the Municipal Corporation. Nearly one-half of the existing slum localities are situated in the Mill Area which is in the heart of the city.

Indore is a multi-functional city and the immigration of people from rural areas, on this account, is quite high. There is a significant migration into the city from the southern districts of Khargone, Khandwa, Dhar and areas adjoining Mandleshwar. Fortunately for this city, the migrants from the northern places thronged Ujjain city and Nagda town, north of Indore, thereby creating the largest slum concentration of the state at Nagda.

The industrial activity in Madhya Pradesh is not distributed evenly but is rather concentrated in some large cities of the state. Indore city is the leading industrial centre of Madhya Pradesh. Coupled with the uneven economic growth is the concentration of rural poor into the slum areas of some cities. Added to this phenomenon is the control of large patches of land in the hands of speculators who sell residential plots of land at prohibitive prices.

The dissatisfaction of life at the places of origin has pushed the rural poor into the city where job opportunities exist. The

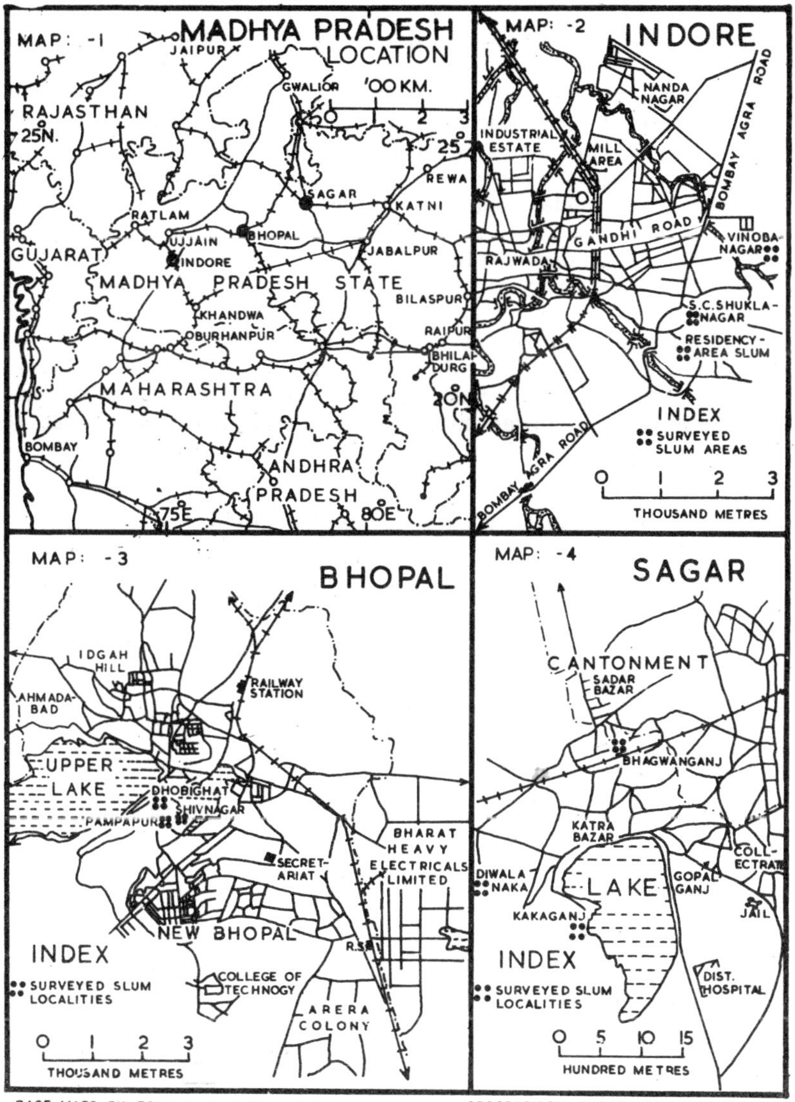


BASE MAPS BY TOWN & COUNTRY PLANNING DEPARTMENT BHOPAL.

GEOGRAPHICAL SURVEY OF SLUMS - P.A.& D.S.S.

migrants are in the know of their potential destination and are in communication with friends or relatives already living there. The pulls of the new area and the pushes of the original area act together as a positive impetus on potential migrants. A rural migrant is a member of a poor family, who is unemployed, underemployed, or may be physically handicapped.

The cases analysed relate to 60 families interviewed at three different economic levels of slum localities of Indore. The surveyed slum area is located in the central part of the city and consists of three slum localities: Residency Area, Shyamacharan Shukla Nagar and Vinoba Nagar.

About 2,800 slum-dwellers live in the Residency Area slum. With 600 houses it covers about half a hectare of land in the eastern part of the city (Table 19.1). This locality can be described as the worst as far as living conditions are concerned. The land on which huts stand is a low-lying area and is poorly drained. Residency slum area has attracted residents mainly from lower socio-economic backgrounds. About 10

TABLE 19.1

**Existing Slums of Indore City, 1980**

| Slum Category | Number of slums | Area in hectares | Number of huts | Population | Density (persons per hectare) |
|---|---|---|---|---|---|
| I. Slums on Govt. land | 30 | 122.57 | 25,365 | 84,395 | 688 |
| Surveyed slums included in the total 1. S.C.Shukla Nagar | | 0.40 | 600 | 2,800 | 1,000 |
| 2. Residency Area | | 0.40 | 600 | 2,800 | 1,000 |
| 3. Vinoba Nagar | | 12.14 | 1,330 | 5,300 | 436 |
| II. Slums on municipal land | 17 | 53.44 | 9,880 | 51,320 | 857 |
| III. Slums on Indore Development Authority land | 4 | 12.55 | 900 | 3,990 | 320 |
| IV. Slums on Housing Board land | 1 | 10.12 | 1,250 | 7,000 | 691 |
| V. Slums on private land | 8 | 28.74 | 3,210 | 16,650 | 5,793 |
| VI. Slums on unidentified land | 15 | 47.72 | 7,705 | 37,240 | 767 |
| Total | 75 | 288.08 | 50,840 | 211,495 | 734.7 |

Source: Madhya Pradesh Slum Clearance Board, Bhopal: Project Report for Indore, 1980.

per cent residents of this slum have migrated to a nearby slum known as the Shyamacharan Shukla Nagar. In this newer slum they now occupy a hut of their own.

About 90 per cent people work in mills and only about 10 per cent are engaged in other services. As these people belong to the low income groups, they cannot afford expenses on transportation and, therefore, want to live close to their work-place. This is the main locational factor for the emergence of this slum settlement.

In a separate section of the Residency slum is a section for 28 leper families comprising of individuals. The number of leper families rose from five in 1970 to 28 in 1982. This increase is largely because of proximity to the "Balaji Temple" from where they earn their livelihood. They are mostly very poor people who live on begging . This slum locality is notoriously in-sanitary and is injurious to health. All other factors, however, seem to sink into insignificance when compared with this dominating cause, i.e. the prevalence of leprosy. The daily in-come of lepers varies from Rs. 1.50 to Rs. 5. The irony of the situation is that the worst hit lepers earn far more by begging than the others. Some of them are married, but a considerable number of the males and females live together without formal marriage. Among the lepers are those who are aged, infirm, chronically ill and mentally sick. Some of these who are not able to get enough by begging live on the collection of waste food. Probably in the past few years, a considerable amount has been spent by the Government to better their conditions. It is understood that the Government gives to every leper a monthly allowance of Rs. 40 and 15 kgs of millet (jowar). Medical aid is also available to them. It is surprising to find two children living with their leper parents.

The Shyamacharan Shukla Nagar is the newest slum settle-ment. The slum, according to the Project Report of the M.P. Slum Clearance Board occupies 0.40 hectare of land and consists of 600 huts with 2,800 residents (Table 19.1). There are inter-mixtures of small shops and workshops with the virtual absence of open space. It is considered as a "high-class" slum locality because the State Government has spent a considerable amount of money for the upgradation of this settlement. An analysis of the data reveals that about a fifth of the residents are engaged in small business, while 10 per cent work in mills and about 70 per cent of the workers are engaged in different occupations.

The Vinoba Nagar slum is the oldest and also the largest among the three slum localities. The average length of residence of its households is 10 years and the oldest household interviewed had been there since 1950. This slum locality presents a rural look. There is no vacant space for new construction of huts. The residents work in the cotton textile mills or are engaged in small household units like incense-stick industry.

The monthly income of the slum-dwellers ranges between Rs. 200 and Rs. 700. This slum occupies 12.14 hectares of land and consists of 1,330 households with about 5,300 residents.

## BHOPAL

During the decade 1971-81 the city has grown by 75 per cent. This explosive growth of urban population can largely be attributed, besides natural increase, to inmigration. The current population of the city is 672,000 persons. The city is expected to grow at a high rate in the near future also because of its importance as the capital of the province and also due to its transport links. The expansion of the city has attracted a large number of persons from adjacent rural areas and smaller towns like Mandideep, Berkheda, Shahganj and Nasrullaganj.

Every increase in population requires extensive provision of facilities of transportation, housing, water supply, sewerage, etc. Even if these provisions could be made the poor population will not be able to afford them.. The poor, therefore, house themselves in high density inner-city slums to get the maximum advantage of living in a central area of the city. To them, architectural design or housing standards are of little interest. Their only need is to get shelter near the places where they can obtain a livelihood.

There are 22 slum localities with 75,470 persons which is 11 per cent of the city's total population (Map 19.3). These slum localities cover an area of 101.68 hectares and have a total of 14,375 huts. The location of slums is conditioned by the availability of vacant land and by the proximity of work places. The sites of the city's slums are not unique but rather seem to be characteristic of slum locations in other two surveyed cities.

The surveyed slum localities are Dhobighat, Shivnagar and Pampapur. The Dhobighat slum settlement is the oldest of the three where the first hut was built in the year 1950. This slum area, with 1,016 persons, is located at the western side of the lower lake. Of the 20 households 10 heads of the families work as washermen, barbers, shoe repairers or as mechanics. Six of the residents sell vegetables and fruits, the remaining four families belong to the service class. Eighty per cent of the residents own their huts which are in very good condition. They have spent Rs. 2,000 to Rs. 3,000 each for the construction of their huts. Twenty per cent are slum-tenants who are the poorest and pay a rent of Rs. 20 per month to hut owners who live in some other localities.

The Shivnagar slum area occupies 2.4 hectares of land where 756 persons live. This locality is newer and rather planned with open spaces. The investigation of the 20 households shows that 55 per cent of the residents are engaged in service while the others are engaged in small business.

Pampapur slum locality is the best of the three settlements. The people have been living here only for the past seven years. It occupies an area of 3.4 hectares where 988 persons live. This slum locality has enough vacant space for other immigrants who might arrive in the city. The slum-dwellers of this locality work at the near-by bicycle shops, tea-stalls and restaurants. Nearly 95 per cent of the workers walk to their workplaces. The slum dwellers of this locality have not been able to find better jobs in the city.

## SAGAR

The current population of the city is 207,000 persons of which 24,500 (i.e. 8.5 per cent of total population) are slum-dwellers who live in 2,488 huts (Table 19.2). There are seven slum localities spread over 5.85 hectares of area.

Sagar presents a case of low-economic development and low urban growth. The backwardness prevails in all the core sectors of the economy. The city is not very well connected by rail, though it has good road links. This drawback in transport and lack of political backing are largely responsible for slow economic and urban development of the city. The sluggish growth of the city, in spite of its importance as a "Bidi" manufacturing centre, is the result of continued neglect of the city by the State. No industry was established, or large-scale construction could take place during the past 20 years.

Most of the slum-dwellers are living in the city for the past 50 years and there has not been any appreciable increase in their number. The study reveals that immigration into Sagar is mainly from adjacent rural areas which started in the fifties. Another important characteristic of the inmigrant population is that those menfolk who have migrated from adjacent rural areas came alone while those who immigrated from distant places came

TABLE 19.2

**Existing Slums of Sagar City, 1982**

| Name of the slum locality | Area in hectares | Number of huts | Population | Density (persons per hectare) |
|---|---|---|---|---|
| 1. Bhagwanganj | 0.75 | 280 | 3,000 | 4,000 |
| 2. Diwala Naka | 0.95 | 380 | 3,500 | 3,681 |
| 3. Kakaganj | 0.85 | 300 | 4,000 | 4,706 |
| 4. Pant Nagar | 1.00 | 315 | 3,500 | 3,500 |
| 5. Subhash Nagar | 1.00 | 318 | 3,500 | 3,500 |
| 6. Vallabh Nagar | 0.50 | 495 | 3,500 | 7,000 |
| 7. Vithal Nagar | 0.80 | 400 | 3,500 | 4,375 |
| Total 7 | 5.85 | 2,488 | 24,500 | 4,188 |

Source: Municipal Corporation, Sagar, 1982.

with their families.

The city being one of class I centres of the State, the housing conditions present a serious problem. Slow growth of accommodation has changed many vacant parts of the city into slum areas. People belonging to low-income groups prefer to live in such areas because of the low house rents. The open drainage, narrow and filthy lanes and insufficient public utility services have made those places most unhygienic.

Surveys were conducted at three slum locallites, viz. Bhagwanganj, Diwala Naka and Kakaganj. These localities occupy 2.55 hectares of land which is half of the total slum area of the city.

Bhagwanganj slum locality occupies 0.75 hectare of land where 3,000 slum dwellers live (Table 19.2). Slum growth of this settlement has exhibited ribbon development, parallel to the railway line and road (Map 19.4). It is located in the low-lying area opposite the Railway Station, and is the oldest slum. It was observed that the older slums have better location relative to employment opportunities and site characteristics. The survey of the 20 households reveals that the residents of this settlement belong to the labour class. They work as unauthorized coolies (porters) and coal-pickers. These people belong to very poor classes who depend mainly on Railway Station for their livelihood. Incomes of people in this slum are less than the subsistence level and range between Rs. 150 and Rs. 250 per month. The economy of this slum locality also depends on stealing and selling coal picked up from the Railway Station. The people involved in these unlawful activities are technically speaking self-employed.

The Diwala Naka slum is the newest settlement. It occupies about a hectare of land with 3,500 slum-dwellers. This area consists of degrading huts located in a jumbled manner. Investigation reveals that the residents are either engaged in small business or in menial jobs. The percentages of business and service classes are 20 and 80 respectively. Their incomes range between Rs. 250 and Rs. 400 per month.

Kakaganj : The slum-dwellers of this old settlement are "better-off" and their socio-economic status is also better than that of the other two slums. The locational advantages of this slum are proximity to markets and work-places, besides the availability of vacant land. It occupies 0.85 hectares of land where 4,000 people live. The average period of residence of the slum-dwellers is 25 years, while the oldest household interviewed had been there since 1940. The residents of this rettlement work in godowns (ware houses) and at different shops. While the womenfolk are engaged in "Bidi" making and earn enough to support the family.

## SOCIO-ECONOMIC STRUCTURE OF THE SURVEYED SLUMS OF INDORE, BHOPAL AND SAGAR CITIES

A total of 208 slum families in the three cities at different functional levels were surveyed. The survey reveals that the unemployment level is generally low. Many people, especially of Indore slums, are employed in mills and are engaged in other services. A large proportion of Vinoba Nagar slum dwellers, of this city have monthly incomes between Rs.500 and Rs.750 (Table 19.3). They, however, appear very poor because of large families, idleness, alcoholism, disease, etc. At the occupational level this is exhibited in menial jobs, lack of seriousness towards their work, frequent job changes and intermittent or persistent unemployment. Learning the skills needed for the job is not difficult for them but what they find hard is to accept the discipline of regular work.

The questions asked at the nine slum localities belonging to different socio-economic levels are :

1. What were their reasons for coming to the city?

TABLE 19.3

**Percentages of Slum Families At The Three Surveyed Cities According To Monthly Income Groups**

| | Monthly income groups (Rupees) | | |
|---|---|---|---|
| | 1 to 250 | 251 to 500 | 501 to 750 |
| **Indore Slums:** | | | |
| 1. Residency Area | 70 | 20 | 10 |
| 2. Shyamacharan Shukla nagar | 10 | 10 | 80 |
| 3. Vinoba Nagar | 5 | 25 | 70 |
| **Bhopal Slums:** | | | |
| 1. Dhobighat | 35 | 65 | - |
| 2. Shiv Nagar | 15 | 80 | 5 |
| 3. Pampapur | 15 | 70 | 15 |
| **Sagar Slums:** | | | |
| 1. Bhagwanganj | 100 | - | - |
| 2. Diwala Naka | - | 100 | - |
| 3. Kakaganj | - | 100 | - |

Source: Based on personal interviews, during August 1982, with 180 families at nine slum localities of the three cities of Madhya Pradesh.

2. Where were they living before coming to the city?
3. Did the entire family migrate at one time, if not, at what later stage did the family join?
4. What were their reasons for selecting a particular locality?
5. Are most residents oldtimers or are newcomers?
6. Do the slum-dwellers welcome newcomers or are they hostile?
7. Do they maintain contacts with their home town by way of marriages or for any other events?
8. Do they have caste and regional affinities or do they live in occupational groups?
9. Are there any fractions or tensions in the slum area?
10. Who are the local leaders and what is the basis of leadership?
11. Where do they go for work? How far off is workplace?
12. Who owns the land on which the hut stands? If not the owner, what rent is to be paid and to whom?

Research shows that residents of slums live in family units. Ten per cent of women slum-dwellers serve as domestic servants. The data obtained through investigation indicate that about two-thirds of the slum-dwellers came to the cities with families in search of employment, while a third belonged to the category of those who moved alone to the city due to family quarrels. The menfolk came first and after building or obtaining huts on rent they brought their families. Almost all the migrants moved directly to the slum locality from their places of birth.

About 95 per cent residents of the surveyed slum localities can be described as isolated individuals as they are cut-off from their relatives. Only 5 per cent slum-dwellers visit their homes on the occasions of marriage or death or just to meet their relatives.

There are two kinds of slum leaders. The leadership of the better class slums is in the hands of those who can read and write, though they may not have any formal education. The leadership of the lower-strata slums is largely in the hands of uneducated ruffians.

## CONCLUSIONS

Slums largely play a negative role in the urban scene but in the developing countries like India, these settlements have an important functional role as well, in view of the increasing city-ward migration of depressed and landless villagers. For such immigrants slums are the only homes in the crowded cities. Slum is not only an expression of extreme population pressure, it has also become a way of life in cities.

With the help of the surveys of the slum-dwellers of Indore, Bhopal and Sagar the socio-economic conditions as prevalent in various localities have been studied. The total slum population of the three cities is 300,565 which is around 3 per cent of the total urban population of Madhya Pradesh State. The area under the 104 slum localities in these three cities is 383 hectares, and the number of huts is 65,173. Of the total city-population 25 per cent in Indore, 11 per cent in Bhopal and 8.5 per cent in Sagar live in these uncontrolled settlements. This study seems to establish that more developed cities have higher slum population. Bhopal has experienced the highest increase (75%) during the decade 1971-81, while Indore has grown by 47 per cent and Sagar's growth was only 34 per cent.

As the cities grow, the increase in the urban population and the resultant unplanned growth of the cities cause many problems. Supply of water and other basic amenities can no longer keep pace with the demand. Prevalence of a greater degree of crime and delinquency, neglect of environmental sanitation and the failure of social controls add to the difficulties. It is in the slum areas that such problems are concentrated.

This paper incorporates findings of the field studies conducted through interviews with about 200 slum-dwellers of the three cities. The persons interviewed were in the age group of 18 and 60 years with five or more years of residence in slum areas. The objective of the survey was to demonstrate the links between the dwellers' perception of their residential environment and observed realities. The answers to field study questions bring out the following socio-economic conditions of the slums.

The reasons for concentration of people into slum areas are varied and complex. Migration from villages to the cities is largely due to the inability of the people to find jobs in villages and hence they are attracted to the cities. Some of the slum-dwellers belong to the category of those who moved to the city due to family quarrels. The findings indicate that many of the migrants moved directly to these cities from their places of birth without "intermediate stops". The pattern of their jobs is largely influenced by the migratory patterns.

It has been observed that slum-dwellers consist of migrants who are both semi-skilled and unskilled labourers. In the sphere of employment the most poorly paid jobs are filled by migrants. Those who migrate from adjacent villages came alone, while those immigrating from distant places came first and after obtaining huts on rent brought their families. Almost all the new inmigrants to slum areas have relatives or friends in these cities. It is noteworthy here that not a single individual has come to live with strangers. Relatives or friends contribute significantly by way of finding jobs and by acquiring huts for the newcomers.

The people of these uncontrolled settlements are segregated by castes, creed and regions of origin. Most of the slum dwellers enter the city without any assurance of employment. The young migrants on their failure to find gainful employment face disillusionment and frustration and are forced to live in these slums where living conditions are worse than those they left behind.

Many slums are located in central parts of the cities to reduce transportation costs. They sacrifice space by accepting high densities so as to reduce the cost per household of occupying such expensive land. Thus they are able to minimize their total combined expenses on shelter and transportation. The land on which slums are located, in many cases are low-lying areas with poor drainage or are otherwise unsuitable for proper urban use. The majority of the slum-dwellers of these cities are old-timers. They are better-off, occupationally and residentially while the newcomers are still struggling for their survival. In other words, the older the migrant, the better adjusted he is. The effect of the length of residence has tended to be stronger than any other socio-economic factor. Better slums have attracted residents from higher socio-economic backgrounds.

Most of the slum-dwellers are slum-tenants though the rental huts are in very poor conditions. Slum-tenants pay on an average a rent of Rs. 20 per month. At some localities, the Government has provided plots measuring 15' x 12' each to slum-dwellers for building huts. In such localities the slum-dwellers are "landlords" and have invested Rs. 2,000 to 3,000 each for the construction of their huts. It was observed that the residents are either engaged in small business or are in menial jobs. The womenfolk also work to raise the family income. The unemployment level is low as many people are either under employed or are employed in marginal economic activities. The economy of some of the slums also depends on stealing and selling coal picked up from railway stations.

The special feature of this finding is the report on leper families isolated in a slum area of Indore. These lepers are aged, infirm and chronically ill. They supplement their income by begging. The worst-hit lepers earn far more by begging than the others.

It is concluded that the slum-dwellers of Indore possess higher socio-economic status than those of the other two class I cities of the State. The growth patterns of slum localities and slum population do not show similar trends in all the three cities. The data show that Indore has the highest slum population (200,595) followed by Bhopal (75,470) and Sagar (24,500). The number of slums in the three cities is 7, 22 and 75 respectively in Sagar, Bhopal and Indore which gives a ratio of 1:3:10.

Civic administration, and sometimes Government, provide for and maintain some services in the slum localities. These efforts, however, do not touch even the fringe of the complex problems of these areas.

## REFERENCES

Abrams, Charles, **Slums, Slums and Urbanization,** p. 9 (Eds.) A.R. Desai and S.D. Pillai, Popular Prakashan, Bombay 1971.

Desai, A.R. and S.D. Pillai, General Introduction, 1970, p. 3, Ibid.

Mumford, Lewis, **The Slum: Its Origins,** 1970, p. 15, Ibid.

Venkatarayappa, K.N., **Slums : A Study in Urban Problem.** Sterling Publishers (P) Ltd, New Delhi, 1972.

Madhya Pradesh Slum Clearance Board, "Bhopal, Project Report for Indore, 1980".

# INDEX